BUSTED FLUSH!
The Thomas Crapper Myth

'My Family's Five Generations in the Bathroom Industry'

Geoffrey Pidgeon

Arundel Books

I have made every effort to acknowledge correct copyright and/or origin of material and images where applicable. Some information came via friends and it has proved impossible to establish the original source or author. Any errors or omissions are unintentional and should be reported to me and I will arrange for corrections to appear in any reprint.

A catalogue record of this book is available from the British Library.

Hardcover Edition ISBN: 978-0-9560515-7-8

Paperback Edition is available: ISBN: 978-0-9560515-6-1

Other books by Geoffrey Pidgeon:

Jane's Railway Family

The Secret Wireless War

Edgar Harrison: Soldier – Patriot and Ultra Wireless Operator to Winston Churchill

To order additional copies of this book or other titles please visit: http://www.geoffreypidgeon.com

Published by: Arundel Books
3 Arundel House, Courtlands, Sheen Road, Richmond. TW10 5AS
Email: info@geoffreypidgeon.com http://www.geoffreypidgeon.com

This book is dedicated to the memory of my dear wife Jane who sadly died early this year just before the work was finished. She wholeheartedly supported me in this project – as she had in every phase of our sixty-six years together.

She played a great part over the years in reading and commenting on each chapter as they were completed. This book is also dedicated to our three sons Laurence, Michael and John – the fifth generation – and to my mother Edith Adelaide Pidgeon (née Humpherson).

Geoffrey Pidgeon
Richmond
October 2014

Preface

In starting to write the history of my family's five-generation involvement in the bathroom industry, I realised how intertwined it is with that of Thomas Crapper, starting with my great-uncle Frederick Humpherson who was apprenticed to him in 1871. I am also conscious of the media constantly reporting that Thomas Crapper 'invented the WC' – whatever that actually meant?

This fabrication, in various forms, has been woven into countless press articles over the years – following the launch of Wallace Reyburn's original 'Flushed with Pride' – first published in 1969. I have responded to these in Chapter 19.

However, I think I should make an initial comment here about the myths that have grown up. The evidence for these being myths is well documented going back many years. I shall also show how my family and Thomas Crapper are linked – in assorted ways – from 1871 right up to the present day. As a result, his name appears in many parts of the book that follows.

If 'WC' means a WC pan, then Thomas Crapper **did not** design a WC pan.
If 'WC' means a WC flushing cistern, then Thomas Crapper **did not** design a WC flushing cistern.

However, he did purchase a Patent for a flushing cistern – from Albert Giblin of Fulham – who had registered it as his Patent 4990 in 1898. Thereafter Thomas Crapper & Co. sold the cistern as being 'Crapper's Valveless Water Waste Preventer (Patent 4990)'.

Frederick Humpherson **did** design a WC pan – the 'Beaufort' in the 1880s.
Acknowledged to be the World's first wash-down pedestal water closet.

Frederick Humpherson **did** design a WC flushing cistern – his 'Humpherson's Patent Syphon Cistern' (Patent 2492) in 1885.

Frederick Humpherson launched his 'Humpherson's Patent Syphon Cistern' at the International Inventions Exhibition held in South Kensington in 1885, for which he received a Bronze Medal as shown overleaf. Details of his other contributions to design and his awards are shown in later chapters.

With the wide misunderstanding and exaggeration by Wallace Reyburn of the part played by Thomas Crapper & Co. in the development of the bathroom – as compared to that of my great-uncle Frederick Humpherson – I felt bound to call my book **'Busted Flush! – The Thomas Crapper Myth'**.

However, as the main object is to record my family's continued part in the bathroom history for over 140 years, the book has a sub-title **'My Family's Five Generations in the Bathroom Industry'**.

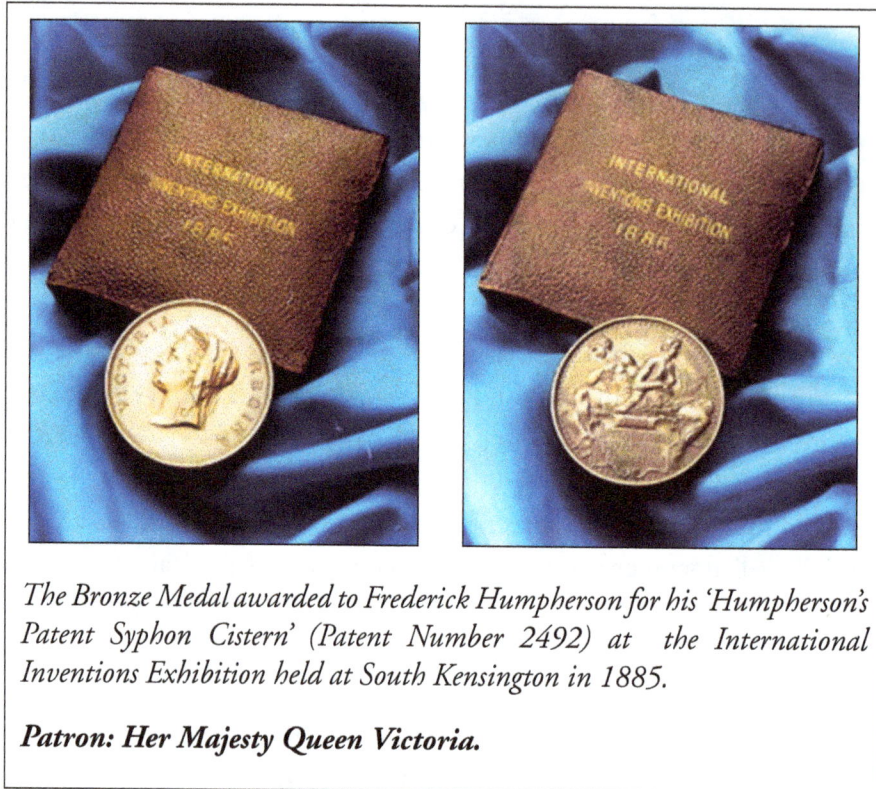

The Bronze Medal awarded to Frederick Humpherson for his 'Humpherson's Patent Syphon Cistern' (Patent Number 2492) at the International Inventions Exhibition held at South Kensington in 1885.

Patron: Her Majesty Queen Victoria.

Geoffrey Pidgeon
Richmond
October 2014

Prologue

My mother, Edith Adelaide Pidgeon (née Humpherson), was born in Fulham in 1897. She liked to claim there had been more changes in her lifetime, than in any previous period of history. Living until 1976, she would certainly have seen some of the earliest motor cars on the road, read about the flight of the first aeroplane, the introduction of wireless and later television. In addition there were huge improvements in medical science, penicillin and so on. She also lived through two World Wars and during World War II, was a nurse in the clinic at Bletchley Park.

The last twenty years of the 19th century into which mother was born was a period of immense technological changes. Invention followed invention in the golden years of Victoria's reign. Importantly, designers were encouraged by the rewards offered by the growing market for their products.

There had been significant improvements in 'public works' with new schools, hospitals, civic buildings and infrastructure of all kinds. Alongside these were the necessary drains, sewer systems, sewage and water works were constructed. These in turn, led to considerable improvements in domestic sanitation, so essential to the growing population, living in the rapidly expanding cities. These developments are regarded as significant steps in man's evolution.

Great benefit was derived from the work of such sanitary engineers as George Jennings, Steven Hellyer, James Duckett, Daniel Bostel, Edward Johns, Alfred Johnson, George Howson, Thomas Crapper, the Johnson Brothers, Thomas Twyford, John Shanks and my great-uncle Frederick Humpherson, amongst others.

It is very difficult for us in Western Europe, to imagine life now without clean, safe drinking water, main drainage and sewers. However, as late as the 1880s there were still many outbreaks of scarlet fever, diarrhoea, and other infectious diseases associated with unsanitary conditions. The urgent need for rapid improvements brought forward the designers and manufacturers – some of whom I mention above.

Although mother was a good communicator, and so full of interest to me as a child, she told us nothing of the part her uncle Frederick Humpherson had played in improving sanitary fitments, as one of the great designers of the late Victorian age. Sadly, she died before I started writing our history, otherwise I could not have had a more reliable 'witness'!

Following Frederick's apprenticeship to Thomas Crapper in 1871, and the formation of Humpherson & Co. soon afterwards by my great-grandfather Edward Humpherson, five generations of my family have continued to work in the bathroom industry, until the present day. Our story runs concurrently with the development of bathroom design and I believe my family have contributed to some aspects of its progress.

This is our story.

Contents

Appendices

These are directly linked to a chapter and referred to within it. They are followed here by stand-alone notes that may well be of interest to the reader.

Notes

Chapter 1

The Background

In early 1947, I returned to London from Singapore after serving in MI6 (Section VIII) from late 1942 until the war ended, then in one of its peacetime replacements, the newly formed Diplomatic Wireless Service (DWS) – a division of the Foreign Office. Father however, wanted me to join the family bathroom business inherited by mother in 1945.

For me to continue with DWS meant (a) probably accepting a dull job in the workshops now located at Hanslope Park – some ten miles north of Bletchley Park and (b) being away from the family all now living in London. So, after a short holiday, I joined the family business Humpherson & Co. Ltd., situated at 188a Fulham Road, South Kensington, (known as 'Beaufort Works') and in a private road called Holmes Place.

On my first day, father showed me my future working space that included a desk so tall that I needed a high stool so that I could reach to work on it. I felt like something out of a Dickens novel and was not best pleased! Fortunately, my father listened to my expressions of horror and allowed me to saw the legs of the desk thus making it normal height – and then the legs of the stool!

Although the expression 'DIY handyman' was not coined then, I was fairly competent with most tools. However, I was never able to get all four legs of my reduced stool quite equal. As a result, I was to spend the next few weeks writing or typing on a stool with a

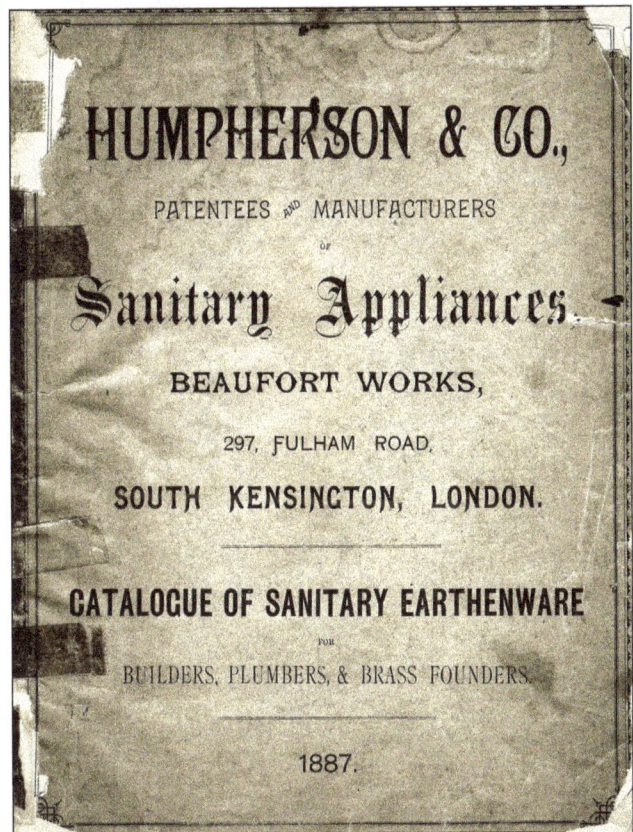

HUMPHERSON & CO.,

PATENTEES AND MANUFACTURERS
OF

Sanitary Appliances.

BEAUFORT WORKS,

297, FULHAM ROAD,

SOUTH KENSINGTON, LONDON.

CATALOGUE OF SANITARY EARTHENWARE
FOR

BUILDERS, PLUMBERS, & BRASS FOUNDERS.

1887.

In the many documents I found in my 'new' desk was the 1887 Humpherson & Co. catalogue. It is rather the worse for wear but it shows pictures of the sanitary ware on offer at the time.

perpetual wobble. It was only after a considerable period that my father finally agreed that I could purchase a proper office chair!

Thus my first days passed, not so much learning the intricacies of the bathroom industry but more in an attempt to bring my future working conditions into the twentieth century. This was 1947 after all!

In clearing out the desk before its long-overdue renovation, I found some old trade catalogues, including a Humpherson one for 1887. I was intrigued by the claims made in a later issue about the 'Beaufort' WC pan and other of Humpherson's patent products There was a Crapper catalogue of 1888 and two from Twyfords: one of 1896 as well as their fabulous '20th Century' catalogue from 1901. There were also others including two of Macfarlane's of Glasgow catalogues showing their cast iron products that are now, like the catalogues of Twyfords, collectors' items.

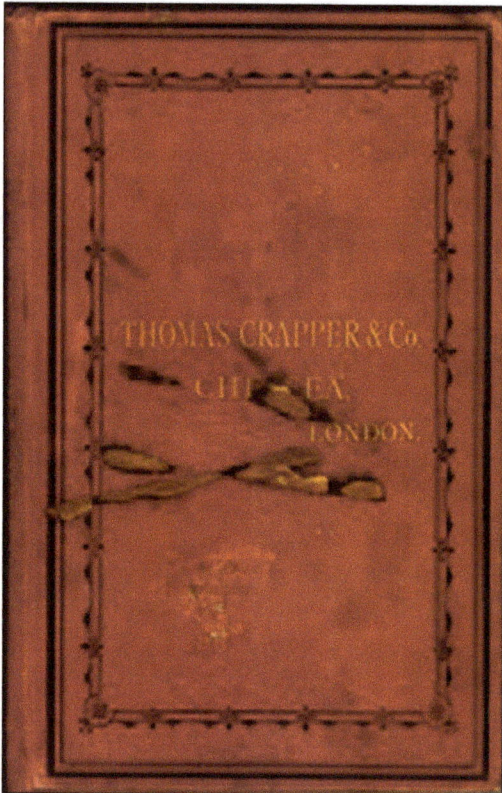
Amongst the other books in the desk was the Thomas Crapper & Co. catalogue for 1888

I spoke to my uncle Sidney Humpherson about them. He told me, with considerable pride, that my great-uncle Frederick had designed the world's first one-piece wash-down pedestal WC pan and *not* Thomas Crapper as people claimed! He said this with some vehemence. As the name 'Crapper' meant little to me – apart from its derivatives – I questioned him further.

Sidney then related the story of how during the period from 1860 to1880 my great-grandfather Edward and his family had lived opposite Thomas Crapper's showroom and works, in Marlborough Road, Chelsea. Apparently, Edward had apprenticed two of his sons, Frederick and Alfred (my grandfather) to Thomas Crapper to learn the plumbing trade. I was told that 'Crappers' had become our rivals and we were simply not friendly one with the other. Therefore, very early on I was made aware of the tension that had existed between the two family firms who had once been neighbours in Chelsea.

Aware of my rising interest, our trade-counter manager Arthur Meadows told me, that not only would senior members of the two firms not speak to each other, they would deliberately actually cross the street to avoid a face-to-face meeting.

Arthur Meadows had joined Humpherson & Co. in 1919, at the age of 14, just before the death of Frederick Humpherson. My uncle Sidney confirmed his comments about the relationship that existed.

In spite of the stories of the past, we enjoyed a growing friendship with Crapper's staff. It started with our meeting George Clarke, (their representative) whose territory covered the Chelsea and Kensington area of west London. Indeed, I had nothing but a growing regard for them and the company. Yes, I agree Thomas Crapper & Co were rivals, but we found they always conducted themselves in the proper and business-like manner of the period.

I became immersed in learning about the company, about plumbing technology and the products being sold. I therefore had little time to pursue the story of the company, Frederick Humpherson, or his 'Beaufort' WC. Very sadly, my father died early, in 1956 – only 58 years old. Consequently, before I was thirty, I found myself fully occupied in running the family business. As a result, I had even less opportunity to think about our history, especially since the company was then beginning to expand in turnover and slowly regaining its importance.

However, following the publication of 'Flushed with Pride' by Wallace Reyburn in 1969, the 'Crapper story' increasingly cropped up in the press with even the daily papers misquoting his achievements, including the wild claim that he had 'invented the WC'! Writers had decided it was a 'fun' subject with wide media appeal, so the claims became more and more bizarre!

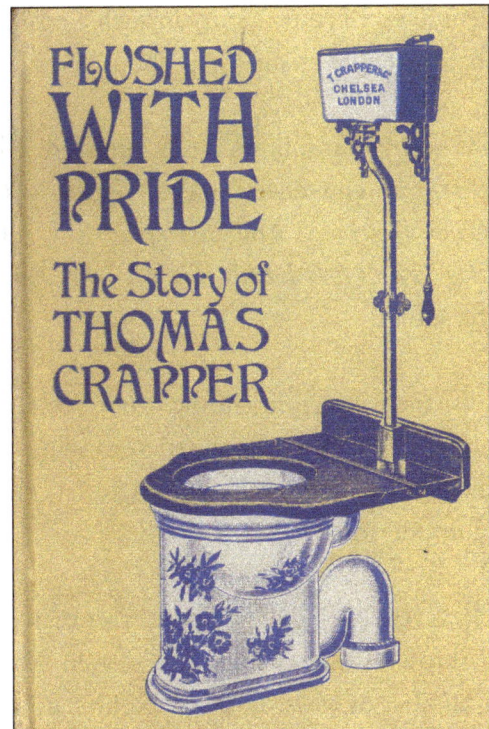

This is Wallace Reyburn's original version of 'Flushed with Pride' that caused so many myths to arise about Thomas Crapper and much concern to me.

Although Reyburn's book angered me – I was not aware of the interest in the United States – until asked if I would speak to Barbara Walters about it in a telephone link up.

I had engaged Chartered Patent Agents, Carpmaels and Ransford of Chancery Lane in London, to examine the information I had available, to find out the truth about the Crapper myth! First and foremost, I wanted to test the family claim that our 'Beaufort' pedestal WC pan was the first of its kind, and the forerunner of millions sold worldwide ever since.

At the end of their study, this eminent company were prepared to issue a statement saying that '...*the world's first one piece pedestal wash down water closet was designed by Frederick Humpherson*'. It was one of the best investments I ever made!

Nevertheless, I had already found support for our claim in the preface to the 1896 Twyfords Catalogue – see Chapter 7 'The Beaufort WC' – so I was already fairly sure of my ground.

When *'Flushed with Pride – The life and times of Thomas Crapper'* was first published in the United States. Barbara Walters, the well-known reporter interviewed me on CBS Radio and was quite charming. However, I debunked Reyburn's story in such a positive way that the interviewer working with Barbara Walters suggested that the euphemism 'Crap' should be to changed to *'Humph'!*

The book that follows is not intended to be the definitive history of the bathroom. Books such as *'Clean and Decent'* by Lawrence Wright, *'Temples of Convenience'* by Lucinda Lambton with its lavish photographs, *'The Water Closet – A new History'* by Roy Palmer, all provide historical detail. I would particularly recommend *'Bogs, Baths and Basins: The Story of Domestic Sanitation'* by David Eveleigh as it so fully covers all aspects of the subject.

I list these and some of the other books of reference in the acknowledgements and bibliography at the back of the book. What I have tried to achieve here is to 'set-the-scene' for the chapters that follow, leading up to the work done by the great Victorian sanitary engineers, including and especially, my great-uncle Frederick Humpherson.

However, leading on from the Victorian era, the book is about my family's five-generation involvement in the bathroom industry up to Chapter 26 'My family today'. Over the latter years I believe we have contributed in a number of ways to today's scene – not least in setting the trend to realistic showroom displays for kitchens and bathrooms.

Whilst not wanting to give offence, I have not hesitated to use the appropriate words where necessary, and make no apology for doing so! It is difficult to explain the appalling state of sanitation that existed throughout Britain until the late 19th century without some fairly graphic descriptions.

So our story starts – as all stories should – at the beginning!

Chapter 2

Evolution

Any book claiming to deal with 'bathrooms' has to deal with two major aspects: that of hygiene – by which I mean personal cleanliness – and the disposal of human waste.

The problem of disposing of human waste worsened, as prehistoric man began to live in closer to his neighbours in the rudimentary tribal villages that developed. A pit dug outside the village was often the only attempt at disposal, with new pits dug as necessary. The stench, associated with constant living in that environment, would have been overwhelming at times, so the siting of the pits would have been an important communal decision. Personal cleanliness was usually the use of a nearby river or stream.

However, some religious systems set out clear rules for hygienic behaviour. In Chapter 23 of the book Deuteronomy in the old Testament of the Bible, instructs Jews '.....*to have a place outside the camp and go out there, and you shall have a spade among your tools, and it shall be when you sit down outside, you shall dig with it and to turn and cover your excrement.'*

The Bible texts found in the Dead Sea Scrolls are more precise: proper hygiene requires Hebrews *'to defecate 1000 to 2000 cubits (1500 to 4500 feet) away from camp and in a north westerly direction'*. Quite why *'in a north westerly direction'* is not made clear!

One sacred Hindu text instructs followers to *'fire an arrow and defecate where it lands or further'*! The Vishna Purana dating from the first to the third century BCE instructs followers *'to defecate at least 150 feet from a source of water, and to urinate 15 feet away from habitation'*.

As civilisation slowly developed and towns and cities evolved, so the need for drainage became more apparent. We frequently read about the advance made in Roman times but in many earlier civilisations attempts were made to provide bathing facilities and a facility for the disposal of human waste. Ancient sites across the Middle East, for

According to an ancient Hindu text – an archer would select a suitable site to defecate well away from a river – by firing an arrow from its bank. Thus ensuring the continued purity of the water used for cooking and drinking.

instance, bear testimony to the ingenuity of their architects. Over 4000 years ago, the Palace of Knossos on Crete had running water, a proper drainage system throughout, with each branch pipe emptying into a major sewage system, thus ensuring disposal away from the inhabitants.

Egyptian's bathing.

In Greece, ancient Egypt, the Mycenaean culture and the Indus valley, amongst others, there are remains of quite sophisticated drainage and bathing structures, dating from those ancient times. However, these were often associated with palaces and grand houses, rather than the homes of ordinary folk. Nevertheless, we should not assume that all the so-called 'primitive' population were necessarily unhygienic or dirty. Examples exist of crude, but effective washing and toilet facilities across many parts of the ancient world.

When it was excavated, they found that the Sumerian palace of Sargon – known as 'King of Kings' – had six privies in it and these were high, rather like modern day toilets, instead of the more usual Middle East variety, known to us as 'squatting closets'.

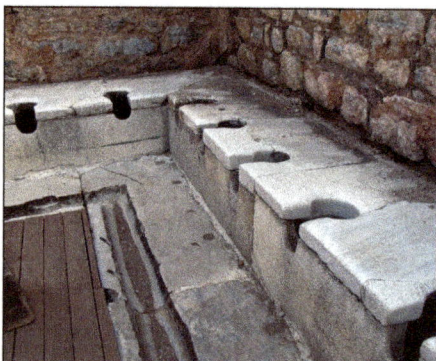

Greek toilets – these were similar to Roman public toilets.

In Egypt, a house belonging to a Court official was discovered dating from about 1300 BC. It contained a bathroom: an anatomically shaped closet carved in marble had a gap front, similar to 'public health' designs, so popular in the 1960's.

One constantly reads of the efficiency of Roman drainage systems, but they were more likely found in palaces, barracks or in larger prestigious homes. Nevertheless, there may well have been a privy in the outhouse of some homes but only a few were connected to an even rudimentary sewer. In most a drainage connection to the privy did not exist. It entailed the removal of waste by slaves to some appropriate site, often an unsavoury pit. There was also a system of 'night men' with pails who would clear the household chamber pots. However, a pot might still be emptied onto the streets below and is recorded in Latin verse.

Roman public baths are well illustrated and rightly deserve praise. They existed in most towns and cities, available for all to use and they were popular meeting places. They were frequently quite luxurious having tepid baths, (the 'Tepidarium') hot water baths (the 'Calderium') cold plunge pools the ('Frigadarium') and often a steam bath. With such a proliferation of public baths there was little need to have private bathing facilities in a more modest home.

Springs or wells could often not support such a large and increasing use of water. However, Rome itself enjoyed the benefit of a stable supply of water, via a series of aqueducts, that were simply a marvel of engineering and essential to the success of the public baths. The aqueduct was a feature across the Roman Empire and was built

A painting showing Roman soldiers in the barrack's toilets. Lacking toilet paper they used a sponge stick washed after use in running water flowing along the channel.

A Roman public toilet. All the details in the picture above can be seen including the water channel to clean the sponge stick!

in most of its major cities. Water flowed both over ground and under ground but the constant flow of fresh supplies meant that the public baths could be emptied, and recharged, overnight. This was very necessary considering the numbers using the facilities – *collectively* – during the day.

It is said that the baths of Diocletian accommodated a staggering 3,000 people whilst those of Caracalla, dating from around 215 A.D., covered an area of 28 acres or six times the area of the site of St. Paul's Cathedral!

Lawrence Wright wrote in his excellent book 'Clean and Decent': *'In the fourth century A.D. Rome had 11 public baths, 1352 public fountains and cisterns, and 856 private baths'.* In addition to private water-flushed latrines, '*....there were plenty of public ones'* (144 is the figure he gives) – and the city supplied water at the staggering rate of *'300 gallons per head, per day'.*

In their conquest of Britain, the Romans brought their concepts of piped running water and bathing with them and built public baths in such places as Harrogate and Chester. However, the most famous was over the

hot springs at Aquae Sulis in Bath. They also brought the idea of 'taking the waters' for medicinal purposes. This happens still at the spas at Harrogate and Bath.

Incidentally, by this time, lead was being used for water supply and drainage, in addition to the long established pipes made from ceramic ware. The Latin for lead is 'Plumbus', from which is derived the name for a 'worker in lead' – a plumber.

The City also provided urinals but this was not altogether done as a public service. The urine was

The famous thermal Roman baths at Bath.

collected for use by the local dye-makers and the tax on their profits eventually added to the Emperor's income. Sometimes, there were just large pots on the corner of a street, rented by the city to those who collected the urine for sale and they too were taxed accordingly.

For centuries, Imperial rule covered the Mediterranean, and most of the countries bordering it, giving many attendant benefits – most especially for Roman citizens. Its rule brought order to everyone within its boundaries and a higher standard of life for all – except perhaps the many thousands of slaves.

The Empire declined in the centuries following the death of Christ as the Byzantine influence grew across the eastern Mediterranean. They too provided aids for bathing and the provision of WCs, if mainly for nobility the priesthood and leading officials of the state. Such WCs, however crude, can be found in castles and palaces in Cyprus and in the countries bordering the eastern Mediterranean coasts. However, most other countries – freed from Roman rule – fell into anarchy and one of the most curious aspects of the period called the 'Dark Ages' is how sanitation became almost non-existent. In Britain, bathing was no longer regarded as an essential daily routine – indeed there are claims that an annual bath was acceptable.

Running alongside the lack of personal hygiene was the return of cesspits and the like, for disposal of waste, in place of drainage into sewers. This state of affairs continued for centuries and so disease became rife in villages and towns throughout the land. It can be said that from the Romans leaving Britain around 410 A.D. the British lost all sense of cleanliness and hygiene for a thousand years.

In the early 1300s, some forms of sanitary facilities were being installed in monasteries and cathedrals such as running water, baths and latrines. At the time of the Black Death in 1350, when tens of thousands died, there were only five public toilet facilities in the whole of the City of London! Perhaps more accurately one could say these were the 'Dark and *Dirty* Ages!'.

Extraordinarily, houses were built with a privy overhanging a river or stream, so that the water below carried the discharge away, thus contaminating the water along its path. An example is that over the River Frome into Bristol. The river is now partially

The River Frome flowing under St John's Bridge in Bristol looks attractive enough in this 1821 watercolour by Hugh O'Neill. However, hanging over the river were privies and raw sewage from them drained into the river underneath – creating a stream of filth. The privies depended on the flow of water to clear it but with low water it lay on the mud. The Frome now runs in a culvert through parts of Bristol.

built over but overhanging privies, discharging body wastes directly into the river below, existed until the early 19th Century. Effectively, using the river as a sewer.

Similar privies were common over the Fleet River in the City of London that lead through the centre of the city. The Fleet rises from various places including Hampstead and Highgate ponds. In Roman times the Fleet was a major river having access to the Thames. By the 13th century, the Fleet river was so choked with the discharge from several open sewers, and numerous overhanging privies, as to be almost solid. Although overhanging privies were so obviously a health hazard and had been prescribed from time to time, you could still instal one – provided you were alongside running water and paid an annual fee of 2 shillings.

It was common practice to empty one's chamber pot from an upstairs window, often regardless of who was passing below. This was banned in Paris in 1395 but the classical cry of 'gardez l'eau' was heard in Edinburgh as late as the 1700s.

Of course, it was not only the contents of pots that were emptied, but household rubbish might well find its way from an upstairs window onto the street below. In 1877, Mr. S. S. Hellyer of Dent & Hellyer, a firm of sanitary engineers in Victorian London, wrote in the first edition of his book 'The Plumber and Sanitary Houses' of the need, *'in years gone by'* to take a guide in the streets at night to avoid *disagreeable accidents from the windows'*. It was the guide's task to call out *'Haud your han'* as he and his party passed along. Hellyer goes on to remark, it must have been a good time for hatters and tailors!

The extensive gardens and grounds in country houses were often recommended as the place to 'pluck a rose' – surely the nicest of all euphemisms! Jonathan Swift in a pamphlet dated 1745, entitled 'Directions to a Servant' condemned women who would not relieve themselves in the garden, thus leaving the servants to clear smelly pots from various rooms in the house. However, most did not own gardens and certainly not of sufficient size to provide an element of privacy, whilst 'plucking a rose!'.

Castles frequently had a 'garde-robe' built into the thickness of the castle walls – a small cupboard-like space with a hole cut into the stone. This sometimes, but not always, had a wooden seat. The privy discharged down a vertical shaft in the inner structure of the wall and then into the moat or stream. It was often left to collect at the foot of the castle wall, there to be occasionally removed by serfs. In larger castles, the garderobe might be off the adjacent 'wardrobe' used for washing and dressing.

In 1969, I worked in such a castle together with my brother Ronald and my son Michael. At Castle Stalker on Loch Linnhe, near Appin in Argyll, we converted a 'garde-robe' into a modern WC area. As the Castle was built on an island we had a variety of problems but the full story is told in Chapter 20.

Bathing in the 'Dark Ages' was quite a rare occurrence so I am not surprised at the attention the lucky man is receiving!

Through the years and on into the Middle Ages, little changed in bathing habits or in the provision of toilet facilities. However, one bright spark ignited briefly. The designs of Sir John Harington could have made a difference – had anybody followed them up.

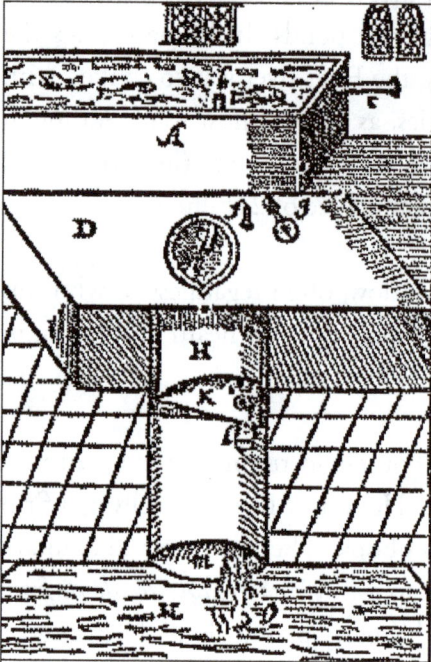

The first known attempt at a flushing toilet in England was by Sir John Harington. He made one for Queen Elizabeth and installed it in Richmond Palace – her favourite home. Apparently it was little used as being too noisy!

There is no doubt that the most famous water closet of the middle ages was that invented by Sir John Harington. He was distantly related to Queen Elizabeth, as well as being her godson. His device was first installed in a new house constructed for him at Kelston near Bath. The estate had come to him as a part of the dowry when he married Mary Rogers. The Queen later stayed in the new house and pronounced herself so pleased with the contraption she ordered one to be built in her palace at Richmond in Surrey.

The Harington designs were not developed in any way, so it was some 200 years before the water closet concept was taken further. The nobility had its padded chamber pots; in the case of Henry VIII it had been covered in velvet and was portable. Similar such unsanitary devices were also used by Charles 1st, his son Charles 2nd as well as James 1st.

Increasingly, a form of chair (complete with armrests) would be used with a ceramic pot placed under a wooden seat. Famous furniture makers like Sheraton and Chippendale made these commodes and which would be sited in various parts of the house – but most frequently in a bedroom. It is said that Louis XIV 'The Sun King' had no less than 260 commodes spread around the Palace of Versailles. Small wonder that men and women of fashion often carried a posy of scented flowers.

Nevertheless, the bowl still required emptying but fortunately there was a plentiful supply of servants for such odorous tasks. It was also fairly common practice, even in society, to relieve oneself behind the curtains, or screens – preferably with a chamber pot!

However, some progress was made in bathing habits. Although the wooden tub of the Middle Ages was still occasionally used in the

I took this picture in Henry VIII's favourite palace – Hampton Court. A velvet seat is hardly the most hygienic but I remember the occasion well. Taking two grandchildren on a tour, I spotted the WC and had to add it to my collection. However, I leant in too far and set off the alarms causing two burly guards to appear – who roundly admonished me. I apologised profusely and thankfully was not led away to the Tower of London!

country, the need to bath more frequently than Queen Elizabeth 1st – 'once a month whether she needed it or not' – became more in vogue. Whilst in the late 1700s proper bathhouses were built in grand homes, a small metal bathtub in front of the fire began to be appreciated, and a small step towards personal cleanliness had been achieved.

At the same time, long overdue improvements in sanitation slowly came about. Ceramic pans were being made for connection to the drain; either to an outside cesspit, or to the fairly basic sewers – where one existed.

These bowls were flushed by a variety of means – from the simple tipping of a pail of water to flush them – to a water connection such as in the simple hopper closet. These were very rudimentary affairs but had the advantage of a trap to contain water, and thus keep noxious smells from returning from the drainage below. It was the 1700s and things were *slowly* moving forward!

There was a long period when a dreadful device called the 'pan closet' was in use. In this, an upper earthenware pan was fitted over a metal bowl containing a few inches of water. After use, the bowl was tipped into the cast iron dish below and thence into the drains.

It needs little imagination to realize why this was later described by S. S. Hellyer) '*….almost the most unsanitary closet in use…….the only bliss being that the public were ignorant of its nature'*. However, the pan closet had a long run and was only gradually replaced by the water closet.

Now at last designers came on the scene, prepared to take a new look at this most fundamental of human activities. The most famous of the early pioneers was Alexander Cumming born in Edinburgh in 1772. He moved to London where he became a renowned watch and clock maker. He had many other interests and produced his patent for a 'water closet' in 1775. This held water in the pan by means of a sliding plate at the bottom of the bowl. When that was removed the contents flowed out. It also allowed the contents of the bowl to then enter an 'S' trap thus creating an element of syphonage – and aiding the discharge to the drains. At the same time the 'S' trap sealed off the foul smells coming back up from the drainage beyond. However, a major drawback to the design was that as fresh water entered to flush the contents from the bowl – *the sliding plate was out of the pan* – so on return remained foul from the previous user.

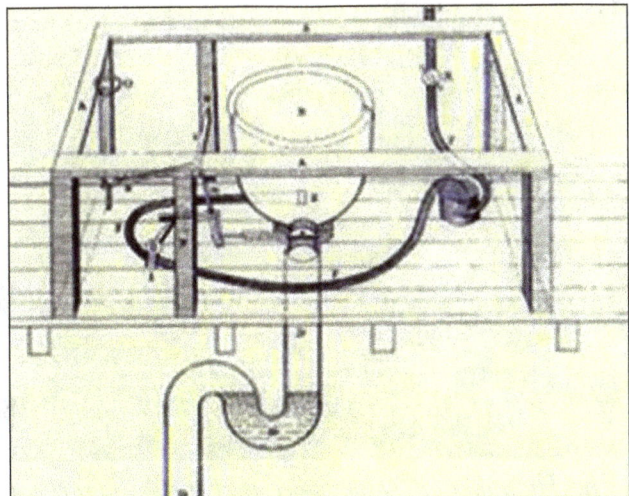

Alexander Cumming was a watchmaker with wide interests. He produced his 'water closet' and patented it in 1775. It was distinctive by having a trap below to keep noxious fumes from the drains coming back.

Lemuel Prosser, who created a rather complicated system of levers, with the aim of having a trap-less WC, quickly followed Cumming's invention. This was patented in 1777 – clearly improvements now seemed to be coming forward more rapidly.

Perhaps the best device of this particular period that we might call the 'first sanitary revolution' came a year later in 1778, when Joseph Bramah patented his own water closet. This turned out to be a huge success, and set the scene for almost a hundred years! His closet had a valve at the bottom of the bowl that worked on a hinge – a predecessor to the modern ball valve. Bramah was a prodigious inventor, being responsible for designing successful products in such varied fields as steam and rotary engines, boilers and of course, the famous locks that bear his name today.

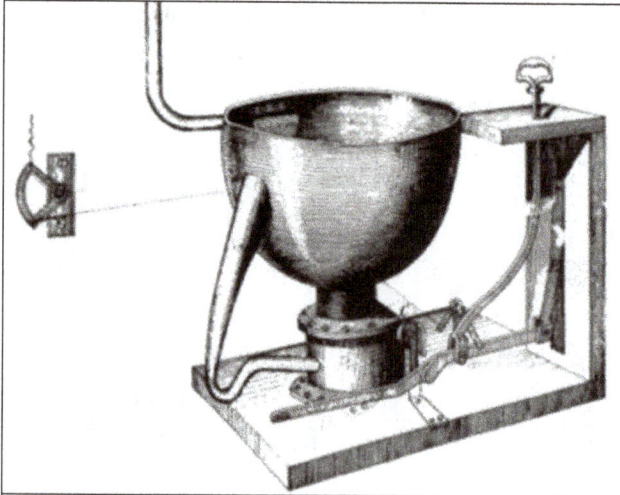

Joseph Bramah's valve closet – patented in 1778 – an improvement on that of Cummings in that the plate hinged and was thus cleansed by the incoming flow of water.

Bramah's closet differs fundamentally, in that the water was held in the WC pan by a hinged plate, instead of the sliding plate in Cumming's design. This idea of a hinged plate continued to be the basic design of the 'valve closet' and the general design was gradually improved by a number of manufacturers. Including Frederick Underhay, a sanitary engineer of Farrington Street London. Similar products were still being in made until the early 1900s – demonstrating the success of his designs.

At the end of World War II in 1945, Humpherson & Co. still had stocks of valve closet parts. Later, from time to time, my brother Ron and I personally repaired valve closets, for special clients. Once we repaired a closet said to come from Windsor Castle. Our stocks were still sufficient, so that until the late 1950s, we were able to supply spare parts to E. J. Margrie & Sons of Dovehouse Street, Chelsea, who also repaired valve closets.

The Humpherson valve closet in Chester Square in London's Belgravia district. When I was asked to check its function, I found it only needed a slight adjustment to the damper arm. The bowl is decorated with a floral pattern. The Humpherson badge and water level can be clearly seen. It might still be in operation somewhere in Chester Square?

Sometime in the early 1960s, I was asked by an architect friend to go to look at a 'Humpherson valve closet' in a house in Chester Square as he thought it needed some adjustment. I was surprised to find the valve was in good working condition and told the grateful owner that it had years of life left in it. I photographed it and then, *rather optimistically,* asked if he would like to exchange it for a new modern water closet of his choice, have the room decorated as he wished plus a generous financial consideration. He thanked me but said he would keep the 'Humpherson Valve Closet just as it was but added *'I will leave it to you in my Will'*. Sadly, I have heard nothing over the subsequent fifty plus years but perhaps one day…..?

One more incident about our connection with valve closets arose at a management meeting at The Savoy Hotel in London, where we were supplying the hotel with sanitary fittings. I should add that we had become a regular supplier to The Savoy and several times I had the pleasure of meeting Dame Bridget Cicely D'Oyly Carte DBE, the owner of the Hotel and the Opera Company that bore her name. At that time, she was still very much in control and closely concerned herself

A close up of a Humpherson unused valve closet bowl from our memorabilia collection. This has its original price sticker on its corner. The figures have long since faded. but in any case it is priceless to me!

with anything to do with refurbishment. We were only supplying the sanitary fittings to the hotel but the plumbing contractors carrying out the installation were also at that meeting – Stitson-White & Co. based in Victoria.

At the meeting, it was mentioned in passing, that valve closets were once in parts of the original hotel. I then said I had just put in a valve closet, still in working order, on display in our showrooms. The following day, Mr Smith, the owner of Stitson-White, telephoned to tell me that they were also carrying out urgent plumbing work at Buckingham Palace – appointed by the Ministry of Works, the Government Department then responsible for the upkeep of the Royal Palaces. Apparently, a damper in a valve closet in a WC – close to where an Investiture was about to take place – needed repair!

Please, would I allow them to collect the damper off our valve closet and use it, rather than attempt to make one? Although I realised I would be now unlikely to receive a Knighthood – I finally decided to decline the request!

This then, is the background to the slow evolution of sanitary fitments and its attendant sewage disposal over centuries – until the reign of Queen Victoria when so much changed! However, these rapid developments were made more urgent by a great rise in disease, so much of which could be attributed to overcrowding, foul drains, hopelessly inadequate water supplies and poor sewage facilities.

**These factors will be explored in the next chapter –
Water supply and the Thames as a sewer.**

Chapter 3

Water Supply and the Thames as a Sewer

In ancient times, towns and villages grew alongside or very near rivers – as it is obviously necessary to have water nearby for drinking and washing. Sadly, however, the waterways were also used as an easy way to take away the daily detritus and sewage created. Much disease arose because 'someone' was further down stream and on the receiving end of the filth, resulting in the diseases it thus encouraged.

Much of this book refers to London so let me use the Thames as an example. I acknowledge it is the largest of our rivers but the same story applies to most of the waterways across the country. What makes it worse than most is the high level of housing and population that grew so rapidly alongside the river in London.

The Thames rises at Thames Head near Cirencester in the Cotswolds. For the first few miles, it meanders through the countryside, very much as it did hundreds of years ago. However, throughout its journey something like forty rivers and small streams feed into it. In the middle ages, the Thames still supported fish of all kinds and salmon ran right up the river being caught at Hampton Court and beyond. Salmon were

This is an open sewer in late Victorian times running through Silvertown (now within the London Borough of Newham) on the north of the Thames.

so plentiful at the time that employers, taking on apprentices in London, had to agree not to serve salmon to them on more than two days a week.

The Thames could cope with the relatively small amount of sewage being discharged into its tributaries when there was a low density of population alongside it. However, the industrial revolution in Britain was linked to a population explosion in the early 19th Century. This was leading people to move away from the countryside to the expanding towns associated with burgeoning industries of all kinds. They were seduced by the higher wages available than working on the land, a break from the seasonal nature of employment and in some cases by better housing than a tied cottage.

In 500 A.D. London's population was in the region 5,000 and that remained the likely level until the Norman Conquest when it rose to rapidly to about 40,000. In 1700 it was estimated to have grown to 700,000. However, the sheer scale of increase in the 19th Century is shown by the following figures.

1841 – Census 1,948,417
1861 – Census 2,803,989
1881 – Census 3,815,544
1891 – Census 4,211,056 Over the Greater London area it totaled 5,633,332.

At the 1851 census it was found that more people were living in towns and cities than on the land. The census showed that the population was growing at a faster rate than any time since the 14th century, the time of the Black Death.

This growth led in turn, to enormous pressures on services of all kinds. Not least, of course, was housing and sanitation. Largely unplanned tenement buildings, cheaply erected to house the mass of people swarming into towns, were teeming but with the very minimum of toilet facilities – often one toilet to a dozen or more families. Washing took place in the kitchen sink that was also sometimes shared. Bathing – if it was undertaken – was in a zinc tub fed by hot water from a kettle over the kitchen fire.

Whilst water closets had started to appear in greater numbers in the late 18th century, they were still being connected to drains that led into sewers, both of which were intended for carrying just rainwater. To make matters worse, in 1815, it became legal to connect house-drains to the sewers.

This is the River Fleet, an open sewer running through the City of London. You can just make out an overhanging privie on the right hand side of the building. It is one of hundreds all discharging into the river below. The river was gradually built over from the 1790s until the 1870s when it was finally covered from end to end.

The raw sewage, now increasingly being introduced into the drains from water closets, was expected to eventually find its way to a river. It should also be noted that the drains themselves were usually either wooden pipes, box-drains lined with porous bricks or open drains. There was a likelihood – some would say a certainty – of the sewage leaking into adjacent building land and watercourses.

Many rivers, wells and springs – many probably contaminated – were used by the local Water Company to extract water for drinking and domestic use!

An outbreak of fever in Westminster led to the discovery of old cesspits and blocked sewers under the Abbey precincts. As a result 500 cartloads of faecal matter had to be carted away!

Is there any wonder that diseases of all kinds flourished – but when cholera struck for the first time in 1831-1832 – the authorities became truly alarmed. To give some idea of the gravity of the outbreak, over 32,000 died in a three-month period of 1832. Cholera struck again in 1848 and 1854.

The prevailing belief amongst the medical profession was that all disease was carried in the air and from contaminated vapours. All fevers and deaths were explained as being 'Miasmas' – arising from decaying waste that poisoned the air.

Today, it is hard us to imagine the stench in a city of those times. London, like many other cities, had very narrow streets with little ventilation between. Horses were used for every form of transport with ensuing piles of manure accumulating. Streets were full of garbage, there were open drains – so it was not difficult to associate illness with these appalling conditions. Typhus, typhoid, diarrhoea and diphtheria were rife arising from flies, fleas and the insanitary conditions.

There was no local authority to ensure overflowing privies and drains were cleared, or the that the heaps of garbage dealt was with adequately. Parish Councils had some responsibility but no real powers or funds to keep in check the amount of filth of all kinds that was accumulating.

The first real attempt to codify the changes needed was by a leading reformer and campaigner of the day, Edwin Chadwick. He was secretary of the Poor Law Commission and wrote a report in 1842 entitled *'The Sanitary Condition of the Labouring Classes of Great Britain'*. He revealed the terrible sanitary conditions under which families were living across the land and advocated, amongst other vital changes, potable water, underground drainage and sewerage, and prompt removal of refuse of all kinds. He also proposed that responsibility for public health works should be in the hands of qualified civil engineers instead of incompetent local politicians.

The steps he put forward were aimed at reducing the large amount of preventable diseases brought about by the low standards of sanitation and water supply. He should also be remembered for putting forward the idea of glazed drain and sewer pipes, instead of the old drains made of brick or porous earthenware. There were a number of pottery firms in Lambeth at that time but of all of them, Henry Doulton saw the potential in glazed pipes and had the ability to manufacture them.

Sir Edwin Chadwick (1800-1890). The Chadwick report of 1842 was a significant step in the movement towards waterborne sanitation.

He proposed there be a Minister of Health and in 1843 a Royal Commission was set up to consider the serious matters he had raised. In 1848 The Public Health Act was passed, including a General Board of Health under Lord Shaftsbury (the pioneer of factory reform). The major problems of London were to be dealt with by a separate body, the Metropolitan Commisioners of Sewers. Much debate then took place, but the money was

PUNCH, OR THE LONDON CHARIVARI, JULY 10, 1858.

THE "SILENT HIGHWAY"-MAN.
"Your MONEY or your LIFE!"

'Death on the Thames.' London's vast increase in population without adequate sewers led to the stagnation in properties across London. It was impossible to avoid the smell in the House of Commons so at last they agreed the works be put in hand to eliminate the causes.

not forthcoming in the volume required to deal with such a vast problem. Chadwick was a most difficult man to deal with, and in many ways, his own worst enemy. His sensible proposals would probably have been acted upon faster, had he been more amenable.

All of this time, the various rivers and sewers leading into the Thames were carrying increasing amounts of raw sewage, giving rise to considerable alarm. In 1858, the crisis came to a peak when the 'Great Stink' of London occurred. The overpowering stench from the Thames was such that at the House of Commons the curtains were soaked in chloride of lime in an attempt to reduce the stink! The smell reached such an intolerable level that sittings at the House had to be abandoned. No surprise perhaps, that at last something was done. A Bill was rushed through Parliament providing money for a massive new sewer scheme for London and an embankment built along the side of the Thames to speed the flow of its water.

The Metropolitan Board of Works had been created in 1855 but funds were not forthcoming until after 'The Great Stink' of 1858. A concerted effort was started in 1859 to contain the city's sewage by constructing massive sewers on the north and south embankments of the Thames, under the supervision of a brilliant engineer Joseph Bazalgette. It is clear that this period of the Victorian era was a time of imaginative engineering. Simultaneously, huge undertakings took place to ensure water supplies with the building of reservoirs and pumping stations on the river to the west of London. The newly built embankments also protected London from flood.

In 1844, Albert, the Prince Consort, had been appalled to learn that there were over forty cesspits overflowing under Windsor Castle. He gave instructions to have all the commodes removed and replaced with water closets feeding into drains. Sadly, they probably ended in the nearby River Thames. However, it is ironic that this pioneer of 'all

The mastermind behind the work was Joseph Bazalgette a civil Engineer who had previously worked on the expansion of the infant rail network. The Metropolitan Commission of Works had ordered all London cesspits to be closed and the toilets to be connected to the sewers emptying into the Thames. As a result, in1848/49 a cholera epidemic killed 14,137 people. In 1853, another epidemic killed 10,738. So in 1858 Bazalgette was given the vast job of building new sewers leading to the east of London and building the Embankment to speed the flow of the Thames.

things scientific' should die in 1861 from typhoid – probably arising from defective drains!

Ten years later, in 1871, his son Edward, Prince of Wales, was near to death from typhoid. He was staying with Lady Londsborough at Scarborough and a fellow guest died of the disease. The cause of the infection was finally traced to defective drains. It is perhaps this event, as much as anything that had gone before, that finally jolted public opinion to hasten wider sanitary reforms.

Harper's Magazine reviewing Hellyer's 'Lecture on the Science and Art of Sanitary Plumbing' states that H.R.H. The Prince of Wales had said – when recovering from the fever that was nearly fatal – *'If I were not a Prince, I would be a plumber.'* Hellyer went on to say *'This illness of the Prince (perhaps from bad plumbing) has done more for the advancement of the principles of sanitary plumbing than could have been accepted from being a member of the craft.'*

It is no coincidence that so many patents in the sanitary field appeared at this time, but running alongside the question of sanitation, was the problem of providing the population with clean, pure domestic drinking water. Unfortunately, this was almost impossible as so much was drawn from contaminated rivers or wells.

The size of the sewers can be seen in this early photograph. Most were cut and covered then building eventually took place above.

This picture shows Bazalgette's foresight in providing capacity for many years ahead. Indeed, it is only now that we are constructing a replacement sewage system for London, after a five times growth in population over that in 1858.

The dreadful cholera epidemic was widely blamed on miasmas – a highly unpleasant and unhealthy smell or vapours. However, a totally different view was about to be put forward. John Snow had first served an apprenticeship to a surgeon in Newcastle, then moved to London and went to medical school for two years, graduating M.D. in 1844. Later he was accepted as a member of the Royal College of Surgeons.

Snow wrote a paper in 1849, declaring that cholera was spread through the body by contaminated water or food. This was entirely the reverse of medical advice of the day – still stuck with the miasma theory. His paper created much ill feeling towards him from the media and from the medical profession.

A repeat outbreak of cholera in 1854 enabled Snow to prove his argument. In the 1850s two companies supplied London's water. One of these took their water from the Thames upstream above the area of major conurbation, whereas the other drew theirs from below the city. It was found there was a higher incidence of

A cartoon showing Death dispensing drinking water from the infamous public water pump in Broad Street (now renamed Broadwick Street) Soho.

A replica of the Soho public water pump erected as a memorial to John Snow. On a nearby corner is a public house called 'The John Snow'!

cholera in the area supplied from downstream – indicating that this water was contaminated by the larger input of sewage.

He was able to pinpoint the cause of a particularly bad outbreak in Soho in August of 1854, when *each day* brought a hundred or more cases of this most dreadful disease. He marked a map showing the homes where the deaths occurred and found they centred on a popular pump in Broad Street where local residents were drawing their water from a well some 30 feet deep. However, close to the well some 25 feet down was a defective sewer and the well was contaminated with infected sewage from that and nearby cesspits. The authorities took the handle of the pump away – and the outbreak in the region started to subside.

The River Thames has served many roles in human history, being an economic resource, a water highway, a boundary, a source of fresh water, a source of food and a sewer at times. However, due to the immense efforts by our Victorian forebears, it has more recently become a leisure facility.

John Burns (1858-1943) was a Member of Parliament for Battersea, a London Borough that lies along the south bank of the Thames. In response to comments from an American visitor, he said of his beloved Thames:

'The St Lawrence is water, the Mississippi is muddy water but the Thames is liquid history.'

Chapter 4

The19th Century – from Squalor to the Great Victorian Innovations

Few will deny that Queen Victoria's reign saw immense changes in Britain's wealth, lifestyle and, for some, a considerable improvement in living standards. Looking around our towns and cities one can still find the splendid town halls, schools, police stations, prisons, sewage plants, railway stations water works, and so on, built in the latter years of that extraordinary period. It was a time of great wealth but the authorities ensured that money was spent on the infrastructure – even enlightened housing schemes were undertaken.

However, the 19th century did not start off like that and its early years saw the desperately low levels of sanitation worsen in the cities. This was because of massive overcrowding due to the population increase, coupled with the influx of country dwellers to the towns and cities. Nor, in truth, did the later improvements in living standards reach right down to the poorest classes. It is no exaggeration to say that the wretchedness of the past continued and especially showed up in sanitary facilities. So the century seems to divide into broadly two halves. From the continued squalor of the past, gradually improving into the second half when so many substantial developments came about.

Before recalling some of the more outstanding sanitary engineers of the time, I think it is as well to remind us of the scale of the problem the authorities faced. I am fortunate to have a leather bound copy of the Parish of Lambeth Annual Report, for the years 1882 – 1884. This is concerned with deaths from various diseases, showing the total deaths in the parish area, compared to those in the Metropolis as a whole. It is comprehensive – giving information about individual roads. It details sanitary conditions and the work of the Parish sanitary inspectors for the year 1881. These cover such varied areas as 'Houses Cleaned 364' – 'Obstructed drains cleared 992' – 'Accumulations of dung removed 228' and some 20 other headings, including a number of 'Cesspools abolished'! Reading it makes one realise how far we have come since.

In passing, I note they also inspected 80 'Slaughter Houses' and 82 'Cow Houses' in the parish. One might be surprised that such activities were still taking place in London. However, my mother recalls there was earlier a licenced slaughterhouse in Fulham Road Chelsea, right opposite Holmes Place where Frederick Humpherson lived, until his death in 1919.

But it is the deaths arising from 'Zymotic' (infectious) diseases in the Lambeth area that should be examined closely and these are shown in the illustration. There were a total of 1030 such deaths in that year, against an average of 1137 in the previous five years.

§ 84

by the presence of large public Hospitals in certain districts, as of the London Fever and Homerton Hospitals in the North, and of the Stockwell Fever Hospital in the South."

In the following Table I have divided the year into 13 periods of 4 weeks each, corresponding with the Monthly Reports to the Vestry, for the purpose of showing the seasons at which particular Zymotics were most fatal, and also to compare the mortality from each disease with the average mortality from that disease during the preceeding 5 years.

Period.	Disease.									
Four Weeks ending	Small Pox.	Measles.	Scarlet Fever.	Diphtheria.	Whooping Cough.	Typhus Fever.	Enteric Fever.	Sim. Cond. Fever.	Diarrhœa.	Total.
1881										
Jan. 29 ...	24	7	29	1	12	...	7	1	4	85
Feb. 26 ...	35	3	18	3	10	...	10	1	3	83
Mar. 26 ...	26	1	11	1	9	...	4	...	3	55
April 23 ...	29	8	14	4	9	...	4	3	1	72
May 21 ...	19	5	15	1	8	...	2	...	3	53
June 18 ...	16	4	14	3	6	2	5	3	5	58
July 16 ...	13	5	7	3	12	5	3	...	42	90
Aug. 13 ...	15	14	20	2	9	2	4	1	83	150
Sept. 10 ...	7	11	16	2	7	3	4	...	29	79
Oct. 8 ...	4	4	13	...	9	1	11	1	8	51
Nov. 5 ...	8	9	30	5	5	3	21	2	7	90
Dec. 3 ...	5	18	19	10	8	2	11	...	3	76
Dec. 31 ...	9	33	10	2	15	1	15	...	3	88
Total ...	210	122	216	37	119	19	101	12	194	1030
Average for last 5 years 1876-1880	172.6	121.8	223.6	50	215.6	22.8	85.6	16.2	229.4	1137.6

Note.—To these may be added 5 deaths from Cholera, which ought perhaps to be included in Diarrhœa.

A page from 'Parish of Lambeth Annual Report' showing deaths from various illnesses – many we now know were due to insanitary conditions and/or overcrowding.

You will see there are deaths from such causes as smallpox, totalling 210 – with 35 in February alone. Diarrhoea caused 194 deaths and the author has added: *'Note. To these may be added 5 deaths from Cholera, which ought perhaps be included in Diarrhoea'.*

All these deaths were taking place in one year in Lambeth – just one of London's many boroughs and actually demonstrate substantial *improvements* over earlier years!

Today, we know that most of the diseases listed had been caused by insanitary conditions and/ or overcrowding. However, whilst waterborne sanitation was now the main direction of the growing sanitary industry, I need to mention first the sanitary fitments and methods of waste disposal widely used in the middle part of the century. We find 'Dry earth and ash privies' – 'Tipper closets' and 'Troughs'.

The Dry Earth Closet and Ash Privy

The Earth Closet

Of the two, the more important was the earth closet designed by the Reverend Henry Moule. The sixth son of George Moule, solicitor and banker, he was born at Melksham, Wiltshire on 27 January 1801 and educated at Marlborough Grammar School. He was ordained to the curacy of Melksham in 1823 and took sole charge of Gillingham, Dorset in 1825. He was made vicar of Fordington in the same county in 1829 and remained there the remainder of his life.

During the cholera outbreaks of 1849 and 1854 he worked tirelessly to help the poor in his parish and surrounding villages – where most lived with appalling sanitary conditions. He feared the disease posed a threat to his family and knowing of the recent discovery of the cause of cholera he decided to do something about the problem. Around the summer of 1859 – it is thought – he decided his use of the cesspit was intolerable, and a nuisance to the neighbourhood.

So he filled the cesspit in and instructed all his family to use buckets instead. At first he buried the sewage in trenches in the garden, one foot deep, but discovered by accident that in three or four weeks 'not a trace of this matter could be discovered'.

He then found that he could recycle the earth, and use the same batch several times, and he began to grow lyrical. 'Water is only a vehicle for removing it out of sight and off the premises. It neither absorbs nor effectively deodorizes. The best agent is dried surface earth, both for absorption and for deodorising offensive matters.' And, he said, he no longer threw away valuable manure but obtained a 'luxuriant growth of vegetables in my garden'.

Deeply impressed by the dirty and unhygienic state of their houses, he turned his attention to sanitary science and invented what is called the dry earth system. He took out a patent for the process (No. 1316, dated 28 May 1860). His system was adopted in private houses, in rural districts, in military camps, in many hospitals and extensively in India. It smothered the odour, kept the flies off and slowly broke down the germs. In the country, the resultant mixture was commonly used as fertiliser.

Moule's design, though following the age-old principle of 'smothering' the intestinal contents with earth – was a mechanical operation. The design was thus a substantial step forward and many were installed, especially in the more affluent households.

As a vicar, Reverend Henry Moule did not approve of the Water Closet. He felt it caused the pollution of God's rivers and seas. Most of all it was a waste of God's nutrients contained in excrement that should be returned to the soil. His Earth Closet allowed human manure to be saved, for return to the soil without the owner having to endure the stink of the average privy or cesspit.

How the Moule Earth Closet works: When the handle is pulled, a little dry earth or peat is spread on top of the human waste to reduce the smell and help it to decay. When the bucket is full the contents are dug into the garden and continue to decay.

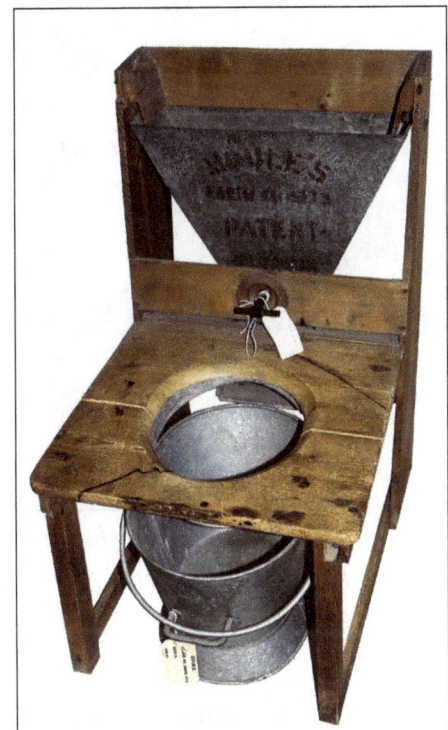

The Revd. Henry Moule designed his 'Earth Closet' to replace the use of a cesspit so common at the time. Instead, he had a bucket underneath the seat and after use a handle was pulled to dump a quantity of dried earth on the 'contents'.

However, whilst the dry earth closet was very suitable to country areas, dry earth was not so freely available in towns and so, there, the Ash Privy prevailed.

The Ash Privy

As an alternative to the earth closet in rural areas, town dwellers could use cold ashes from the fires instead – but the principle was the same. A shovel was used to spread cold ash from the fires over the excrement to make it less odorous – and hopefully – less likely to cause diseases. Later quite complex appliances were designed to make the ash deposit take place mechanically – rather than to use a shovel!

One of these designers was John Conyers Morrell, who became an inventor and manufacturer of ash closets. Bear in mind that coal was plentiful and, due to the expanding rail system, was cheap across the whole country. Many homes had a fireplace in each room and the occupants depended on coal for warmth, as well as cooking in kitchen ranges. As a result, there was a daily output of cold ash that had no other use and needed to be disposed of in some way. Clearly the concept of using the ash to first 'smother' the excrement to reduce the odour and then make it more easily disposable – found many willing to become involved in the rapidly expanding 'industry' that built up around it.

LONDON NIGHTMEN.

[From a Daguerreotype by BEARD.]

The night cart man collecting buckets of from homes with ash privies instead of earth closets.

However, 'Night Carts' would still have to collect the contents of the pails or empty the ash pit on a fairly regular basis, with some local councils requiring the ash pit to be emptied once a week.

The 'Night Cart' was a contractor who would go round with a horse and cart at night and remove the foul waste, for a weekly fee. Such men operated in towns and villages and were essential in the absence of waterborne sanitation. The 'Night Cart' was a long established part of living and they cleared privies of all kinds, including the 'pail privy' (or bucket) that was used before the earth closet. The clear cesspits and ash pits were cleared on a regular basis.

In large towns and cities the municipal authorities sometimes supplied a 'Night Cart' service but otherwise these were 'freelance' operators who had to be paid by those who used the service.

Cesspit (or Cesspool)

A cesspit is a sealed tank for the reception and temporary storage of sewage. As it is sealed, the tank must be emptied frequently – in many cases as often as weekly. Because of the need for frequent emptying of cesspits the cost of maintenance was quite high.

In rural areas, the builder of a cesspit sometimes breached the floor of the pit so as to allow liquid from the tank to escape into the ground. Such incidents often gave rise to local pollution and possible contamination of the drinking water supplies.

A cesspit or cesspool was usually constructed like a dry well and would generally be lined with loose-fitting brick or stone. Liquids leach out if soil conditions allow, while solids decay and collect as a composted matter in the base of the cesspool. As the solids accumulate, eventually they block the escape of liquids, causing the cesspool to leach out more slowly or to overflow. Then the 'Night Cart' became needed – *urgently!*

As these rather different concepts in toilet design, the Earth Closet and Ash Closet, were in such widespread use, is right to mention them before returning to waterborne sanitation. However, before doing so we must look at one other form of closet – the humble Chamber Pot.

The Chamber Pot

Until the 18th century, the chamber pot was the usual form of household toilet that had to be emptied into the nearest open sewer or cesspit. The chamber pot remained in most households for night time use as a urinal, until inside toilets became more common. The pots were often placed behind the curtains in a room and men would 'retire' behind the curtain to relieve themselves, in special cabinets, or in 'night stands'.

Where servants were employed, it was the Scullery Maid's or 'Tweeny's' job to empty the chamber pots – a constant task throughout the day. In Victorian times, such a servant was expected to work up to 15 hours a day at this, and other menial tasks, for which she received £13 per annum i.e. £0.25p – or 25 pence per week.

The chamber pots of the working-class were sometimes made of copper, although later ones were usually crockery. Chamber pots were a big part of the pottery industry as most houses had a pot for each bedroom, usually under the bed, as well as numerous ones around the house – in strategic places. The designs and quality improved over time and now these are regarded as collector's pieces. The chamber pots for the very rich and royalty might also be of silver. In the Victorian period there was even a musical chamber pot that played when the lid was opened.

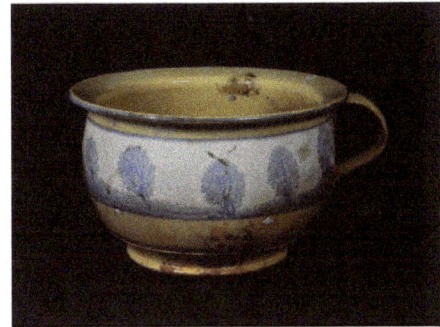

The chamber pot. This was a very common item in every household. In earlier times they would be placed around the house, behind curtains, in a cupboard, indeed anywhere just out of sight. It would be a servant's job to empty them and ensuring a clean one was put in place. In Victorian times they were more likely to be 'in emergency' or more usually under the bed to save going out to the backyard privy. They were often called a 'goesunder' meaning they go under the bed.

The 'Tipper' or 'Slop' closet

Although these depended on water to clear the contents, they could be said to come between the ash or earth closet and the proper water closets that follow. These devices were an attempt to improve sanitary conditions and called the 'Tipper' or 'Slop' closet. The best-known exponent was the firm of Ducketts of Burnley. Founded in 1859 by James Duckett, a builder who specialised in high quality work, such as churches. He had noticed during a train journey that a railway cutting went through soil suitable for brick making.

He purchased the nearby land and commenced making bricks. Later, following the example of Henry Doulton, he started making salt-glazed pipes. Factory production developed into urinal slabs, sinks, closets and other sanitary fittings.

However, his best-known product was the 'Duckett Tipper closet'. It found favour in towns where water was in short supply. Whilst it used water to clear the bowl, that water was sourced from the kitchen sink, or the rainwater pipes.

The closet cleaned itself automatically, based on a tilting bucket on the inlet to the base. It was so hinged as to tip incoming water from the kitchen or rainwater pipe down onto the pan contents, and wash it *(or most of it!)*, into the drains below.

Whilst not using town water supplies, it should be noted that there is no trap in the 'pan or receptacle'. The user was dependent upon someone washing up, or on rain occurring, fairly soon after use! The only trap was *after* the receptacle – between it and the drains below.

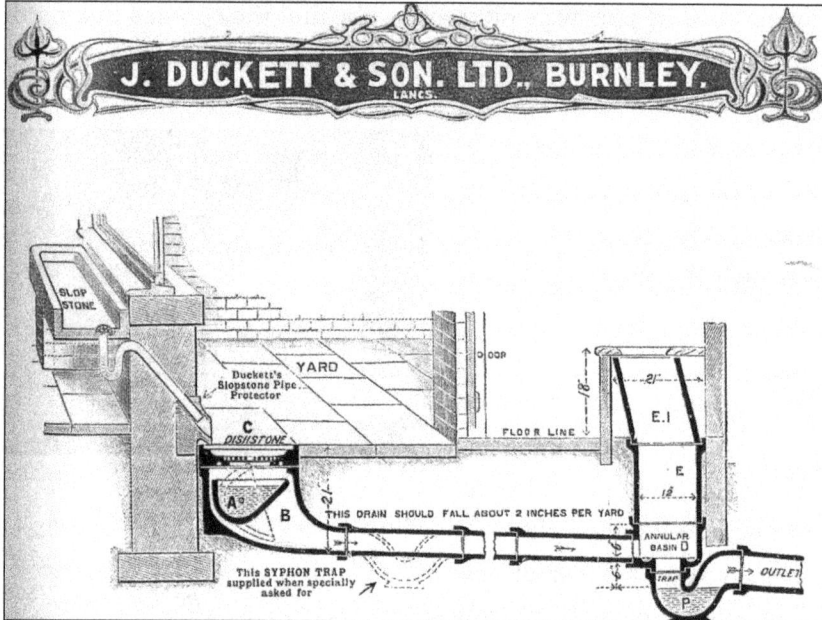

Ducketts Tipper WC. This is from the original advertisement but several modifications were took place. These can be seen in the drawing below.

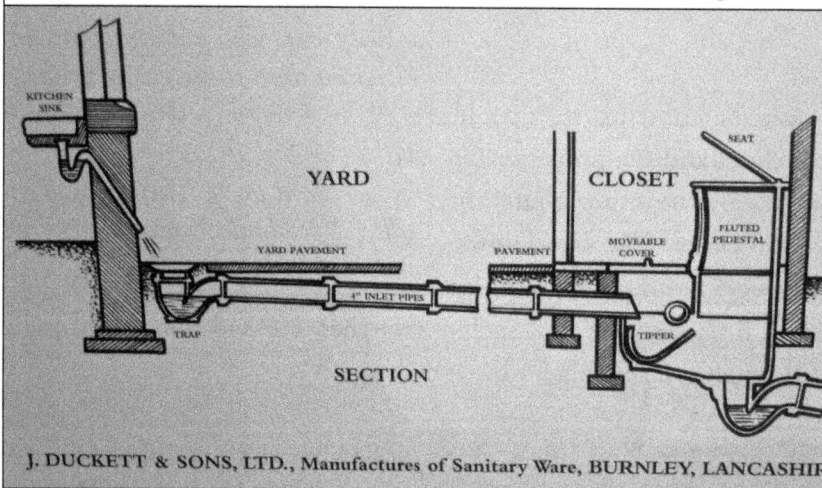

J. DUCKETT & SONS, LTD., Manufactures of Sanitary Ware, BURNLEY, LANCASHIR

Designs varied but they had also produced a 'Trough' version that I regard as one of the most revolting pieces of sanitary apparatus ever devised. It was rather like a horse trough, with a wooden rail along one side as a seat and the water passed along in the trough beneath. There were four, five, even up to eight 'Seater Troughs' available and prices went upwards from £8 for a four-seater. Should you require them, luxury extras were available, like ring or hinged seats!

The picture of their more popular 'Individual Tipper Model' was taken in my earlier showrooms some years ago then later given to the Science Museum. In 1980, I paid £300 to a builder from Kent to dig it up from a house he was rebuilding. In 2005 I presented it to the Science Museum in South Kensington. It is of particular interest in this environmentally conscious age – since it makes no demand on fresh water supplies.

In the modified WC the tipper was moved from near the sink outflow to close to the WC itself. They found that having the tipper near the sink lost velocity on a long run. Secondly, instead of one feed i.e. the kitchen sink, they added multiple feeds and these went directly onto the tipper. They might be from another washing facility or rainwater downpipes. In other words, there was more chance of the soil being flushed away. However, the Tipper closet had a major drawback. On its way down soil was likely to adhere to the sides of the walls, and that area was not cleansed with water!

Cast iron troughs by
Walter Macfarlane's of Glasgow

I said earlier that the Ducketts 'Trough' was revolting. However, just how loathsome a trough could be, is shown graphically in the two illustrations in the catalogue from Walter Macfarlane & Co. of Glasgow. I have shown the illustrations almost full size so that the details can be more easily read, thus giving a real insight into typical public sanitary arrangements of the period.

Note: These fitments were for use in public places such as: Streets, Parks, Schools, Railways, Factories and Institutions – amongst others.

The concept of a utilising a hole in a cast iron trough – with or without a seat, and in a public place – makes one realize the great achievements of the Victorian sanitary engineers in the latter years of Queen Victoria's reign.

The author is standing beside a complete Duckett WC showing the depth it was buried. That was to be sure the water feeding it could thus be some distance away

Demonstrating the action of the tipper. Any inrush of water would fill the tilting bucket and it deliver the water onto the soil and hopefully, into the drain. Of course, it was important that water arrived soon after use otherwise the smell from the 'contents' soon become unpleasant. Obviously there is nothing to stop the smell rising, unlike the Beaufort wash-down WC where the soil is immediately covered with water.

80   MACFARLANE'S CASTINGS — DRY PAN CLOSETS

FOR STREETS, COURTS, PARKS, RAILWAYS, WORKS, FACTORIES, SCHOOLS, INSTITUTIONS, &c.

These are intended for public use in places where there are no sewers or where it is desirable to keep the excrement out of them, and to save it for manuring or chemical purposes. The pans can be supplied in either of two forms, first for collecting fæces and discharging urine into a drain or tank; second, for collecting both fæces and urine. Note the distinguishing numbers of these on each illustration. A close fitting lid is applied to the pan before removal, thus preventing smell and danger of spilling.

Please insert in Specification "**To be Macfarlane's Castings, from Saracen Foundry, Glasgow,**" to prevent an inferior article being supplied.

DIRECTIONS FOR ORDERING.

State No. and for how many persons, and when wanted combined with our other Sanitary Appliances or modified to suit the nature of the site, give rough sketch indicating the proposed arrangement.

No. 21 for collecting fæces and discharging urine.

No. 31 for collecting both fæces and urine.

Nos. 21 and 31 Pan Closets each consists of a galvanized wrought iron pan and seat with cast iron bearers for fixing to walls, and guide bar for placing pan. The seat is of cast iron covered at front with wood, and hinged so as to be easily lifted and brought to rest against the back wall, giving access to the pan for removal when required. When seat is down it is secured by a lock, and fixes the pan in position that it cannot be tampered with. The pan in No. 21 has a portion partitioned off to receive the urine and conduct it through an opening in bottom and a syphon trap in ground to a drain or tank.

No. 22 for collecting fæces and discharging urine.   **No. 32** for collecting both fæces and urine.

Nos. 22 and 32 Pan Closets are same as Nos. 21 and 31 respectively, but with the addition of iron partitions and back guard plates, dividing the range and preventing standing on the seats. Nos. 21 and 31, 22 and 32 Closets are intended to be fitted up inside buildings of brick or other suitable material.

The above are selections from MACFARLANE'S CATALOGUE OF CASTINGS.

Walter Macfarlane's cast iron WC troughs. It is difficult to believe today that these were installed in public places like parks, streets, schools and railway stations. The 'shroud' over each WC is also made of cast iron and is intended to stop the user from standing on the seat!

MACFARLANE'S CASTINGS — WATER CLOSETS

PATENT AUTOMATIC FLUSHING TROUGH CLOSETS.

FOR STREETS, COURTS, PARKS, RAILWAYS, WORKS, FACTORIES, SCHOOLS, INSTITUTIONS, &c.

These Closets have no gearing or mechanism. They discharge their contents periodically into the sewers, and by adjusting the rate of the water supply can be regulated to act at any desired intervals, requiring no further attention from any one.

DIRECTIONS FOR ORDERING.

State No. and for how many persons, and when wanted combined with other Sanitary Appliances, or modified to suit the exigencies of the site, give rough sketch of the proposed arrangement.

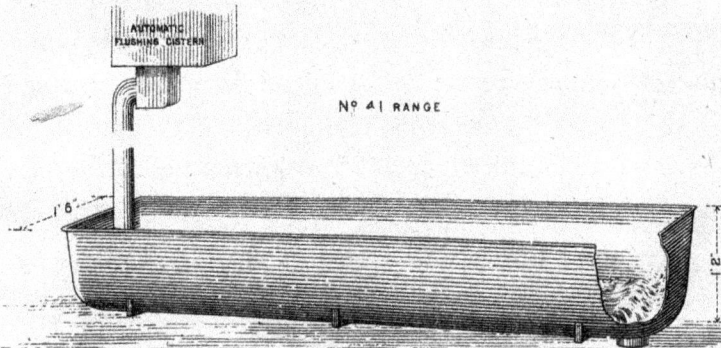

No. 41 consists of a parallel trough, with outlet at one end, and connected at the other by a pipe with an automatic flushing cistern, which can be regulated to discharge its contents into the trough at any desired intervals. The trough is formed so as to retain a few inches depth of water, which receives and deodorises the excreta, and as the water from the cistern rushes through with great force at the regulated intervals, it carries all foul matter before it to the sewer, leaving only the required amount of clean water in bottom of trough.

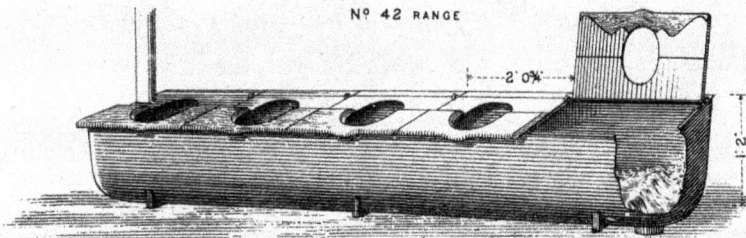

No. 42 is the same as No. 41, but with the addition of hinged seats, consisting of iron plates covered with wood at the front only, which, being thus raised by the thickness of the wood, keeps the clothes and the person clear of the back part of opening in seat, and gives greater comfort and cleanliness than the ordinary flat seat. Partitions can be added of any suitable material.

TROUGH WATER CLOSETS.

FOR ONE PERSON

Nº 1 WITHOUT SEATS.
Nº 2 WITH SEATS

Nº 1 RANGE WITHOUT SEATS
Nº 2 „ WITH SEATS

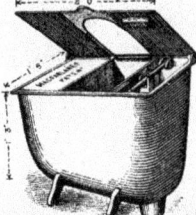

No. 2 W. C. is the same as No. 1, but with the addition of hinged seats M, consisting of iron plates, covered with wood, having an oblong opening, terminating at the back with an iron cope, thus giving a degree of cleanliness not attainable by the usual oval opening. The discharge gearing is inclosed by a portion of the end seat with lock N. Partitions may be added of any suitable material.

The above are selections from MACFARLANE'S CATALOGUE OF CASTINGS.

Another view of Macfarlane's cast iron 'Trough' water closets. Apparently there was a ready demand for them but without privacy they are not much better than the public toilets of Greek or Roman times.

The Water Closet and improvements begin

Now we move on into the period of the WC or Water Closet.

Various Acts of Parliament and local laws were put in place to remedy some of the worst problems arising from the increased use of water closets. Laws passed in the 1820s insisted that cisterns should have ball floats and stopcocks to conserve water. In 1848 a public health act was passed requiring new houses to be fitted with a WC, privy or ash pit. But the real breakthrough came with an Act of 1875 whereby:

"It shall not be lawful newly to erect any house, or to rebuild any house pull down to or below the ground floor without a sufficient water closet, earth closet or privy and an ash pit furnished with proper doors and coverings."

The Chadwick report of 1842 and the Health Act of 1875 arising from it were responsible for giving impetus to an already accelerating movement that had now accepted the concept of waterborne sanitation.

It added commercial incentive to the need to provide sanitary fitments in line with the new laws. Many designers, engineers, and potteries joined those already working in this field. Patents for new designs of cisterns, cistern valves, ball valves, pipe-joints, water closets, indeed the whole gamut of fitments, abounded.

At the same time, water supply itself was not overlooked. The feeble elm-wood water supply pipes used in water distribution could not withstand the pressures needed to supply cisterns on the first or second floor of a dwelling. The water pipes in the streets were gradually being replaced by cast iron or fireclay stoneware. Patent taps, and improved quality water fittings, all kept pace with the drive to generally improve standards.

There can be little doubt that **George Jennings** (1810 to April 1882) was the first major influence on the design of the water closet in Victorian England. He was a sanitary engineer and plumber who, although renowned for inventing the first public toilets, was a brilliant designer and inventor.

George Jennings, whose full name (though seldom used) was Josiah George Jennings, was born in Hampshire in 1810. He was the eldest of the seven children of Jonas Joseph Jennings and Mary Dimmock.

At 14, after his father's death, he was apprenticed to his grandfather's glass and lead merchandising business, before moving to his Uncle John Jennings' plumbing business at Southwick, Southampton. In 1831 he became a plumber with Messrs. Lancelot Burton of Newcastle Street, London where his father had been a foreman before him.

One of the greatest of the early sanitary pioneers was George Jennings. His wash-out water closets were installed at the Great Exhibition of 1851 and the charge for use was 1 penny. Hence the euphemism 'Going to spend a penny'!

Jennings quickly moved on to designing water closets. He was the first to realise that the growing population in our cities needed public toilets. As a result of his work, we all know – and at times have appreciated – the underground 'public convenience' that he designed and promoted. They gradually became quite elaborate affairs with cast iron railings around the entrance and considerable use of slate floors and ceramic tiles.

In 1847 Prince Albert presented George Jennings with the Medal of the Society

No. 32—MONKEY CLOSET.

Patent or Fan Rim.

Jennings 'Monkey Closet' used throughout the Great Exhibition alongside his Trade Mark

of Arts for his fittings. By this time Jennings was running a considerable size business manufacturing his water closets, salt glazed pipes and sanitary ware of all kinds.

At The Great Exhibition at Hyde Park held in 1851, George Jennings installed his water closets in the 'Retiring Rooms' of The Crystal Palace. These caused considerable interest as they were the first public toilets. During the exhibition over 800,000 visitors paid one penny to use them. In return for their penny, they had a clean seat, a towel, a comb and a shoeshine. Coming directly from this event in 1851 arose the euphemism 'to spend a penny'!

In August 1852 Jennings Patented:
1. "An improved construction of water-closet, in which the pan and trap are constructed in the same piece, and so formed that there shall always be a certain quantity of water retained in the pan itself, in addition to that in the trap which forms the water-joint." *[Note: This is the forerunner of the wash-out **closet** that dominated the industry for so many years before the advent of the **wash-down closet** created by my great uncle Frederick Humpherson and launched in 1884.]*

2. "An improved construction of valve for water-closets and other uses, and several arrangements of valves and other apparatus for like purposes. The novelty of the valve consists in its spindle being prolonged downwards, so as to be capable of being acted on by a lever that opens and closes it, and thus admits water without (in the case of water-closets) the use of wires, etc. The other arrangements include a similar valve, but provided with a waste-pipe and an arrangement of the same with a ball- cock for governing the supply of water to water-closets and their cisterns; also an improved stand-pipe, and a sluice-valve for steam and fluids, the novelty of which consists in the manner of fitting and fixing the facings against which the slide works."

During the period 1860 to 1880 Jennings built up a substantial export business across Europe and into Egypt and the Middle East.

In 1872 George Jennings supervised the public facilities at the thanksgiving service for the Prince of Wales at St Paul's Cathedral to celebrate his recovery from typhoid. That he had become a favourite of the Prince Consort was recorded by 'The Sanitary Record' in these words:

'The Prince Consort greatly encouraged this indefatigable Engineer. In sanitary science he was avant coureur [forerunner] in his day and generation, and was among the first Engineers to practically carry out the theories of the wise men of the time. 'Sanitas sanitarium' was Mr Jennings's motto before Disraeli adopted it as his political maxim and he implored a shocked city of London to accept his public lavatories free, on the condition that the attendants whom he furnished were allowed to make a small charge for the use of the closets and towels.'

George Jennings died on the 17 April 1882, aged 72 following an accident on Albert Bridge that leads across the Thames from Chelsea to Battersea. The 'South London Press' reported the accident as follows:

'It is with feelings of regret, which will be joined in by all who knew him, that we have this week to record the death of Mr. George Jennings of Ferndale, Nightingale Lane, Clapham, universally known as the celebrated engineer of Palace Wharf, Lambeth. Mr Jennings' death occurred under the following painful circumstances: On Thursday evening, according to his usual custom, he, together with his son George, drove home in his gig. The horse, of a very restive character and hard in the mouth, whilst crossing over the Albert Bridge, shied and threw Mr. Jennings and his son against a dustcart.

Mr. Jennings Jnr. escaped with only a shaking, but Mr Jennings' collarbone was fractured. He was conveyed home and attended by Dr Edmonds and two other physicians. His recovery from the injuries proceeded favourably up until Sunday, when against his doctors' order, he would get up. On Sunday night a relapse and congestion of the lungs set in, and he expired on Monday evening, about 6 o'clock. He was 72 years of age.'

Apparently the family firm continued until 1967. I met the Mr Jennings Junior (also named George) mentioned in the 1882 accident report, in or around 1957. At that time a group of pottery companies had formed themselves into ACI Limited (Associated Clay Industries). The companies represented were selling sanitary ware in both china and fireclay. Due to the export drive by the major pottery companies, there was then a general shortage of products available from our normal suppliers. In our case, this was exacerbated by our rapidly growing sales performance.

Associated Clay Industries had purchased a large complex of offices and warehouse space in Holman Road Battersea, across the Thames from our premises in The Royal Borough of Kensington and Chelsea. On learning of the prodigious quantity of fittings they had built up there, and in need of supplies, I approached their Sales Director and was invited to visit them. Our own showrooms and offices were then at Holmes Place in Fulham Road. We were therefore within easy walking distance to Battersea Bridge and the nearby Albert Bridge, scene of the accident to George Jennings back in 1882.

When I arrived at the ACI offices in Battersea, I met the Sales Director and was then shown around the property to see their very impressive stocks of WCs, washbasins and fireclay sinks – indeed the whole gamut of sanitary fitments. One part of the building however, was devoted to the manufacture of drain rods – in those days made exclusively of cane. Knowing my family background in the industry, the Sales Director introduced me to an elderly gentleman who seemed to be in authority – whether just over the manufacture of drain rods or ACI itself – I did not establish.

It transpired he was *the* George Jennings who had been injured at the same time as his father – Josiah George Jennings back in 1882. I was told, in a whisper, that he was 'well over ninety years old'. He had a large brass ear trumpet with an ivory earpiece and my host tried to explain who I was and our long family connection with the industry – going back to Victorian times. He failed to get the story over to Mr Jennings so my host suggested I try to explain. I spoke fairly loudly to him directly into his ear trumpet, to which he replied *'Speak up sonny – I can't hear what you are saying!'*.

I am pleased to say that I finally established a 'connection' with him and he showed great interest in our history but I can only wish our meeting had been recorded on film. Following my visit to ACI, we ordered a full truckload of washbasins and WCs – something over 300 pieces and a load of fireclay kitchen sinks. However, we quickly discovered why they had stocks available.

Some of the waste holes to the basins were out of line, and if you put them onto the ground too sharply, glaze actually fell off WCs. They took back all the faulty pieces and later sold off the rest of the considerable stocks, at a knockdown price, to a firm in Upper Thames Street in the City of London. I think much of it ended up somewhere in the Middle East. Associated Clay Industries closed down soon afterwards.

A footnote to the story: A major paint manufacturer, bought the property in Holman Road Batterea consisting of over 25,000 sq ft from the liquidators and then built quite prestigious offices in some 20% of it – using the rest for warehousing. In 1974, I purchased that block and some nearby buildings to become our 'Humpherson Group' headquarters.

I met George Jennings son (also named George). This is not a picture of him, though he looked similar. However, the ear trumpet is exactly as described in the text.

In looking back at the earlier pioneers in sanitary engineering, we have briefly examined the work of great men such as Cummins, Bramah and their affect upon the infant sanitary industry. Now we are well into the Victorian period, where so much more pressure was put upon the frail drainage infrastructure by the massive increase in population.

I might start by mentioning some of the luminaries of the period: George Jennings, Edward Johns (his company later became Armitage), Henry Doulton, Daniel Bostel, Thomas Crapper, S. Stevens Hellyer (Dent

& Hellyer), Joseph William Twyford and his son Thomas Twyford, John Shanks of Barrhead, and Frederick Humpherson, were to become literally 'household' names, whilst many others have been lost to us, together with some of their more bizarre ideas.

Drain pipes

Before reverting to the main stream of WC design, one must stop to appreciate the great strides made in drainage by Henry Doulton with his introduction of salt glazed stoneware drain pipes and fittings. Until then, drains and sewer pipes – *where they existed* – were frequently brick lined and porous.

You will find salt glazed drainpipes and fittings were used for the drainage in homes built before the mid 1970s. More correctly speaking, they are actually under ground carrying away the discharge from WCs, baths, basins and sinks as well as rainwater – from the home to the main sewers in the road. However, one can see 'brown' salt glazed fittings when you lift a manhole cover in houses before that time.

There can be little doubt that Hellyer's company Dent & Hellyer played a substantial role in the general improvement. His 'Optimus' was essentially a valve closet but all valve closets, of whatever design, gradually had to give way to the wash-out, and wash-down, closets that appeared. Here, I will illustrate the main types of WC in use.

The closet supplied to Queen Elizabeth 1st by Sir John Harington was essentially a valve closet, as were the later designs of Alexander Cumming and Joseph Bramah. They were complicated and expensive to make and as most had numerous working parts, they were difficult to maintain. They fell into disuse as the sheer simplicity of the washout and the washdown closets took over. However, some small quantities were still in production at the beginning of the 20th Century.

No. 303. Tall Hopper.
(Right Hand.)

	Inches.
Size of Top	15¼
,, Outlet	4⅛
Depth	20¾
,, to floor line	17

Cane.	White.	Printed.
6/0	7/0	9/0

Hopper closets

These had been available for a many years but the earliest models were in metal so they were hard to keep clean, as well as being unhealthy. Later on models in glazed earthenware came into use and Wedgewood

Far Left: Tall (or long) hopper from our catalogue dated 1887. This met the continued demand for a choice of hopper – that then had to be connected to a separate trap.

Sketch showing connection of tall (or long) hopper to trap. Flushing depended upon an input of water near the top, spiralling down and hopefully, cleaning the bowl. The water came via a nearby tap operated when the trap required clearing.

No. 305. Short Hopper.
To fit Traps 431 to 438.
(Right Hand.)

	Inches.
Size of Top	14½
„ Outlet	4¼
Depth	16¾
Height fixed on Trap.....	20

Cane.	White.	Printed.
4/0	6/0	7/0

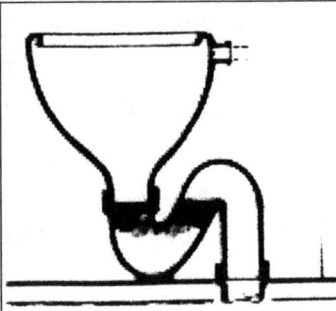

Above: Sketch showing connection of a short hopper connected to a trap. Left: Short hopper closet from our catalogue dated 1887.

No. 336. Servants' Basin.
To fit Traps 431 to 438.
(Right Hand.)

	Inches.
Size of Top	14¾
„ Outlet...........	4¼
Depth	13¼
Height fixed on Trap......	16¾

Cane.	White.	Printed.
5/0	6/0	8/0

No. 306. Servants' Basin.
To fit Traps 431 to 438.
(Left Hand.)

	Inches.
Size of Top	14¾
„ Outlet	4¼
Depth	13¼
Height fixed on Trap......	16¾

Cane.	White.	Printed.
5/0	6/0	8/0

for example, had begun making them by the end of the 18th century. At first the 'long hopper' or 'long pot' was in demand and it was flushed by a jet of water fed into the top that was intended to spiral down the bowl, thus cleaning it during its descent. However, with a long bowl – and a feeble flow of water – they were generally regarded as unhygienic.

Still later, the 'short hopper' closet appeared with a shorter bowl depth and was a real improvement. With a separate trap fitted below to prevent the return of noxious gases, and water fed from near the rim, it was moving towards the wash-down closet that followed.

The illustrations come from the Humpherson catalogue of 1886 showing various models. It is interesting to note that there were also models for 'servants' available. The hopper continued to be popular right into the early 20th century, appearing in many manufacturers' catalogues.

Wash-out (or flush-out) closets

This form of closet has a shallow tray holding a small quantity of water, somewhat above the trap. After use, the contents of the tray are flushed into the lower part of the pan and out through the trap.

Servants' basins from our 1887 catalogue. A mark of the social differentials that existed in almost every sphere of life. The basins were simpler and cheaper to manufacture. In it simplest form 'Cane' – it then cost 5 shillings (£0.25) about £28 today.

Far right: A typical wash-out closet of the period – this from my copy of the Thomas Crapper catalogue of 1888. The wash-out was far and away the most common WC of the period

This sketch of the wash-out closet shows the shelf holding a shallow amount of water.

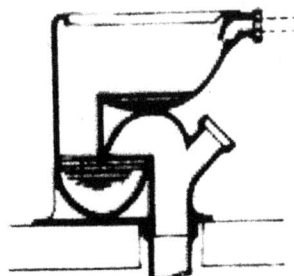

₃₈ THOMAS CRAPPER & CO.,

"Wash-out" Closet.
(NEW PATTERN)

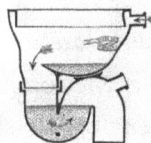

No. 94

No. 94. ... Cane colour outside, white inside,	...	12/6
„ 95. ... White outside and inside	....	14/6
If printed inside, extra		3/-

There are a number of claimants to the design of the wash-out closet including George Jennings, P. J. Davies. Daniel Bostel of Brighton exhibited his 'Excelsior' washout closet as early as 1875. Hellyer produced the 'Artisan' that was given a US Patent in 1879 and Twyfords make a claim as well with the 'National' of 1881.

Twyfords were based in the 'Potteries' in Stoke-on-Trent and started by making domestic ware such as teapots and washbowls. As an established family pottery, Joseph William Twyford, and his son Thomas Twyford, saw the opportunities that the rapidly rising demand for sanitary ware would bring and in the 1870s turned their considerable skills into making sanitary fittings. It seems the 'National' washout closet by Twyfords came *after* the 'Excelsior' by Daniel Bostel – who is now generally given the credit for its design.

This type of pan rapidly lost popularity in Britain, as the Frederick's designed wash-down closet took over. However, it remained in use in Germany for years, and can still be found in a few places.

Syphonic WCs
The basic idea is that the contents of the bowl are carried away by syphonic action. A number of these appeared in the 1870s and some seemed to suggest that the more complex the mechanism the better.

Early models were not popular here but later versions were extensively used in the United States and remain in widespread use today. In the 1960s, I started to represent the merchant organisations of Great Britain, on various bathroom orientated committees of the British Standards Institute (BSI). At one of the first meetings I attended, mention was made of the models of syphonic WCs manufactured in the United States. They utilise an inflow of water into the bowl from below, thus raising the level of the water over the invert of the trap, causing a syphonic action to take place *sucking* out the contents.

In those days, a Mr Clancy represented the all-powerful LCC (London County Council) on the BSI Committee. His full, explicit remarks on the subject – *if ever published* – would have destroyed any 'special relationship' that existed between the United Kingdom and the United States. He told us that he regarded the fittings as 'foul' and said that even if acceptable over there, the design was unacceptable to him. Therefore, as a result of his edict, they could not be used in the whole Greater London area. The BSI Committees were in such dread of his pronouncements – that his ban in London would automatically have become a *nationwide* ban!

That strongly expressed viewpoint was useful to me. Shortly afterwards, I was approached by the Crane Corporation, then a major manufacturer of sanitary ware in the USA, to see if it were possible to import their bathroom fittings into the United Kingdom. I was able to say, with great authority, that they could not bring fittings in without a radical redesign.

Wash-down closets
In 1849, a Metropolitan Commission suggested pans be made with traps attached, perhaps a natural development of the short hopper pan on a trap. Despite this the infant sanitary industry continued By producing hopper pans, etc., *on separate traps*. Earlier catalogues show a multitude of pans – of all shapes and sizes but all needing a trap to sit on.

Though now universally described as 'wash-down' – but Frederick earlier called his 'flush-down'. This is the most common design in use today, not only in Britain but also in most other countries across the world.

The first **one-piece pedestal wash-down closet** – in use worldwide today – was the 'Beaufort' designed by my great-uncle Frederick Humpherson. It was based on his earlier two-piece 'Flush-down closet' (also called the 'Beaufort') that received a Certificate of Merit from the Sanitary Institute of Great Britain in 1885. He had brought the two parts together and added a front, thus entitling him to say:

'This Closet, unlike the ordinary form of basin, is not cased with woodwork, but forms a solid fixture by itself, so that the enclosure under which a receptacle is so often formed for dirt and filth is entirely dispensed with; free access is thus given to all parts so that both the floor and basin can easily be kept clean, while the air can circulate freely around it. The mahogany seat being hinged, may be lifted, and the basin used for either a slop sink or urinal, and thus a wet seat, which is so objectionable, can be easily avoided.'

Top left: This is Frederick Humpherson's 'Flush-Down WC (later he described it as Wash-Down). The WC was awarded a Certificate of Merit' by the Sanitary Institute of Great Britain in 1885. Its merit was the flush was concentrated on the area of the pan that was usually corroded. That alone was a great step forward – over hoppers and pans or all shapes and sizes – that had gone before.
Top right: Frederick's 'Beaufort' wash-down one piece pedestal closet – the WC pan as we know it today and used world-wide. More details in Chapter 7.

The launch of Lucinda Lambton's second book 'Temples of Convenience and Chambers of Delight' took place at a flat in Tite Street, Chelsea. In her research for her books, she had tracked down descendants of the four leading WC designs and invited them to attend the launch. This is from the leaflet handed out to those attending:

Serena Harington-Barrow
A descendent of Sir John Harington – designer of a flush cistern in the reign of Queen Elizabeth 1st – around 1576.

Edward and Jeremy Bramah
Descendents of Joseph Bramah inventor of the valve closet from 1778.

Richard Bostel
Descendent of Daniel Thomas Bostel, designer of a 'wash-out' closet of around 1870.

Geoffrey Pidgeon
Great nephew of Frederick Humpherson, who in 1884 launched the worlds first pedestal wash-down WC pan – the WC – as we know it today.

WC Cisterns
One of the major problems of the period was the provision of water for the many new WCs being installed and, as we have seen, distribution pipes able to cope with either the volume or the pressure, needed to lift the water up to just the first floor of a house – did not exist.

Slowly, new main water pipes were laid, mostly of cast iron. However, it was realised that it was imperative to hold water supplies in each household since a regular supply could not be guaranteed. Hence domestic water cisterns for storage became standard practice in the loft or on the roof. As a result, we ended up – perhaps uniquely in Europe – with what is known as a 'low pressure system'.

The flow from taps and into ball valves was therefore dependent on the pressure exerted by the height of the storage cistern from the fittings. The rest of Europe had direct water supplies coming from their newly laid mains water network, giving greater pressure to fitments from the beginning. Having low-pressure water in one's house was a cross we had to bear for nearly a century, the result of Britain being first in the field of modern domestic sanitation.

Nevertheless, water was in very short supply. New reservoirs and pumping stations were only commissioned in the latter part of the 19th century – instead of drawing water from rivers and wells – that were often contaminated by sewers and/or cesspits. Accordingly, great stress was laid on water preservation. The sanitary industry coined the phrase 'Water Waste Preventer' (WWP) to describe WC cisterns designed to supply only sufficient water to adequately flush the closet. In an Act of Parliament (The Metropolitan Water Act 1871), the legal norm was set at 2 gallons (9 litres) and all kinds of inventions were put forward to ensure cisterns conformed.

Again, all the leading designers made their own contribution. Jennings, Davies, Boldings, Hellyer, Tylor, Humphersons and so on but they were all intent on conforming to the legal limit – except Hellyer who ranted against it on every possible occasion! Typically he says in his book 'The Plumber and Sanitary Houses'. *'Every sanitarian should lift up his voice against the limitation of water to such sanitary fixtures and never cease crying, like Oliver Twist, for more water until a quantity double or even treble the present amount is allowed for WCs.'*

Hellyer's plan would have meant 4 gallons (18 litres), or 6 gallons (27 litres) each flush and thankfully, was never enacted. But, until the 1950s, certain water authorities in England allowed 2.5 gallons per flush and 3-gallon cisterns were common in Scotland. This is very different from the current UK maximum of 7.5 litres (1.65 gallons), with valve fittings saving water and energy – by working very satisfactorily on 6.25 litres (1.38 gallons) and even less. (See Note: H)

Because of the benefit to public health, the improvements in sanitary fittings must hold pride of place in any record of the Victorian bathroom industry. However, one must not ignore the design changes and improvements in associated products like baths, basins and taps. They contributed substantially to the well being of a population increasingly aware that the high rate of disease was associated with the need for cleanliness.

Baths

Bathing, the immersion of the body in water is an important part of various religions as well as for healing and medicinal purposes, for recreation – as well as cleanliness.

Our interest here is in the cleanliness aspect and the improved hygiene that follows from it.

The earlier times, both the Egyptians and Greeks generally bathed frequently and it reflected the high level of civilisation they reached. However, it was the Romans who raised the standard of bathing higher with private baths in the more prestigious households and public baths for those of more humble means. These baths were not for show but were regularly used as part of the Roman culture. It was helped by their design of bathhouses with hot water available, steam rooms and cold plunges. Perhaps the best-known baths in England are the Roman baths in the city of Bath. There, the citizens had the advantage of a thermal spring bringing hot water into the bathing complex.

Sadly, in the 'dark ages' that followed the Roman departure from Britain, the idea of regular bathing and any kind of control of sanitation seemed to have departed with them. There were, of course, exceptions and some improvements arose from time to time but only amongst the more affluent.

As well as seeing the need for improvements in sanitary fittings (the WC, cisterns, pipe work and sewage disposal) the Victorians increasingly recognised the importance of personal hygiene. Fading were the days of *'having a bath once a month – whether one needed it or not'*. Now, with the installation of internal pipe work connecting the WC to the drains, it became obvious that the pipes could be used to connect baths and washbasins to the drains in the same way.

Before the 19th century the bath was usually freestanding. The servants brought up the hot water by bucket and emptied the bath in the same way after use. This often took place in the bedroom, in front of the fire, so as to keep warm after bathing. The carrying of water and emptying the bath was fairly irksome for the servants but the whole operation meant that it was quite an event for all concerned – but bathing was not as frequent as hygiene might have required!

However, in 'working class' homes it was quite common for 'bath night' to involve the entire family. They would use the same water – one after the other. Considering the work needed to heat the water and fill such a vessel, one can hardly blame them. The baths were often of zinc or occasionally of copper and, at the cheaper end of the market, just about big enough to sit in – with one's knees up.

One would be pleased to have the space and hot water facility to have the luxury of a zinc bath tub. However, the hot water usually came from saucepans on a stove so it was common routine for a whole family to use the same water.

The new era introduced baths made of enamelled cast iron with the water fed into the bath through brass taps, mounted either over the bath rim, or later on the bath itself. The bath was emptied from a waste outlet connected to the drains – now being widely installed.

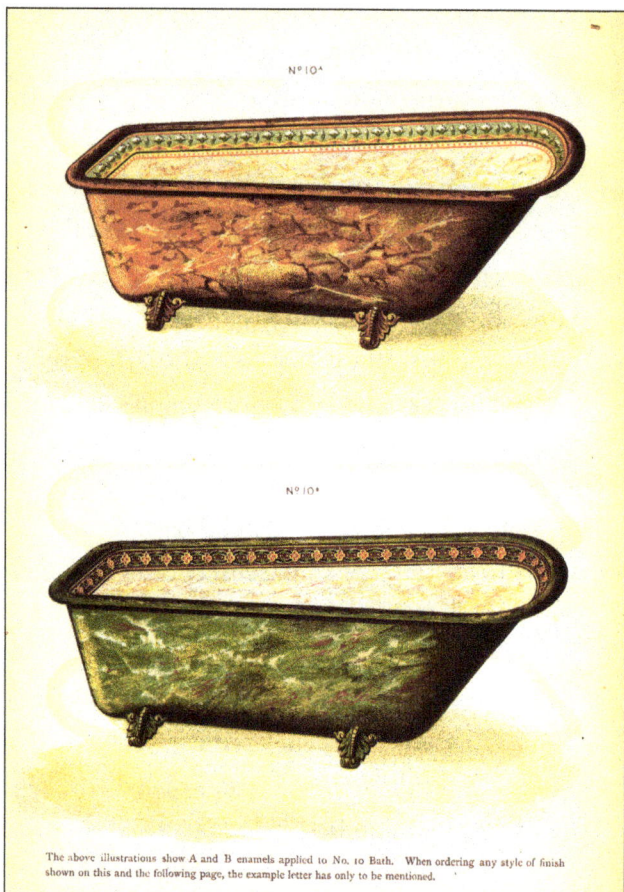

The above illustrations show A and B enamels applied to No. 10 Bath. When ordering any style of finish shown on this and the following page, the example letter has only to be mentioned.

Again, I am grateful to Walter Macfarlane's catalogue, for illustrations of cast iron baths from the late 1800s. A number of firms claim to have made the first cast iron bath and they include Standard Sanitary Manufacturing Company and Kohler – both in the United States. Standard Sanitary claim their first model dates from 1883. Clearly, Macfarlane's baths existed from the same period and they were able to offer a wide range of decoration early on.

However, there were cast iron bath plants in operation in the UK before 1883! Indeed, several foundries were making them from the late 1850s. It is believed that T. & C. Clark of Wolverhampton were producing enamelled cast iron baths in their Shakespeare Foundry – *before* 1850!

These are examples from the Macfarlane catalogue of the finishes available. In our catalogue a 5'6"bath enameled inside and with 'fancy decoration' on the outside was £5. 15. 0. complete with taps.

In Scotland, Shanks & Co. 'Sanitary Engineers' had an extensive factory making sanitary ware – WCs, washbasins for the domestic market and for ships being constructed in the nearby Glasgow shipyards. They built a foundry to make the iron fittings, brackets and washbasin stands to complement their ranges and quickly added cast iron baths to the goods offered.

Scotland had many iron foundries. As the demand for bathroom fittings grew in the late 1800s, so they added domestic fittings to their ranges. This is included Carron of Falkirk, Ballantines of Boness, Govan Iron Works, M. Cockburn & Co., Callender Iron, McDowell Steven & Co., Falkirk Iron, amongst others. However, my favourite is the splendidly named: *The Forth & Clyde & Sunnyside Iron Company!*

The hot water for the bath, basin and kitchen sink increasingly came from a domestic boiler. In a large house there would be a freestanding unit in the kitchen or basement, heated with coal or coke. In others a boiler section was built into the kitchen range.

By the turn of the century, in many small homes, there was a 'back-boiler' fitted behind the fireplace. Thus, the usually constant fire was also heating water for domestic use. These had to be fed with water from a storage cistern higher in the house.

CAST-IRON BATHS.

"COMBINED CASCADE BATH," with Hot and Cold Water Fittings and Waste Arrangement complete, with Trap. Flange Rim for use, with Wood Enclosure.

The "BEAUFORT."

PRICES.

No.						£	s.	d.
100	5-ft. 0-in.	3rd Class	Sienna Japanned Bath & Fittings			3	0	0
101	5-ft. 6-in.	3rd ,,	,,	,,	,,	3	5	0
102	6-ft. 0-in.	3rd ,,	,,	,,	,,	3	12	0
103	5-ft. 0-in.	2/2nd,,	,, Enamelled	,,	,,	3	18	0
104	5-ft. 6-in.	2/2nd,,	,,	,,	,,	4	2	0
105	6-ft. 0-in.	2/2nd,,	,,	,,	,,	4	15	0
106	5-ft. 0-in.	2nd ,,	,,	,,	,,	4	6	0
107	5-ft. 6-in.	2nd ,,	,,	,,	,,	4	10	0
108	6-ft. 0-in.	2nd ,,	,,	,,	,,	5	5	0
109	5-ft. 0-in.	1st ,,	,,	,,	,,	5	3	0
110	5-ft. 6-in.	1st ,,	,,	,,	,,	5	10	0
111	6-ft. 0-in.	1st ,,	,,	,,	,,	6	5	0

Nickel Plated Fittings 4/6 extra.

112 Fitted with Polished Wood Capping for use without Enclosure, and Bath Japanned outside, £2 5s. extra.

HUMPHERSON & CO.,
297, FULHAM ROAD, LONDON, S.W.
43

An early cast iron bath from our 1880s catalogue. Again the trade name 'Beaufort' as the showroom was on the corner of Fulham Road and Beaufort Street, Chelsea.

However, if the water supply was stopped for any reason – frozen pipes for example – the back boiler could explode (and frequently did). Nevertheless, these were very common installations and brought constant hot water to a family home, where it had not existed before.

Towards the end of the 19th Century, firms – such as Ewart & Co – introduced gas water heaters. As a small child in the late 1920s, we had a Ewart gas water heater over the bath in our home in Fulham. The roar of the gas was quite terrifying when it lit up – and accidents did occur!

However, in spite of the improvements in design and the availability of hot water, the idea of 'Friday night is bath night' continued well into the 20th Century.

Incidentally, by the 1950s, enamelled pressed steel baths became popular – being cheaper and lighter than cast iron. They were often a bi-product of factories making enamelled kitchenware and/or pressed steel sinks. The downside is that they are more easily chipped than enamelled cast iron – although some makers now claim they have reduced the likelihood of chipping.

As one of the first firms in the UK to show acrylic (Perspex) baths, you would expect me to be in favour of them. That is certainly the case. For a time, I was Chairman of the British Standards Institute (BSI) Committee on acrylic baths. However, we found a major problem was the comparative ease of manufacture with low capital costs. One enterprising gentleman was making them in his – albeit large – garage. This, coupled with thinner and thinner sheets being used, began to create a poor image for the early acrylic bath market.

My firm was amongst those promoting the benefits of acrylic baths with articles in the press and I gave personal demonstrations to the directors of major builders, like Wimpey. However, it needed firms like Hoesch from Germany to show that the material – properly made and properly installed – was *at least* as good as any other form of bath material.

Basins ('Lavatory basins' or 'Washbasins')

Designs have varied over the centuries but it was the Victorian era that saw the most rapid changes. This was largely due to the creation of numerous pottery companies, mostly in the Stoke-on-Trent area of Staffordshire. The city's history is intimately bound up with that of the ceramics industry; the Stoke-on-Trent area is, in fact, generally known as the Staffordshire Potteries, or just the 'Potteries'. The production of pottery in the region dates back to at least the 17th century.

By the time Josiah Wedgwood started his business in 1759, in the village of Burslem, the area was supplying a wide variety of earthenware and stoneware, produced in and around all the villages of the area. Pottery production was also in the process of changing from a cottage-based to a factory-based industry, a transformation that placed the potteries at the forefront of the Industrial Revolution.

With growing affluence and the need for WCs and washbasins, many of the potteries involved in making tableware started to manufacture sanitary fittings. Twyfords are a good example, having moved rapidly away from making tableware, teapots and the like.

The industry's growth was also aided by the opening, in 1777, of the Grand Trunk Canal (now the Trent and

A Victorian wash-stand. These were frequently in a bedroom before the advent of the bathroom with washing facilities. Its top and would be of marble but the stand illustrated has one of mahogany. It has a complete set of china accessories. A washbowl, jugs for hot and cold water, and a soap dish. Underneath is a chamber pot with lid, two tumblers for toothbrushes and a slop bucket. It is dished so water does not easily spill.

Mersey Canal), which provided an outlet to the ports at Hull and Liverpool which allowed the transport of raw materials into the city and the export of its finished products.

Washbasins were originally bowls on specially designed 'Washstands' with a marble top and a row or two of tiles behind. The water would be in a jug alongside it. These 'Washbasin Sets' were big business for the potteries and most homes had at least one and, in more affluent homes, there would be a washstand in every bedroom.

A full 'Set' would comprise a wash bowl, a jug for hot water and a smaller one for cold, a soap dish, two tumblers, a chamber pot and a pail – all in pottery. They were easy to manufacture and most potteries offered them for sale. The best were usually colourful and highly decorated.

In larger households, it would be the job of the 'skivvy' – the lowest rank of maid servant – to ensure that hot

A close up of a slop bucket showing the dished lid

water was provided in the jugs, that the 'slops' were emptied from the bucket, the chamber pot was emptied and returned clean!

With the introduction of basic internal plumbing to a house in later Victorian times, the bowl would be let into the washstand top, often made of marble. Having a waste pipe from it to discharge outside the bowl became known as a 'Plug bowl' from the need for a basin *plug* to close off the waste whilst washing.

There are obviously few restrictions in designing washbasins. There was a rapid growth in sales, once basic plumbing could provide piped water to the basin and waste pipes to empty the bowl to the drains. In fact, the range of designs offered was extraordinary. Period catalogues from the late 1800s and early 1900s demonstrate by comparison just how clinical patterns had become.

The Bidet

Until recent times, few Britons or Americans ever saw a bidet unless they stayed at French hotels, and then were either puzzled because they did not understand it, or embarrassed because they did! That the bidet serves to clean one's 'private parts' has given it an aura of indelicacy and its contraceptive role one of downright immorality. About the turn of the 20th century the Ritz Carlton in New York fitted them in some bathrooms but apparently there was an outcry in the press.

A number of well-known visitors actually asked me to describe its use but I refrain from naming them. Several writers referred to the bidet being so evident in our displays. However, I think it was Alice Hope of the Daily Telegraph who described me a being the 'King of the Bidets' that caused some hilarity amongst my friends. However, my favourite story from those early days arose from that article. I received a letter from Ireland from a gentleman who had read the Alice Hope piece. He wrote to ask me, as he was too embarrassed to ask others, *what exactly is a bidet?*

I replied in a fairly detailed letter and two weeks later received a reply. In the envelope was a fairly fulsome letter expressing his thanks and a brown 10/- shilling note to thank me. His letter contained these, never to be forgotten words, *'…I can now hold up my head in polite society'!*

The bidet always seemed to me to be a necessary adjunct to the WC. When we were able to extend our showrooms in Beaufort Works, I ensured that many of the new bathroom displays had a bidet adjacent to the WC. However, years later I now recognise the increasing use of the walk-in shower and the extraordinary growth of wipes – both help to avoid the feeling of being 'unclean'!

Taps
Here too, the Victorian era saw rapid changes from the simple tap design of earlier periods. Before this time not much had changed since Roman times. Most were of the 'Plug' type – i.e. a plug of metal inserted into the pipe with a central through-way in it – that allowed the passage of water (when turned 90 degrees).

During the 18th century running water was rare in households and only became more widespread in the latter half of the 19th century. Fresh water from the mains, either direct or from a storage cistern, meant that tap water in a household could be called 'potable' (fit to drink), as opposed to water from rainwater collection, village pumps, streams, rivers or lakes.

The manufacture of brass taps in the UK sprang up in factories in and around Birmingham in the late 1800s. By then, they were dealing with higher pressures and more constant use, requiring renewable washers. Again, Frederick Humpherson was in the forefront of tap design and his 'Quick Turning Hot Water Cocks' were awarded a Silver Medal by the Society of Architects in 1886 and their 'Star' Certificate in 1887. ***Note:*** The Society of Architects became the Royal Institute of British Architects (RIBA) in 1925.

The Bathroom
The idea of 'The Bathroom' gradually evolved in the 1870's – arising from the multitude of improvements that took place in the latter part of the 19th century. The period saw proper drainage and sewers installed, thus eliminating many of the illnesses rife at the time, alongside a growing understanding of the benefits arising from improved hygiene.

The development of a circulating hot-water system meant that hot water was available around the house and along with the new cast iron baths and taps – the bathroom as we know it today began to evolve. Nevertheless, to begin with, the fitments were usually encased in panels, often of mahogany to make the new bathroom resemble other furnished rooms in the house. That was taken further since there would be a fireplace with mantelpiece and heavy curtains to the windows.

Our joiner's shop kept several carpenters busy and I remember seeing the old stocks of mahogany, even in the 1930's in Charlie Keen's workshop in Beaufort Works, Holmes Place. Such bathrooms were the norm in 'upper class' homes throughout the 1880/90's – until the turn of the century when more tiling was used.

However, there was still a pronounced difference between classes, in the facilities available to them. The poorest homes had to share whatever kind of toilet was available. That might be a dry pan closet needing emptying by the 'Night Cart' men and, even if the

A typical late Victorian bathroom. Note the extensive use of timber paneling, thus giving a 'furnished' appearance to the room. The coal-burning fireplace was essential since central heating was rare indeed. No WC is visible in the picture but it might well have been on the adjoining staircase and shared by others.

home enjoyed its own toilet, it would seldom be connected to the drains. So far as washing was concerned, that would mean a bowl in the kitchen sink, while taking a bath probably meant a 'Bath tub' in front of the fire.

Things did improve in the second half of the century with the new laws beginning to take effect but again that left great differences between the classes. In middle class and more affluent homes there would already be a washstand in the bedroom but a WC – be it a privy or ash pit – became required by law in new houses from 1848. However, the real break-through came with the 1875 Act of Parliament mentioned in the previous chapter.

So the 'bathroom' as we know it today took time to evolve with only builders of high quality homes installing a bathroom as part of the original design.

Of course, those occupying mansions were used to having such facilities inside the home – to use a WC – they certainly did not have to go outside to a shed in the yard. Sometimes, one was sited by the staircase so those in nearby bedrooms could share them.

In middle-class homes, one expected the WC to be inside the house but quite separate from the bathing area.

But, gradually a spare room became utilised as a bathroom, containing a WC, a washbasin and a bath. So gradually the bathroom became a social indicator to the point that by 1904, the German architect, Herman Muthesius, wrote: 'England has led all the Continental countries in developing the bathroom.'

The late Victorian period was truly one of enormous progress in bathroom design for the benefit of all.

Chapter 5

Apprenticed to Thomas Crapper

In the basement of the Fulham Road premises in Holmes Place there was a large walk-in safe built into the cellars. It had been a source of curiosity since I was a child visiting Alfred my grandfather with my two brothers, but always slightly sinister. It had a 6ft high steel door with the name of the maker embossed on a large brass badge: Hobbs Hart & Co. By appointment to Queen Victoria.

I recall grandfather sometimes going there for our pocket money when we visited and no matter what our age, he always gave us the same amount of money – two shillings and sixpence known as 'half a crown' – now expressed as 12 pence. I have no idea why great grandfather Edward or Frederick felt it necessary to own such a huge safe. So far as I am aware, neither had especially valuable items to store. Nor incidentally, do I know why grandfather sometimes found it necessary to pay pocket money from a tin box kept there, instead of putting his hand in his pocket – *but he often did!*

Inside, the cellar was about 8 feet high and some 10 to 12 feet deep. It also had a very damp and musty smell and was not a favourite place for us children. Certainly, we did not play our games of hide and seek in the basement or anywhere near it.

This is the impressive Coat of Arms on the 6ft door of the walk-in safe in the basement of 'Beaufort Works' Holmes Place, Fulham Road. Here we found Frederick's apprenticeship papers. Holmes Place is now part of the Royal Borough of Kensington and Chelsea.

A few months after I joined the company in 1947, father resolved to clear out the back end of the safe that was filled with old files and ledgers – some going back to the 1890s. On close examination he decided that its damp, cobweb covered walls should be cleaned and whitewashed. Lying on the damp shelves were many old documents. Amongst them, we found two folded sheets of parchment but sadly the outer layer fell apart in our hands.

The inner document turned out to be the original apprenticeship papers of Frederick Humpherson to Thomas Crapper and was dated 1871. It is one of the few existing examples of Crappers signature and is countersigned

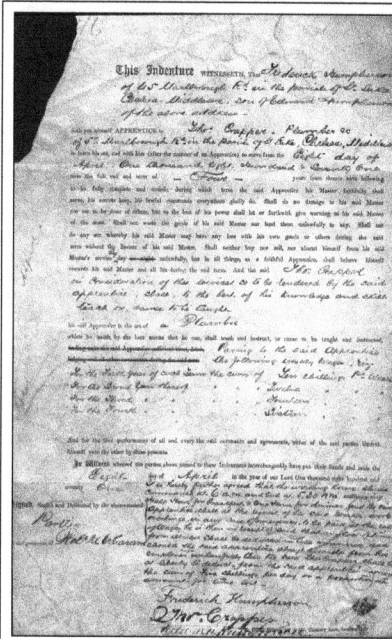

Robert Marr Wharam

Thomas Crapper

Indenture whereby Frederick Humpherson is apprenticed to Thomas Crapper for four years 1871 to 1875. It is signed by Thomas Crapper, Frederick and his father Edward Humpherson. It is witnessed by Crapper's partner – Robert Marr Wharam. It is shown as a full page in Appendix 2 – together with a transcript that may be easier to read.

by the apprentice Frederick Humpherson and Edward his father. We could just decipher from the remains, that the outer layer had been the apprenticeship paper of his younger brother Alfred, also to Thomas Crapper.

The witness to the document was Thomas Crapper's partner Robert Marr Wharam, who was also the Secretary to the company. He had brought financial and accounting skills to Crapper and he became the owner on Crapper's death. It is likely he had brought finance into the company as well. On *his* death, his son Robert Gillingham Wharam inherited the firm and later he sold it in 1963.

Frederick Humpherson was born on 2nd April 1854 at 29, Castle Street in the district of South St. Giles-in-the-Fields, Middlesex. On his birth certificate it was also listed as the residence of his parents. His father is shown as Edward Humpherson and his mother Matilda (neé Farmer) and Edward entered his profession as Silversmith.

In the Census of 1871 for the Parish of St. Luke's in Chelsea, residing at 45, Marlborough Road we find: Edward Humpherson aged 40, his wife Matilda aged 36, and their five children:

Frederick aged 17 – Plumbers apprentice to Thomas Crapper & Co.
William aged 14 – Zinc workers mate. (Likely also apprenticed to Thomas Crapper & Co.)
Alfred aged 9 Scholar (My grandfather. Later apprenticed to Thomas Crapper & Co.)
Charles aged 7
Elizabeth aged 3

The 1871 Census for 45 Marlborough Road, in the Parish of St. Lukes, Chelsea. It shows my great-grandfather Edward, his wife Matilda and their five children. The eldest is Frederick aged 17 and a 'Plumbers apprentice.' As we know, he was apprenticed to Thomas Crapper whose works were across the road.

I note that in the 1871 Census (Appendix 3), Edward now lists himself as a 'Carpenter' and not as a 'Silversmith' as he had done in Frederick's Birth Certificate in 1854.

On the apprenticeship document, Crappers premises are shown as being at 54, Marlborough Road, Chelsea and were opposite Edward Humpherson's home at No. 45. Thomas Crapper called his premises 'Marlboro Works' and that name was used both for these premises and later on in the Kings Road. It also served as a trademark for many of their fittings. Notice the use of the shortened word – 'Marlboro' instead of Marlborough.

We do not have a record of Frederick's actual progress as an apprentice with Crappers, nor do I know for certain why he only started his apprenticeship at the age of 17. It was normal to start apprenticeships at the age of 14, on leaving school and the full term was seven years. In view of his obvious scholarship in his examination results from **'Science and Art Department of the Committee of Her Majesty's most Honourable Privy Council for Education'** listed below, I can only surmise he continued his education, though I cannot trace where that took place.

Thomas Crapper's shop front in Marlborough Road.

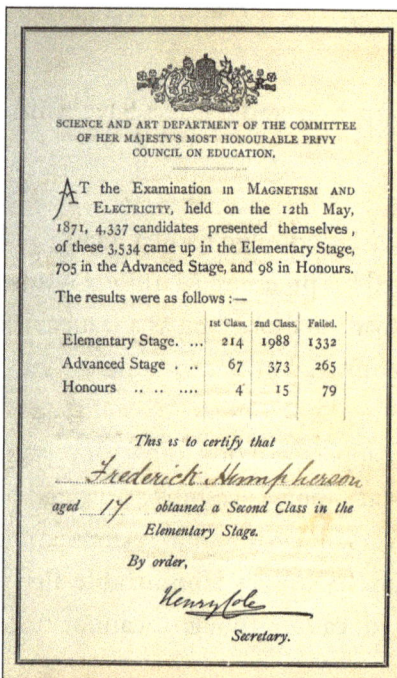

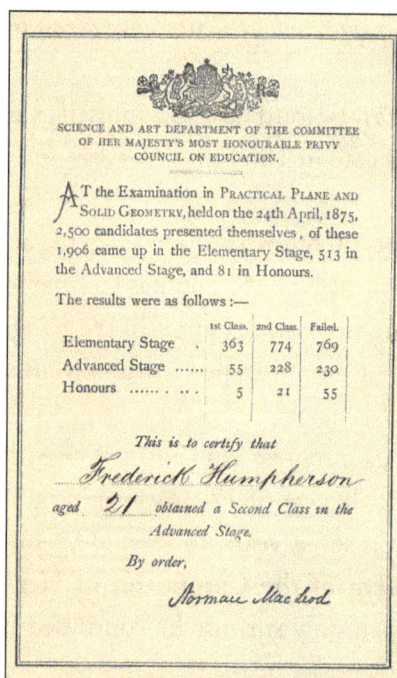

Far left: One of the Certificates awarded to Frederick Humpherson by Science and Art Department of the Committee of Her Majesty's Most Honourable Privy Council on Education. This, on Magnetism and Electricity, was taken on 12th May 1871. He also sat and passed examinations on 10th and 16th May 1871.

Another of the Certificates awarded to Frederick Humpherson. This, on Practical, Plane and Solid Geometry was taken on 24th April 1875 and he also sat and passed examinations on 1st and 11th May 1875.

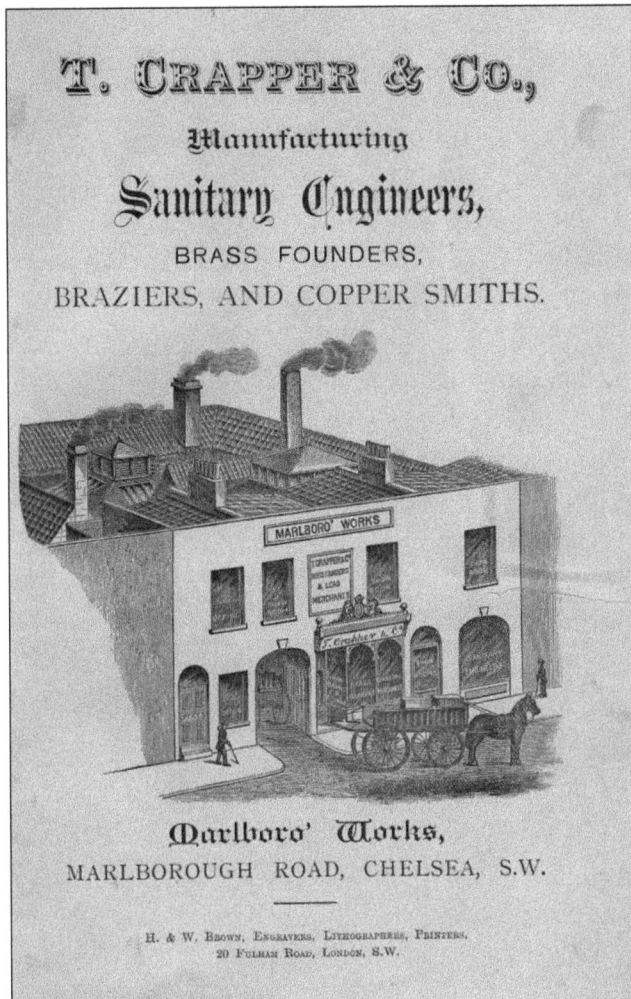

Thomas Crapper & Co.'s Marlboro' Works, 50-54, Marlborough Road, Chelsea. My great-grand father Edward Humpherson lived opposite in 45 Marlborough. The road later became Draycott Avenue.

education in a leather bound book containing twenty-three Examination Certificates from this august body. I suspect these might equate to something like 'A Level' examinations today.

They cover a wide variety of subjects from, Inorganic Chemistry / Acoustics Light and Heat / Magnetism and Electricity / Theoretical Mechanics / Metallurgy / Practical Plane and Solid Geometry / Physical Geography / Machine Construction and Drawing / Geology / Vegetable Anatomy and Physiology / Building Construction / Applied Mechanics. (See example Certificates in Appendix 4).

Frederick passed these examinations at Elementary, Second and First class levels, between the ages of 17 to 21. This would be a remarkable and scholarly achievement at any time. However, it is truly extraordinary – considering he was working at the same time, five days a week from 6.30 am to 5.30 pm. It is clear from the results of these examinations, that they indicate a very receptive and intelligent individual. It also suggests that he had indeed continued his education between the years 14 to 17. However, it does suggest Thomas Crapper allowed Frederick time off – at least for the two or three examinations – involved each year. Whether he deducted wages or not we shall never know.

At the same time, we should bear in mind he had to travel to and fro from his home in Chelsea, to any site where he was working - wherever that happened to be at the time. For example, the site might be at Hampstead - about six miles from Chelsea. With public transport so limited at the time, the chances are he might have to walk, yet be on site ready to work by 6.30 am and not leave for home in Chelsea until 5.30 pm. This left little time for studying, especially with such a variety of complex subjects.

Frederick's pay was to be ten shillings a week (£0.50) and this must be regarded as quite good apprentice pay for that period. It rose to sixteen shillings (£0.80) a week in his fourth year by which time he was 21.

In view of his subsequent achievements, there can be little doubt that Frederick was the outstanding apprentice of Thomas Crapper's company. Perhaps this success was partially responsible for the enmity that arose between the two companies – Crappers and Humphersons.

Chapter 6

1876 and the Chelsea Years

We know that Humpherson & Co. was already trading in 1876, based at 331, Kings Road, Chelsea. That is the western end of Kings Road – whereas Thomas Crapper's final premises were at the eastern – and more affluent-end of the road. We also know that later, Humpherson & Co. had a showroom at 297, Fulham Road on the corner of Beaufort Street, Chelsea. This lasted until 1902, when they transferred everything to their new purpose-built offices, showrooms and workshops at Holmes Place, 188a, Fulham Road.

For most of its history until 1902, the company offices were at 331 Kings Road Chelsea, just a few yards away from Beaufort Street. The picture is of one of our exhibition stands of the period and shows the office address and a range of products.

Their company catalogue of 1887 claims they are 'Manufacturers and Patentees' and this growing success, in ten years, was due entirely to Frederick. However, his father Edward had clearly financed the start up of Humpherson & Co., since Frederick had only been earning a maximum of sixteen shillings (£0.80) a week (£40 per annum) until 1875.

In fact, there was a partnership between Edward and two of his sons Frederick and William that existed *before* 1876 – the date the family have always regarded as the 'start-up' year. Edward's role had been to provide financial support to the infant company. However in 1876, Edward left the partnership to concentrate on his own building company further along Kings Road, towards the 'World's End' the name of a public house that gave its name to the western end of Chelsea.

Frederick and his younger brother William then ran Humpherson & Co. until 1882 when they parted company, thus leaving Frederick as sole owner.

We next hear of William down in Newton Abbott in Devon – as part of Hexter-Humpherson & Co. manufacturing clay products, including drainage pipes and fittings, tiles and bricks. He soon had a flourishing business and later acquired other firms in the same industry.

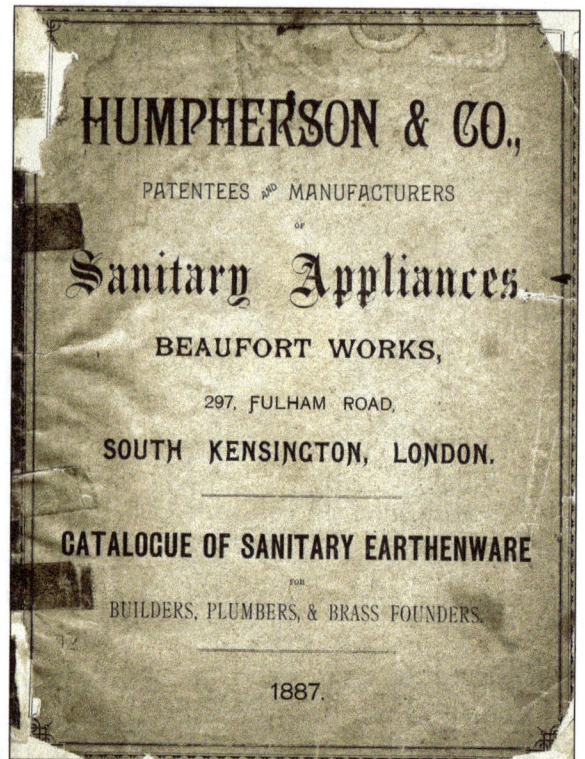

The cover of Humpherson & Co. 1887 Catalogue, proudly claiming they were 'Patentees & Manufacturers' and giving the address as 297 Fulham Road which is on the corner with Beaufort Street, Chelsea. The 'Beaufort' name was thereafter used for our various premises. Many of our products also used the name or its derivatives like 'Beauline' taps – 'Beauseal' – bath sealing strip – right up until 2006 were derived from it.

Mother remembered Edward well and told me that he was a 'Victorian' grandfather in the strictest and more unpleasant sense of the word. One must bear in mind she had positive likes and dislikes; this man was on the 'dislike' side of her barometer. Although she was quite young when Edward died, I nevertheless found she was seldom wrong in her judgement of people.

Humpherson & Co., run by Frederick, was increasingly successful. Bearing in mind he was so young at first, the progress was astonishing. This led to great prosperity for the firm. It enabled them first to occupy the showroom and workshops near the corner of Fulham Road and Beaufort Street Chelsea, then to make the very substantial move across the Fulham Road to Holmes Place – a turning off the main road.

There he had to finance the demolition of the three cottages on the site and erect what were by far the largest premises in the area. Not only that, he designed some of the building fittings himself, even the detail of the staircase and the windows. These alone would have been more expensive than standard production. His strong financial position came from his proficiency in all the spheres he undertook. It also brought a series of awards presented to him for improvements and inventions connected with the sanitary field and some of these were very prestigious.

As we have seen, one of the most famous cisterns of the Victorian period was by Frederick Humpherson, called 'Humpherson's Patent Syphon Cistern'. It is plainly shown above the illustration of the 'Beaufort' WC pan. Besides winning a Bronze Medal at the International Inventions Exhibition in 1885, the cistern was also awarded a Certificate of Merit from the Sanitary Institute of Great Britain in the same year.

The Sanitary Institute of Great Britain held an annual exhibition from 1877 to 1887. Frederick Humpherson exhibited his products at its 'Leicester Health Exhibition' of 1885. Here he showed his patent products and other wares.

'The Builder' Magazine in Volume LII January – June 1887 reports on another such an exhibition and describes Humphersons stand with these words:

"Messrs. Humpherson & Co. exhibit another tour de force in lead-working, some plumbers' brasswork of excellent quality and finish, and some good water-closets, including the 'Beaufort', which combines in one fixture a w.c., urinal, and slop-sink; this closet, like one or two others in the Exhibition, is of the pedestal-type and consists of an improved form of hopper, with a good flush."

What expands the Humpherson story is the reference to '*lead-working*' as we are in danger of overlooking Humphersons wider contribution in taps and lead work – so important at the time. The lead workshop produced quite stunning rainwater heads some for exhibition, but it was a regular part of its work. A few graced quite grand establishments but the bulk were for ordinary houses. The family still have some of the special heads but none as important as that requested by the Ministry of Works for 10 Downing Street – nearly a century after it was made. (See Notes: I).

During the latter part of the 19th Century the company continued to expand. It was increasingly concerned with the Home Office contracts supplying fittings for prisons and police stations. At the same time, its lead workshop produced large quantities of lead products. It became famous for special rainwater heads for both grand and domestic housing. Perhaps the supreme example of its work was its lead head shown above. (Its full story is told in Notes: J).

At the earliest one, he proclaimed Humpherson & Co. as 'Sanitary Engineers' of 331 Kings Road Chelsea. On a later stand he advertised his company more boldly, but perhaps more accurately, as being 'Patentees & Manufacturers of Sanitary Appliances'.

However, Frederick's most famous product remains as the 'Beaufort' wash-down WC pan and that is dealt with in the next chapter.

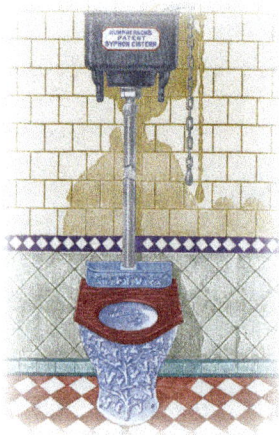

Chapter 7

The 'Beaufort' WC

In the Preface, I described how I engaged Chartered Patent Agents, Carpmaels and Ransford of Chancery Lane in London, to test the family claim that our 'Beaufort' pedestal **'Wash-down'** WC pan was the first design of its kind and the forerunner of many millions sold worldwide ever since.

However, I already had some initial support for the claim after reading the preface to Twyfords 1896 catalogue – much of it printed in colour. This is an extract from that Preface:

'In 1889, 'Wash Out' W.C. Basins were most in favour but there has been a gradual demand for an efficient and really reliable W.C. Basin on the 'Wash Down' principle, of which the 'Cardinal' and 'Deluge' are the best types.'

Here, we have the mighty Twyfords admitting that the 'wash-down' WC had taken hold in the sanitary industry.

Frederick Humpherson's 'Beaufort' Pedestal wash-down closet is the forerunner of most WC pans made today. Bear in mind this illustration is from our 1890s catalogue and yet millions of homes have an identical looking pan in use today. Indeed, it could be said that the DNA of the 'Beaufort' is present in all modern WC pans. However, the price at £1.16.0 (£0.60) is now somewhat different! The address of 297 Fulham Road is on the corner with Beaufort Street from which it derives its name.

PEDESTAL

CLOSET.

THE "BEAUFORT"

H. & CO.

TRADE MARK.

SECTION.

PRICES (either S or P Trap.)

All white basin and trap in one piece	...	...	...	£1 16 0
Blue Printed Inside ...	...	...	...	2 2 0
Blue Printed inside and outside	...	...	...	2 6 0
Flown color inside ...	...	..	...	2 4 0
Flown color inside and outside	...	...	...	2 10 0
Cane outside and white inside	...	...	...	1 8 0
All white with fixed slop top	...	...	...	2 12 0

If with vent socket add 1/- each.

When ordering please state if S or P trap is required.

HUMPHERSON & CO.,

Patentees and Manufacturers of Sanitary Appliances,

297, FULHAM ROAD, LONDON, S.W.

9

Pedestal THE "BEAUFORT" H.&CO. Closet.

TRADE MARK.

This Closet, unlike the ordinary form of basin, is not cased with woodwork, but forms a solid fixture by itself, so that the enclosure under which a receptacle is so often formed for dirt and filth is entirely dispensed with ; free access is thus given to all parts so that both the floor and basin can be easily kept clean, while the air can circulate freely round it. The mahogany seat being hinged, may be lifted, and the basin used for either a slop sink or urinal, and thus a wet seat, which is so objectionable, can be easily avoided.

All connections being **above** the floor and **within sight**, any leakage can be at once detected, and if the joint to the soil pipe is made with our **Patent Pipe Joint** an escape of sewer gas becomes almost an impossibility.

The basin and trap are constructed similar to our well-known **flush down closet**, which gained the Certificate of Merit of the **Sanitary Institute** of **Great Britain, 1885**, and has met with such general approval wherever fixed.

The outside of basin may be had with a raised ornamentation of ivy leaves, either plain or coloured.

Far excels any washout closet, and it has been highly recommended by Architects, Sanitary Engineers and others. It is made in one piece with either **S** or **P** trap.

Our Syphon Cistern is specially suitable for this closet, as it has a full $1\frac{1}{2}$-in. water way so can be used with either $1\frac{1}{4}$-in. or $1\frac{1}{2}$-in. pipe, and has no valves to get out of order.

HUMPHERSON & CO.,
Patentees and Manufacturers of Sanitary Appliances,
297, FULHAM ROAD, LONDON, S.W.

8

The Humpherson & Co. catalogue in the late 1880s makes these claims for its Beaufort Closet and the first paragraph alone is worthy of note. Further down it rightly boasted that it 'Far excels any-wash out closet and has been highly recommended by Architects, Sanitary Engineers and others.' When you realize that most of the world now use closets based on the 'Beaufort' – then such claims were clearly justified.

Then, as a result of the Carpmaels and Ransford research, I was able to state that my great uncle Frederick Humpherson designed the world's first one-piece wash-down WC pan, called the 'Beaufort' in the 1880s. The WC pan – as we know it today. His 1890 catalogue described it as being 'The Original pedestal wash-down closet.'

Below are quotations from books by four eminent writers in this field, confirming our claim. Then the final authentication came from 'The History of Twyfords' written by John Denley in 1982.

1. Roy Palmer - 1973

This is taken from 'The Water Closet: A New History' by Roy Palmer, published by David and Charles in 1973. Its jacket describes it thus: 'This is the most detailed examination of the development and variation of the WC, its place in society and in literature and its sudden popularisation in the nineteenth century.' The extract reads as follows:

'The proudest claim of Humphersons, and indeed the most important, is that they produced 'The Original Pedestal Wash-down Closet'. This claim is worth examination in detail because the wash-down or flush-down closet (the terms are synonymous) is the direct ancestor of the type in principal use all over the world today. The original 'Beaufort' scarcely differs in detail from many modern appliances, a tribute to the skill and inventiveness of the Humpherson family.

A comprehensive search of British Patent rights filed in the 19th century revealed the fact that a patent was granted to Frederick Humpherson for his 'Triune'. The current handbook of 1891 states that 'the basin is of the same shape as the well-known 'Beaufort' Closet thus showing that the 'Beaufort' was the earlier model. But events are often not as simple as they seem. The firm of Thomas Twyford has put forward a serious claim that 'the first pedestal wash-down water closet basin in one piece was introduced by Thomas Twyford in 1899 – the 'Deluge'. This would appear difficult to sustain in view of a pamphlet still in existence and from which is pertinent to quote. Advertising the 'Beaufort Pedestal Closet' in 1892 it is quite specific:

"The basin and trap are constructed to our well-known flush-down closet which gained the Certificate of Merit of the Sanitary Institute of Great Britain,1885. The outside of the basin may be had with a raised Ornamentation of Ivy leaves, either plain or coloured all white basin and trap in one piece £1–16–0."

As if this was not enough to dispense with claims, other than Humphersons, to have produced the first wash-down closet, further research was undertaken by Messrs Carpmael and Ransford, Chartered Patent Agents of Chancery Lane, London. In a letter dated 18th March 1970, they wrote:

"....we have conducted a subject matter search under the general heading water closets and more particularly under the heading of personal water closets of the wash-down type, and from the results which the search revealed together with information gleaned from the publication....... we have no reason to doubt the correctness of the statement 'The Original Pedestal Wash-Down Closet' appearing on the advertisement entitled The 'Beaufort Pedestal Closet."

Another claim by Lawrence Wright in his book 'Clean and Decent' that the wash-down closet was invented by D. T. Bostel in 1889 will similarly carry no more weight than that of Twyfords, and Humpherson's evidence seems irrefutable.'

2. Lucinda Lambton - 1978

The following is reproduced from 'Temples of Convenience' by Lucinda Lambton, published by Gordon Fraser in 1978.

'The firm of Humpherson & Co of Chelsea first patented the wash-down closet with their 'Beaufort' in 1884. Edward Humpherson had founded the firm in 1876, who was later joined by his two sons Frederick and Alfred, who had each served four-year apprenticeships with Thomas Crapper at his Marlborough Works in Chelsea.

Humpherson, at their Beaufort Works, produced a number of patented inventions, winning prizes and medals at exhibitions, but their greatest achievement of all was the 'Beaufort' of which so many millions have since been copied.'

3. David Eveleigh – 2002

The following is reproduced from page 130 of 'Bogs Baths and Basins – *The Story of Domestic Sanitation*' – by David. J. Eveleigh and published in 2002 by Sutton Publishing Limited, above a photograph of the 'Beaufort' WC pan.

'The Beaufort' wash-down closet was introduced in 1885 by Humpherson & Co. Chelsea. This was almost certainly the first fully enclosed pedestal wash-down closet and the precursor of the standard wash-down 'toilet' of the twentieth century. This unadorned example is in cane and white ware, but it was also made with oak leaf decoration in relief around the outside of the pedestal.'

4. 'Ceramic Water Closets' by Munro Blair

Munro Blair is an authority on the subject having worked for Twyfords, Armitage-Shanks and English China Clay. He has lectured and broadcast around the world on the technology, design, marketing and history of ceramic sanitary ware. In his book he says, under the heading 'Wash-down WCs':

'In 1884, Frederick Humpherson introduced the wash-down WC, considered to the first of its type.'

5. 'The Hidden Room – A Short History of the 'Privy' by Johnny Ragland

Johnny Ragland is a well-known designer now living and working in Austria. This is an extract from his book published in 2004.

'The wash-down W.C. followed the same pattern of development as the wash- out. However, Frederick Humpherson of Humpherson & Co. re-designed it and marketed the 'Beaufort', a pedestal flush-down water closet, from their workshops and showrooms in Chelsea. The 'Beaufort' was exhibited in 1885 and it was not long before other firms began to design their own flush-down/wash-down closets including Twyford whose 'Deluge' was a fairly inexpensive two piece closet with an exposed trap. However it was the wash-down that was finally adopted as the 'British loo' and which stood the test of time; today's wash-down closets bear a very close resemblance to the models of the last decade of the 19th Century.'

Authors Note: Frederick Humpherson called his initial design on the wash-down principle 'Flush-down' but by the end of the 1880s he was already describing it as 'Wash-down' and so it has continued since. Flush-down and Wash-down are the same thing.

6. 'A History of Twyfords 1680 – 1982'

Final confirmation comes from the most authentic of sources. It is contained in the book 'A History of Twyfords 1680 - 1982' – written by the historian James Denley, in collaboration with Harry Barclay – Chairman of Twyfords.

Twyfords were then one of the leading manufacturers of sanitary ware in the United Kingdom. The book was published in 1982 and this is an extract (but the emphasis is mine):

'Somehow, amid the chaos of building Cliffe Vale and establishing the fireclay factory, Twyford managed to continue the work of new product development. The 1889 catalogue was published as the new Works was coming on stream, with the mortar barely dry. Yet it was nevertheless a very significant one and ushered in the final frenetic decade of 'the Golden Age', when all but a few of the sanitary devices we know today were created in one long burst of invention.

Open the pages of this and succeeding catalogues almost at random, and you will nearly always find a new pattern, some important new design or improvement that has come down to us, with only the styling substantially changed.

For Twyford this was the year of the 'Deluge'. Since the early days of the 'National', the wash-out, in one form or another, had become the dominant WC (in some parts of the world, it still is). But in 1884, just as Thomas William [Twyford] had perfected the 'Unitas' **a completely new type hove into view, when Humpherson's of Chelsea introduced the 'Beaufort' - as far as we know, the first wash-down WC.**

The wash-down is the closet that most of us in the Western world are familiar with. *As its name perhaps suggests, it works on 'the Niagara principle' - like a waterfall. The flush falls directly from the cistern and gushes down the sides of the pan to sweep away the soil and clean the bowl by sheer force of water. This was the system that Twyford was to improve and help popularise with the 'Deluge', created while Cliffe Vale was still being built.'*

'This, coming direct from Twyfords official history, confirms the other authoritative statements. James Denley had the benefit of the unlimited research facilities and historical material of one of the oldest and largest pottery manufacturers in the country.

When Frederick Humpherson introduced his 'Beaufort' in the 1880s, he proudly called it **'The Original Pedestal Wash-down Closet'** – a claim that nobody thought it wise to challenge at the time. Roy Palmer's **'The Water Closet – A New History'** published in 1973 is regarded as the most exhaustive examination of the subject and his findings have also never been challenged.

I regard it as conclusive that Frederick Humpherson designed the World's first wash-down WC pan the 'Beaufort'.

Its DNA can clearly be seen in the design of every WC pan made today.

The full story of the design of the 'Beaufort' WC pan and press comments at the time are shown in Appendix 5.

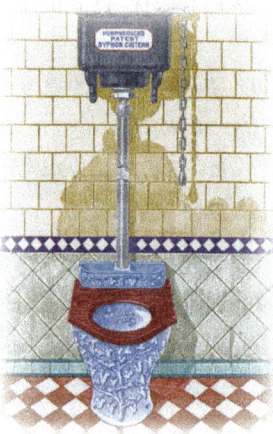

Chapter 8

Humpherson's Patent Syphon Cistern and Water Waste Preventer

My initial reason for writing this book was to ensure my great-uncle Frederick Humpherson was properly acknowledged as the designer of the 'Wash-down' water closet – the 'WC' as we know it today. I believe that has been dealt with fairly in the previous chapter 'The Beaufort WC'.

However, in the years following the publication of 'Flushed with Pride' by Wallace Reyburn, I became increasingly concerned with the suggestion that Thomas Crapper's 'Patent Valveless Water Waste Preventer' was the forerunner of syphon cisterns. Indeed, Reyburn suggests in his Chapter 3 'Pull and Let Go is Born' – that Crapper *perfected the cistern as loo users throughout Britain know it today*. We know, of course, that the design was nothing to do with Crapper but was a patent of a gentleman by the name of Albert Giblin.

That was some twelve years after Frederick Humpherson launched his award winning Beaufort 'Humpherson's Syphon Cistern and Water Waste Preventer' at the International Inventions Exhibition in 1885.

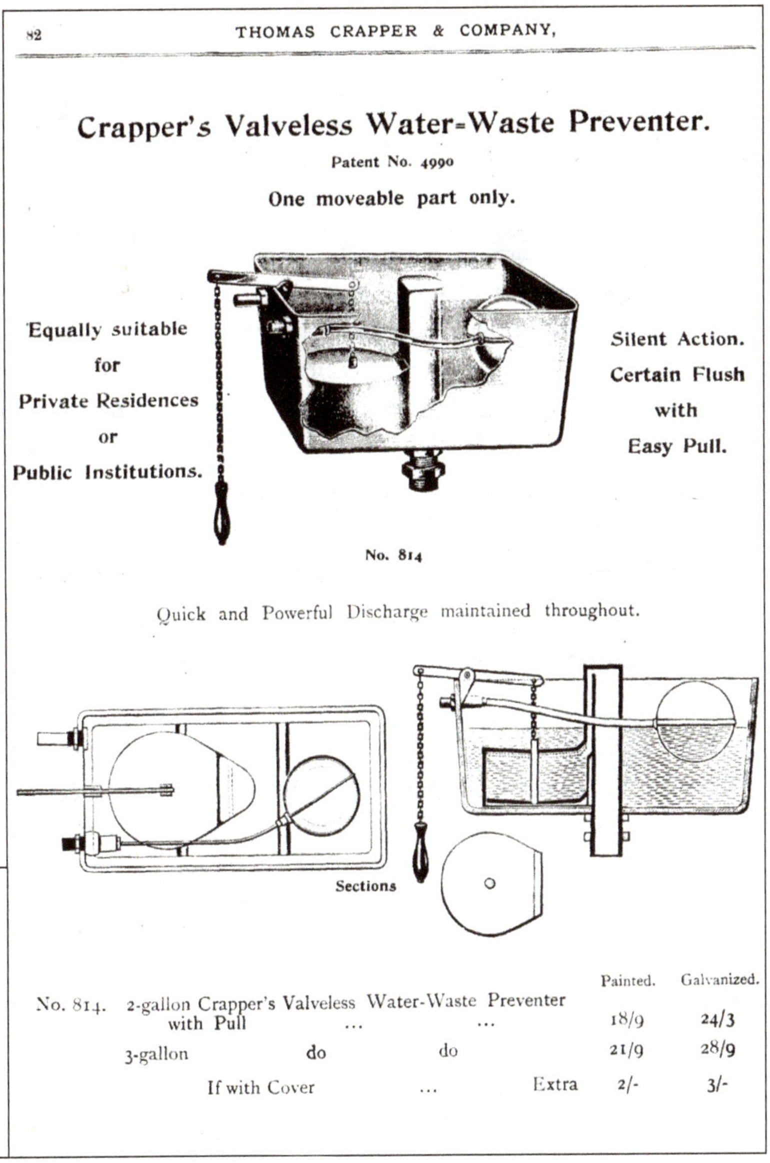

A page from a Thomas Crapper & Company catalogue (believed to be 1902) showing Crapper's Valveless Water-Waste Preventer Patent Number 4990. The patent was actually purchased from Albert Giblin. Thomas Crapper did not design the cistern as implied.

THOMAS CRAPPER & COMPANY,

Crapper's Valveless Water=Waste Preventer.

Patent No. 4990

One moveable part only.

'Equally suitable for Private Residences or Public Institutions.

Silent Action.
Certain Flush with
Easy Pull.

No. 814

Quick and Powerful Discharge maintained throughout.

Sections

			Painted.	Galvanized.
No. 814.	2-gallon Crapper's Valveless Water-Waste Preventer with Pull		18/9	24/3
	3-gallon do do		21/9	28/9
	If with Cover ...	Extra	2/-	3/-

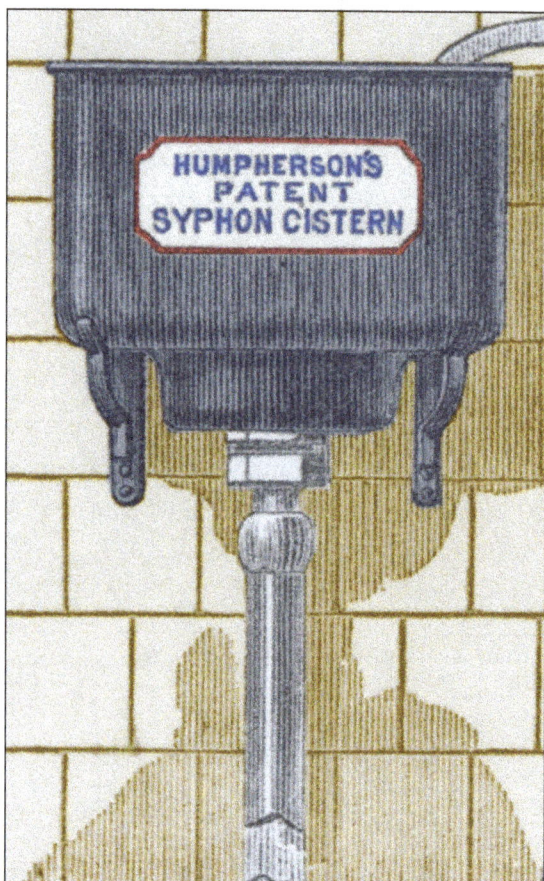
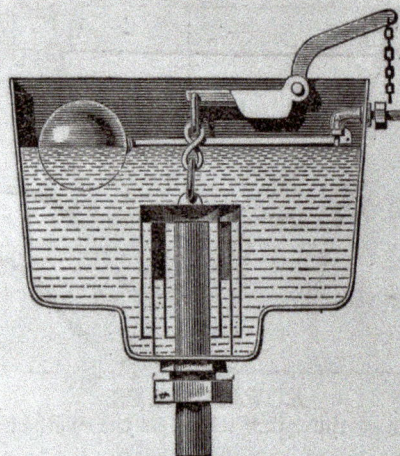

HUMPHERSON'S
PATENT
SYPHON CISTERN

HUMPHERSON'S
IMPROVED SYPHON CISTERN
And WATER WASTE PREVENTER.

Awarded the only Prize Medal for Flushing Cisterns at the International Inventions Exhibition, and Certificate of Merit by the Sanitary Institute of Great Britain.

Over 12,000 of these Cisterns are now in use.

Simple.

Strong.

No Rubbers.

No Valves.

Possesses the following Advantages:—

It is extremely simple in its action, and has great flushing power. It flushes well at a low head of water. The flush is certain, whether lever be held or not. There are no valves, excepting ball valve, to get out of order, thus dispensing with rubbers, washers, leathers, &c. Flushes well at height of only 2ft. Adapted for all kinds of Closets and Urinals.

This is Frederick Humpherson's Syphon Cistern Patent No. 2492 launched at the International Inventions Exhibition in 1885. It received a Bronze Medal from the Exhibition and a Certificate of Merit from the Sanitary Institute of Great Britain. Frederick's cistern worked on the bell syphon principle. When the chain is pulled the bell draws the water upwards and then it is syphoned down the flush pipe into the WC.

Many companies, including Thomas Ventom and Son (originally based in Burlington Road Fulham), later marketed a similar design. They called it 'The Burlington' and that became the generic name for the well bottom cistern – or 'water waste preventer'. Iron foundries up and down the UK sold millions of cast iron 'Burlingtons' from the early 1900s and soon Ventom were forced to sell theirs as **'The Original Burlington'**. Sales of cast iron water waste preventers continued well into the late 1960s.

In my early days as Humpherson's lorry driver, I often called at 'Tommy' Ventom's warehouse to collect 50 or so of their ordinary Burlingtons, that had been badged specially for us as:

The Beaufort
Humpherson & Co. Ltd.

Sometimes near me in the queue, might be Crapper's lorry, collecting *their* Burlingtons badged:–

The Leverett
T. Crapper & Co. Ltd, Chelsea SW.

At other times, drivers from other leading merchants would be there, collecting Burlingtons proclaiming *their* own name for example, Froys of Hammersmith and John Boldings.

I should add that I knew 'Tommy' Ventom (the 'Son' in the title) and his well known, much liked sales director Ernest 'Ernie' Adams. Sadly, the cast iron 'Burlington' trade was eclipsed by manufactures like Shires – producing similar products in plastic. Nevertheless, one can still purchase high – level cisterns – now more usually in vitreous china and 'period' designs!

The cisterns we have been describing here were called 'high level cisterns' since they were not close to, or connected to the WC pan. Instead, there would be a 5' 6" flush pipe on the wall feeding water from the cistern into the WC. Clearly, the inrush of water from that height was much more likely to clear the pan than a 'low level cistern' but the noise is considerably greater.

No wonder some WC pans were named Niagara, Torrent, Deluge or Tornedo!

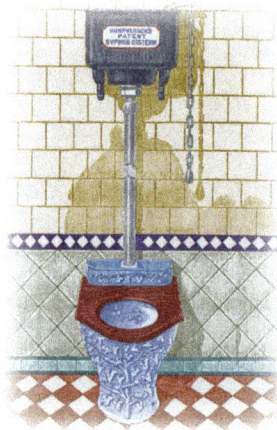

Chapter 9

Holmes Place

By 1901, the rapid and still rising success of Humpherson & Co. meant that their existing premises were no longer suitable. The offices were at 331 Kings Road, whilst the showrooms were on the corner of Beaufort Street and Fulham Road, with the workshops at the rear of the premises. These were all in the same general area of Chelsea but Frederick wanted to bring all his main activities together.

Fulham Road is a long thoroughfare, going across a large part of west London. It extends all the way eastward from Putney to Kensington. Its eastern end now forms part of the Royal Borough of Kensington and Chelsea.

Holmes Place was a cul-de-sac with three cottages with extensive grounds behind that came up for sale. It was large and ideal for his purpose being only some 500 yards from Beaufort Street. He then negotiated the purchase of its lease from the Gunter Estates. I have the original parchment deeds in which Sir Robert Gunter (Gunter Estates) allowed Frederick Humpherson to purchase the cottages and build his new premises. The lease for the entire site was for 80 years from 1901, with the ground rental fixed for the full duration of the lease, at £80 per annum!

The original lease from the Gunter Estates for Holmes Place is on parchment and in many pieces. However, some extent of the size of the property can be seen from this Indenture between Frederick Humpherson and Humpherson & Co Limited in 1919. Then Frederick sought a rental between the limited company he had just set up – and himself. Whilst the rent he paid to the Gunter Estates continued at £80 per annum fixed for 80 years – he charged the company £250 per annum – well he did have a controlling interest!

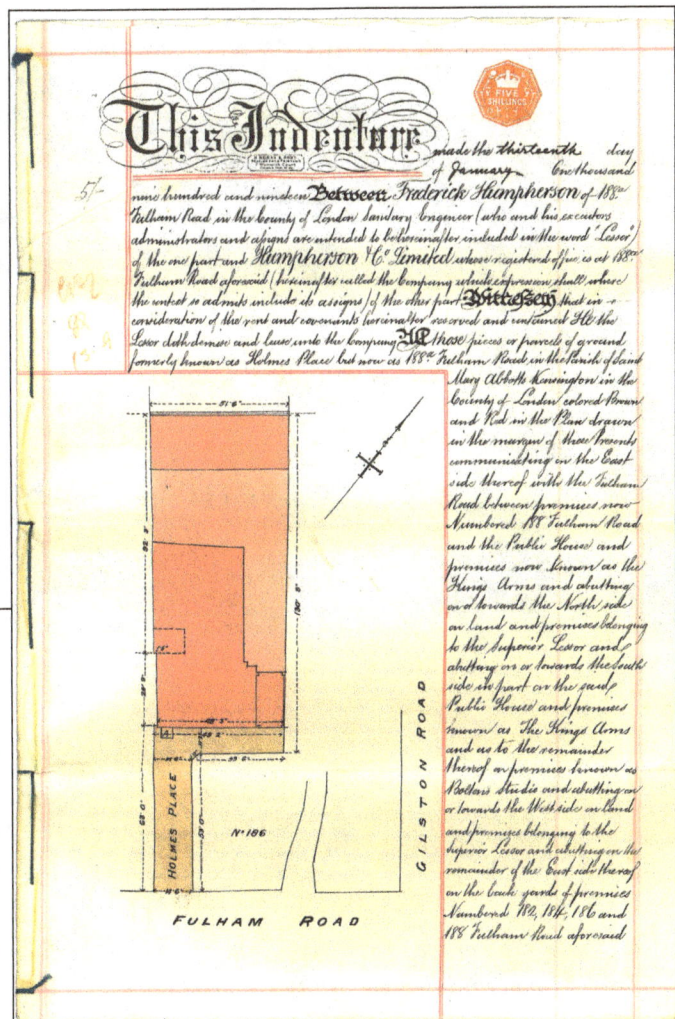

HUMPHERSON & C⁰ L^TD SANITA

This photograph of the showroom window of Humpherson & Co. was probably taken in the early 1920s. The title clearly has had an insert added '& Co. Ltd' following its formation as a limited company in 1919.

The Gunter Estate owned the freeholds of extensive areas of West Brompton (an area of Kensington) and it spread over into parts of west Chelsea.

As part of the contract, Frederick, obtained consent from the Estate to demolish the cottages and (in their place), build substantial showrooms, several offices, workshops, warehouse and stables. The extensive workshops at the rear of the property were for the many plumbers, fitters and carpenters, then employed on his special contract work – such as prisons and police stations.

In addition, he added a large apartment above the front of the property as his London home. It included four bedrooms, staff-room, pantry, extensive kitchen, scullery, toilets, bathroom, dining room 'drawing room' and central heating. There was also a well-equipped workshop with two lathes and workbenches, plus a darkroom where he could pursue his hobby of photography. Frederick took a close interest in every detail of his new home, particularly as he was to live above the firms' premises. He even designed such details as the shape of the banisters and handrails.

The tenant of cottage No. 3 Holmes Place ran a poultry and fish shop nearby in the Fulham Road – and he kept ducks and chickens in the rear garden of his home. When we sold the property in 1972, you could still see the cement fillets on the adjacent wall that would have sealed it to the roof of his chicken (and duck) coops.

In the 1960s, an elderly man called at the showroom and asked to see 'the Manager'. He told me that he had known the original cottages in Holmes Place when he was a child. Apparently, in addition to the poultry in No. 3, one of the other cottage owners kept goats in the garden and their milk was for sale. He recalled being sent to the cottage by his mother for goat's milk as she was having difficulty nursing his younger brother!

My mother told me that before World War I, cattle and sheep were regularly driven into Holmes Place, prior to being taken to the butchers shop across the Fulham Road. At that time, it had an abattoir licence and animals were slaughtered there. Over the years, the place must have had a quite rural air to it.

When the contractors were excavating the ground for the new buildings, they found that it consisted almost entirely of high quality sand suitable for construction. As a result of the find, it was used throughout the development with a considerable saving in costs. Bearing in mind the main part of the building was to have a full basement, they had to dispose of many tons of sand elsewhere. Apparently there was another major construction site in the region at that time and the sand was actually sold to them.

When Frederick died, he left most of his estate to his younger brother, my grandfather Alfred Humpherson. He soon moved into the flat in Holmes Place with his wife Jane, and his three children Sidney, Ernest, my mother Edith and continued to live there after his wife died in 1926.

After the death of Alfred in April 1945, my mother and father took possession of the apartment and they moved in at the end of 1945 with my older brother Ron. I was still working in Calcutta at the time and returned to London from my later posting to Singapore in early 1947.

The famous 'Finch's' pub on the corner of Holmes Place the haunt of the Chelsea 'In-crowd' in the 1960's. Our property can be seen at the back to the right hand side of the picture.

By 1954 we were living in the two bungalows I had designed and built in Caterham in Surrey - one for my wife Jane and our sons, and one for mother, father and my brother Ronald. My father sadly died early in 1956 and I became responsible for the family business.

The King's Arms Public House - widely known simply as 'Finches' – was on the west side of Holmes Place. Now that the flat was unoccupied there was considerable misuse of the right-angled road by its clients, especially on busy Friday and Saturday nights. In 1957, I obtained permission from the Council to shut off the road when we were closed. They actually granted the freehold of Holmes Place itself to us, on our written undertaking to illuminate the property in perpetuity. I readily agreed and shortly afterwards fitted gates across the entrance. As a result, we could close the road each evening and over the weekends.

I suspect their prompt agreement to our taking over the road, had something to do with their existing commitment to lighting Holmes Place as public property. Over the years, sending a gas company 'lighter man' at dusk and dawn must have been a considerable expense to the Council. We took on responsibility for lighting the road with an electric light – on a time switch!

I became increasingly concerned about the leasehold situation. In 1962, I telephoned the Estate agents, who by then purchased many of the Gunter Estate freehold properties. With our lease having less than twenty years to run, I asked if I could purchase the freehold? The man I spoke to sounded surprised at my request and put me through to the senior partner. He asked how I came to know that the company was winding up? Of course, I had no idea it was happening but did not tell him.

He telephoned back the following day and suggested they would transfer the freehold to us for £10,000. I might have had trouble finding even £1,000 at the time but bravely suggested £7,500 and we settled on £8,750. Having agreed a deal, I then had to quickly find a way of raising that amount of cash for the property and to fund the rapid growth of the company. In the end, our accountants Lord, Foster and Partners of King William Street in the City of London, put us in touch with the Eagle Star Insurance Company and we soon raised £30,000 (today that would be about £560,000) on a life insurance policy on me.

Thus, we became the freeholders of Beaufort Works – a large Kensington property. Plus, we had money in the bank as well as now owning the roadway – Holmes Place. All that was necessary now was for the business to continue to grow, as I had predicted in my cash flow projections to Midland Bank. Our first need was for office space for the increasing number of staff we employed and the empty apartment above the showrooms was my immediate target.

However, I was able to show that part of the flat had been used as offices at times. My argument being that the annual audit took place in the privacy of its dining room, as well as our board meetings. It was rather tongue in cheek but it was accepted and I moved my office up there.

I then demonstrated that the workshop in the flat had clear connections to the business and obtained permission for our use of the whole first floor. In 1963, having demonstrated that – as the first floor was now offices – the second floor could not be regarded as domestic dwelling. I had engaged a planning consultant to make our case and we finally received formal consent to turn the whole flat into offices for our rapidly growing company. This was quite a coup, since it also added immensely to the value of the site.

This picture gives a better idea of the width of the property – yet further to the right was an archway over the road, leading to the workshops and the earlier stables. The window display shows our period of transition when I also established the company as engineers suppliers. Fortunately, that set us on the path to profitability. Note, we had removed the earlier sign reading 'Sanitary Engineers' and now declared ourselves to be 'Plumbers' and Builder's Merchants.

By that time, due to an amalgamation, the local authority was now 'The Royal Borough of Kensington & Chelsea'. However, it troubled me that the Council's name tablet existed on the flank wall of Holmes Place and wrote to them. The Town Clerk of the Council at the time was Leslie Holmes and I received a letter from him dated 28th January 1970 in reply (Appendix 6), confirming they claimed no rights over our private road. I was grateful for his statement that '*The existence of official name tablets does not in any way imply that the Council have, or would seek to claim, any such rights.*'

On one occasion, Gilbert Harding, a well-known but rather bombastic TV celebrity, challenged our right to close the road! His driver had parked their car in Holmes Place just before we closed at 12 noon – then our usual closing time on Saturdays. I told the driver to move the car or it would be locked in. He went into 'Finches' public house next door and fetched out an irate Gilbert Harding. He said I could not close the road, as there was a street sign still on the wall saying 'Holmes Place' – with the local authorities name on it!

I told him it was now a private road but we had a fierce argument. However, although he was a large and daunting character – he clearly did not like the idea of his car being locked in behind our new gates – his driver parked elsewhere. Gilbert Harding returned into the pub with much muttering!

I had a copy of Leslie Holmes letter with me on the following Saturday – all ready for Gilbert Harding. However, we had no further challenges to our rights over Holmes Place.

I sold the entire property to the Peachey Property Corporation in 1972 for a considerable sum. They offered to give us 25% more if I were to take payment in the Corporation shares. I refused and took a cheque instead. The company's share value collapsed shortly afterward – one of my better decisions.

Two years later it became the first of some 65 'Holmes Place Health Clubs'.

Chapter 10

Tall, Dark, Handsome – *and Enigmatic!*

When I started to write about Frederick Humpherson I found so little documentation that I thought it would be difficult to build a personal picture of him.

In mother's papers, I found a collection of letters from Frederick to his wife, Jean Swan Dunbar whom he had married in Chelsea on 20th December 1877. These letters are obviously drafts in Frederick's handwriting to his wife regarding their final separation in 1885. There are also letters to and from a Priest – Andrew Mearns of the London Congregational Union who claims in his letter to *'..still be a friend of both..'*. The letter is dated the 29th July 1885 but clearly his plea *'to return to the happiness of bygone days'* was in vain. They signed the formal separation on 30th July 1885.

Their separation is amongst the few papers that still exist as **'A Deed of Separation'** and this indenture shows him living at 331, Kings Road, Chelsea. He describes himself as a 'Plumber' although he was clearly no longer simply a plumber. You will recall his father called himself on birth certificates and census returns variously, a silversmith, a carpenter and later a builder.

This is Frederick Humpherson around 1900 when he would have been in his mid-forties.

Frederick finished his four-year apprenticeship to Thomas Crapper in 1875. Two years later in 1877 age 23, he married Jean Swan Dunbar and was already a partner in Humpherson & Co. The company had been founded as a partnership in the early1870s between his father Edward, brother William and himself. Almost the only records remaining about Frederick is this rather unpleasant correspondence about his separation. His attitude in it, towards both his wife and daughter Amy, can charitably only be described as severe.

He was a well-known and gifted photographer and a 'dandy' (my mother's description), so it is also strange that no photograph remained of him, until one was discovered by chance. I have to ask why – *considering the breadth of his interests* – no other records should exist after his death in 1919?

I can only assume everything else was then destroyed by his brother, my grandfather Alfred. My mother and her part of the family clearly did not really like Frederick, but perhaps this was merely reflecting a dislike for his lifestyle.

When Frederick formed Humpherson & Co. into a Limited Liability Company in 1919, he owned 100% of the firm. Looking at Alfred's life after his brother's death, I have to say he had every reason to be grateful to his brother for bequeathing almost everything to him.

There were comments on Frederick's gregarious lifestyle from mother and from my uncle Sidney Humpherson. They both said, in careful language, that he was a 'Ladies man'. I know that his housekeeper Minnie Dodds was prominent in these comments but the implication was clear that there were 'others' as well. He apparently owned a house in Merton, not far from Wimbledon Lawn Tennis Club mother suggested it was bought for a 'Lady friend'. Mother would never have used the word 'Mistress'.

In Frederick's Will, Minnie Dodds was left £52 per annum until her death, or unless she married. Her address is shown as being 188a, Fulham Road, the same as his, but she was his housekeeper – described in earlier census returns as 'Servant'!

Now I come to a recent discovery. I was looking through the few papers left intact by Alfred and there is an envelope marked 'Mr Humpherson's Grave' in Brompton Cemetery in the Fulham Road. I had seen this many times before; it has a plot number mentioned on it but I had never bothered to open the envelope.

However, in view of the importance of my research, I looked closer and found that the envelope actually reads '*Mrs* Humpherson' – and not as I earlier thought '*Mr* Humpherson'. The lettering is far from clear. Inside are the details of the burial of 'Eleanor Sarah Humpherson' in 1913.

I then assumed that it was a joint grave in Brompton Cemetery for '*Eleanor Sarah Humpherson – died in 1913*' and '*Frederick Humpherson – died in 1919*'.

In June this year (2014), I visited the cemetery. It occupies some 40 acres between Old Brompton Road on the north, Fulham Road to the south, and only a short distance from Chelsea Football Club. I was well received by Jay Roos, the Cemetery Manager. He located the grave from a plan and we set off to find it. I was shocked by the state of part of the grounds. Apparently due to staff cuts, large areas are overgrown with grass, weeds, nettles and brambles – much of it four feet tall.

Mr Roos casually mentioned that there were four people buried in the Grave 53910. That came as a complete shock to me. I assumed it contained just Eleanor Sarah Humpherson and Frederick Humpherson!

Brompton Cemetery in West London. It was quite impossible to precisely locate grave 53910 in the tangled brambles and weeds. Two slabs exist side by side in the general area but neither has names remaining on them. There is a cross and a headstone – again now without markings.

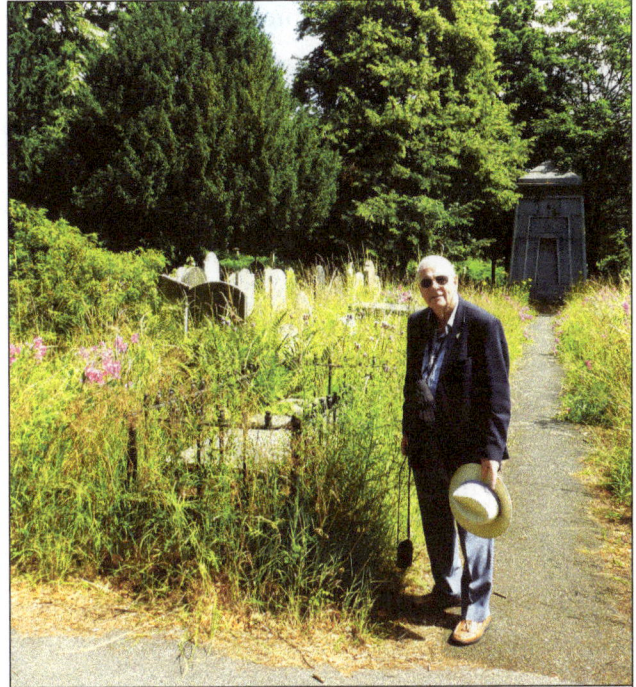

Myself visiting Brompton Cemetery in June 2014. The grass and weeds are mostly 4 feet but in the left background is one of several widespread bramble bushes standing up to 6 feet, spread over a large area.

I have found a sale document for Plot 53910 from a Mary Anne Moore '*...the registered owner of Private Grave 53910 in consideration of the sum of Eleven Pounds eighteen shillings and six pence [£11.18s.6p] by Charles Edward Scarse to hereby bargain, sell and assign....*' **This is dated 11th April 1899**. Then I have a very similar document between the same Mr Scarse to Frederick Humpherson dated 19th June 1913, assigning his rights to Grave 53910 to Frederick but now for the sum of Ten Pounds. (£10.00). What I did not expect was that they each had already buried relatives in the grave. Is it conceivable that Frederick did not know at the time?

I have read the cemetery list for Grave 53910. A 'Mary Young' was buried in it on 2nd November 1868 after the ground was dug down to 13 feet, 'Mary Ann Scarse' was buried in it on 11th April 1899 at 12 feet and Eleanor Sarah Humpherson at 11 feet and finally my great-uncle Frederick Humpherson was buried at 9 feet from the surface. It seems the gravediggers stopped when they struck 'something'! I have emphasised the dates above as they show that Charles Scarse sold his rights to the grave to Frederick Humpherson – on the same day he buried his wife!

The depths puzzled me but Jay Roos explained the depths recorded by the gravediggers were approximate. Nevertheless, they were not likely to be wrong by more than 6 inches or so!

The only explanation is that the lower coffins collapsed due to the great weight of soil piled on top. Remember, these graves are not the accepted 6 feet deep. Apparently in Victorian times, Brompton Cemetery usually dug graves down to 17 feet. That must have been difficult for the gravediggers, given the small area involved.

The picture gives an idea of the difficulty faced in locating the grave. Many upright gravestones made of stone have shed the names of those interred over the 130 – 150 years since they were put in place. Only those of granite seem to be have remained intact and the lettering on them is still legible when it is of lead.

Frederick describes Eleanor Sarah as his 'Wife' in the 1891 Census returns for Woodhall Spa near Horncastle in Lincolnshire. He described her as his 'Wife' in the 1901 census and again in 1911. In both the Census for 1901 and 1911, the address is 188a Fulham Road – also known as Beaufort Works.

However, in the 1891 Census return for St. Peter's Parish in Fulham, 'Jean S. Humpherson' appears as 'Wife' status 'Married' – 'living on her own means' with her daughter Amy – as 'Teacher of Piano Forte'. In the 1911 Census she and Amy are shown again in similar terms. Jean Swan Humpherson died in the 1930s.

This is the 1891 Census for Woodhall Spa in Leicestershire. In a 'The Fairlawn Lodging House' we find an entry for Frederick Humpherson – status married, Eleanor Humpherson – status married and 'Hannah Dodds' servant. She later became their Housekeeper and as 'Minnie' Dodds appears in Frederick Humpherson's Will in 1919. All this is after Frederick's separation from his wife Jean Swan in 1885 – who was never divorced from him. She continued in all subsequent census to enter herself as 'Married' as indeed she was – to Frederick Humpherson!

Frederick died in 1919 and left his daughter Amy Humpherson £52 per annum – although the Will does not show their relationship. My grandfather Alfred Humpherson paid that until he died in 1945. Then mother continued the payments and in latter years it became my responsibility until Amy died. By comparison, he left the company secretary £104 per annum and Minnie Dodds his 'faithful Servant' £52 per annum. Everything else was left to my grandfather Alfred Humpherson.

We know Frederick was legally separated from his wife Jean Swan (née Dunbar) in 1885. However, after exhaustive searches we can find no record of a divorce from her, or a marriage to 'Eleanor Sarah'. Thus, Eleanor Sarah was continually entered as Frederick Humpherson's wife in repeated census and buried as 'Mrs Eleanor Sarah Humpherson' though they were never married. I am advised that it was not unheard of for a partner to be described as 'Wife' in a census and even to be buried under that false surname.

As an interesting aside, Frederick's solicitor James Allward of 10, Gray's Inn Square in the City of London, drew up the 'Deed of Separation' in 1885 and my present solicitor, is his great-grandson Alasdair Allward.

A Pro-Forma receipt always intrigued us for the 'Woodhall Spa Water Company' from 'The Collector Mr F. Humpherson' and the Collectors Office address is given as Beaufort Works, Woodhall Spa. It is marked 'Cheques payable to Capital and Counties Bank Horncastle'.

WOODHALL SPA WATER COMPANY.

Mr. ....

Mr. F. HUMPHERSON, Collector, applies for payment of ....Quarter's

Water Rate to ....

The Collector will call .... £

Water Rates received at any time at the Collector's Office, **BEAUFORT WORKS, WOODHALL SPA.**
Cheques and Post Office Orders to be crossed " CAPITAL AND COUNTIES BANK, HORNCASTLE."

N.B.—The Company's Official Receipt, signed by the Collector, will alone be recognised in discharge of the payment of this demand.

Amongst the papers I found in the desk was this further indication of Frederick's great interest in Woodhall Spa. Here he is acting as the 'Collector' for payments due to the Woodhall Spa Water Works – payable at Beaufort Works.

The Woodhall Spa Cottage Museum found this picture of 'Beaufort Works' Woodhall Spa. It reminded me of Arthur Meadows oft' told story – that Frederick had a 'bicycle works' in the Midlands. It certainly looks as if the group of men are associated with the premises in some way.

With the great help of the Woodhall Spa Cottage Museum, I now have a picture of 'Humpherson & Co. Beaufort Works' in Woodhall Spa. Clearly, Frederick was dividing his time between his business in Beaufort Works in Chelsea and another, by the same name, in Lincolnshire! One can only assume the choice of location had something to do with his affair with Eleanor Sarah?

The Humpherson & Co at Woodhall Spa – seems to have had a multiple role. Firstly, it was involved with bicycles to a fairly substantial extent. The photograph shows a number of men standing alongside the building – could they be the works staff all dressed up for this formal photograph?

Bicycles were very important in rural England as very few yet owned a car. However, the enterprising Frederick, also catered for cars with his 'New Motor Car Garage' with *Accommodation for Chauffeurs including pit and washing stand with water laid on'*.

He was also advertising this Humpherson & Co. – as 'Ironmongers, Sanitary, Heating & Electrical Engineers' and at the same time selling *All kinds of Golf, Tennis and Cycling requisites'*. A truly diverse enterprise!

The Woodhall Spa library found an advertisement for Humpherson & Co. 'Beaufort Works and Garage Woodhall Spa' – and in small print 'And at London'. There is a motley collection of bicycles in the picture including basket weave chairs to be pulled by a bicycle.

The early claim by my mother that Frederick Humpherson was 'tall dark and handsome' puzzled me. I had visions of Frederick being 6ft tall and towering over everyone in the office. Finding his portrait has made me reconsider the matter and I realised why she made the point that he was tall.

Height is of course, relative and from mother's point of view he would appear to be tall. I should explain that she was 5ft 2½" (*and absolutely insisted we remember the ½ inch*). Her brother Sidney I would guess, was 5ft 5" and his father Alfred, around the same. Certainly, neither was over 5ft 6". I only met mother's brother Ernest Humpherson once as I explained earlier, but he was a similar build to Sidney in every respect – including his height.

I have found some old family photographs. In one you can see Alfred with William Hedgecock, Humpherson's chief designer until World War II, and he seems to tower over him, even allowing for some camera distortion.

My grandfather Alfred with Humpherson's general manager – William Hedgecock. I barely remember him but he was probably 6 feet tall – again suggesting that Alfred would hardly be 5 feet 6 inches. Of course, there is an element of distortion with William being nearer the camera.

Mother insisted that Frederick was tall. Here she is at her then home at 30 Bovingdon Road Fulham, with her brother Sidney. As we know mother was 5 feet 2½ inches and Sidney seems only a little taller. You might note his dress sense – even then the title 'Dandy' fits!

There is a picture of mother and Sidney taken at their home in Bovingdon Road Fulham before they moved into Holmes Place in 1920. I would put her age then as around seventeen so it must have been around 1914. She certainly appears almost as tall as Sidney and we know she was only five feet two *'and a half'* inches. I vividly recall Sidney wearing spats over his shoes, winter and summer. He always carried a walking stick, wore gloves and a black Homburg hat. I am sure he was emulating his uncle Frederick Humpherson whom in conversations with me, he clearly admired.

In Chapter 14 there is a picture of Alfred playing bowls at Barnes Common Bowling Club only a short distance from Richmond. He can best be described as 'stocky'. I recognise the cigarette holder as one of the many he machined for his own use out of the stocks of ivory. At the turn of the century, all the best 'Beaufort' WC cisterns were supplied with brass chains having 'Ivory Pulls' so ivory offcuts were plentiful.

Looking again at these pictures of the Humpherson family, it is not difficult to see why mother should consider Frederick tall. By comparison to her father and brothers he would appear so, even if he were only average height.

I started these notes on Frederick thinking that I knew very little about him except that as my mother said, 'he was tall, dark and handsome' and 'he was a ladies' man'! The more I have written, the more I realise that we actually do know quite a lot about this extraordinary man. Frederick was:

* Self educated to remarkably high and broad technical standards.
* Designer of the world's first one-piece pedestal wash-down WC pan – the pan as we know it today.
* An accomplished engineer.
* An inventor with awards and patents to his name.
* A successful businessman with interests in design and manufacturing.
* A member if the Chelsea Arts Club.
* A member of the Chelsea Photographic Society and winner of numerous prizes.
* A Fellow of the Royal Photographic Society.
* Mother would have added – *'and a ladies' man'!*

Yes mother, perhaps it was a good description – 'Tall, dark and Handsome'
but I would add – *enigmatic!*

Chapter 11

Cop Shops and Prisons

As small children, my brother Ronald and myself used to delight in visiting my grandfather's business in Holmes Place, especially when it was open and the staff was about. However, I am not so sure the staff shared the same sense of pleasure! In the early 1930s, the task of keeping an eye on us during our visits fell to Arthur Meadows, who was then the assistant manager of the Trade Counter.

To us the showroom, workshops and warehouse were a huge, exciting warren. On one visit, I remember finding a pile of, what appeared to be, glass bricks, about 6" x 4" and around 1" thick. Arthur told me that they were glass from prison windows and that Humpherson fitted out all the 'cop shops and prisons' in London and the South East of England!

I realised later that his statement not only contained slang that we were taught to avoid but was a slight exaggeration. However, it is undoubtedly true that the many prison and police station contracts obtained by the company in the 1890s and early 1900s were one of Frederick Humpherson's greater achievements.

In the warehouse basement, a dark and forbidding place for small children, were stacks of other prison materials. Airbricks of all sizes, ventilators, cell-bed bearers, even window frames and a few cell doors. On the warehouse top floor, was an assortment of gullies for police station stables, heavy-duty pans for their WCs but most interesting of all, some thirty of Frederick's patent 'Triune' WC pans. These WC pans were enamelled cast iron and designed to be built into the cell wall. Arthur assured us with some pride, that no prisoner had ever smashed one!

Frederick Humpherson had created all these products. The prison and police station contracts were a major part of his success that now turned to supplying military installations. Hence his price list of 1905 listing 'The Triune' enamelled iron Pedestal Closet (used in Cell W.C's)' at the top of the page.

Further down we read of two versions of his 'No 2 'Beaufort' Pedestal Closet' the first as *Used in Officers and Married Quarters W.C's)* and then below it the similar closet and seat but of a lesser standard as *Used in Men's W.C's).*

Much has rightly been made of Thomas Crapper & Co. purchasing a patent then passing it off as their own. Therefore, I note with some satisfaction, that Fredrick once purchased a patent air ventilator for prison use.

It appears in a blue-print we have of prison fitments as an 'Arnolds Ventilator' – acknowledging the name of the original designer.

Humpherson employed specialist plumbers and fitters in those days – mostly used to install our own products. Certainly, that was the case with the prisons and police stations. When I joined the company in 1947, we still had a few men who had worked on those contracts - my uncle Sidney Humpherson, George Williams and Jack Herbert, to mention a few.

Amongst the many Police Stations containing Humpherson's products was Bow Street pictured here. We supplied the complete range from standard WC's, cell WCs, cell doors, remote flushing levers and indeed all the plumbing and sanitary work involved.

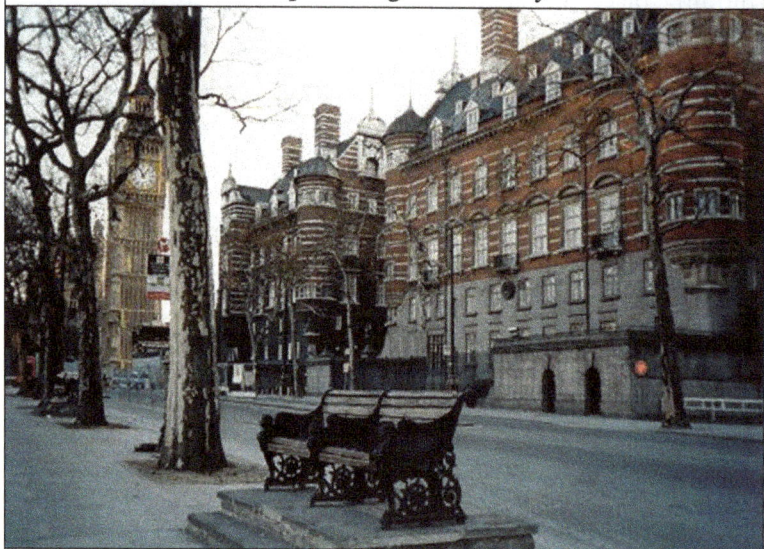

New Scotland Yard the headquarters of the Metropolitan Police until 1967 when it moved to Broadway in Westminster, with its well-known revolving sign outside.

They told me that, among the many police stations in the Metropolitan Police area supplied by Humpherson & Co. were Bow Street, Notting Hill Gate, Battersea and most importantly, New Scotland Yard. I suspect that most of this was in the period before World War I, although we were involved with the contracts until 1926.

I can be positive about the date, because of a tale told to me by George Williams who was present at the time. Apparently, the chief architect (or surveyor) for the Metropolitan Police area, was very partial to good Havana cigars. For many years, he had received a box as a Christmas gift from the firm.

On visiting a police station contract in January 1926, my grandfather Alfred Humpherson happened to meet the great man and asked if he had enjoyed the cigars. In reply he expressed his thanks but added that unfortunately, the box had arrived broken in the post and the cigars ruined. My grandfather's immediate response – and I can quote the words from George Williams, was a gruff – *'What do you want me to do about it – give you another box?'* Breathtaking tact and salesmanship!

Perhaps, through superintending the firm's men and its contracts, rather than assisting in the management of the company, this demonstrates that Alfred was not trained to take over from his brother Frederick. Needless to say, we never again supplied the prison or police service, except for jobbing repairs. The major contracts went elsewhere and gradually, different patterns of fitments were incorporated in prison and police station design.

My own specific knowledge of this aspect of Humperson's work is limited to the period after I joined the company in 1947. We were occasionally asked for some of the various items we held in stock but these orders were few and far between.

For a few years, we received regular orders for the springs used in the lever to operate the WC cistern. Obviously no chains could be installed in case a prisoner committed suicide with them. The famous company Terry made the springs for us and we ordered them a hundred at a time – an indication of the volume of work we had carried out through the earlier years

The lever mechanism for cell or remote operation of the WC was entirely Frederick's design – just one of many he used in this very specialised work.

From time to time, we were asked for cell airbricks or vents that had been broken. However, the last call we had for a major prison fitment was for a cell bearer for Reading Gaol, where Oscar Wilde had spent his two-year sentence.

With our expansion in the late 1950s, it was quite difficult to justify the space devoted to the stable gullies and special prison WC pans – all of which were dormant stock. We did try to sell them but found no buyers and so they were dumped. In the 1960s we sold off the remaining cast iron airbricks, vents and cell bearers as scrap, in our bid to find space for more current stock.

Thus, we came to the sad end of what had been a major source of trade for the company and a matter of great pride for the family.

The Police Station work included New Scotland Yard on the Embankment at Westminster and it would have had the whole range of Humperson's products. The cast iron soil stacks were renewed and one of our soil pipe inspection covers is illustrated. Note it has the name 'Humpherson & Co London' cast on it.

The last item of Humpherson's prison range supplied was a corbelled bed-bearer for a cell in Reading goal. I would think it would be in the mid-1950s. Soon afterwards, due to the pressure on space, we decided to collect all remaining stocks of cast iron fittings from the range and sold them as scrap.

Chapter 12

Humphersons at War

When I joined the company in 1947, we were still employing Charlie Keen. He had joined the company in the late 1890s, to make our wood products in the company workshops at Beaufort Works, Beaufort Street, Chelsea. Then these included such items as WC seats, bath panels, sink brackets, WWP boards, toilet paper boxes, etc. He was a joiner by trade and, over the years, gradually took full responsibility for our increasing turnover in these products.

One of the many interesting items made over this period were our teak toilet-paper boxes. These were rectangular boxes that fitted at the back of the WC pan with two compartments each side of the flush pipe. In this was placed torn newspaper for use as toilet paper or, in more affluent households, some of the new toilet tissue paper.

Extensive use was made of mahogany and teak in our works and large stocks were carried in the joinery shop at the back of the premises. Mahogany was used for seats and bath surrounds and teak for our range of seats and toilet boxes.

It was during World War I that Charlie Keen became such an important member of the company. This was due to our range of WC seats being in such demand for army camps throughout the London area and the south. Most of these were of hardwood, such as teak and mahogany. The joinery plant above the back workshops was extended, to facilitate the production of these in large quantities. A number of men were employed under the management of Charlie Keen. Sidney Humpherson told me that we made 'thousands' of seats between 1914 and 1918.

One of our toilet paper boxes made in Beaufort Works both before and during World War I when the demand was very substantial. They appear in our 1905 catalogue as 'Polished teak paper boxes' under the heading for our No. 2 Pedestal 'Beaufort' Pedestal Closet (used in Officers and Married Quarters WC's).

For many years we had specialised in army contracts. Indeed, in 1905 one of our Nett trade price lists refers to 'The No. 2. Beaufort Pedestal Closet with fixed seat' to be *used in men's WCs.'* Just above it, is another price for the No. 2. Pedestal Closet but this one is the model *used in Officers and Married Quarters WCs'.* The difference? The officer's version has a hinged seat!

HUMPHERSON & CO.,
Merchants & Manufacturers,
BEAUFORT WORKS,
188a, FULHAM ROAD,
LONDON, S.W.

Telegraphic Address—HUMPHERSON, LONDON.
Telephone—1233 KENSINGTON.

PATENTEES & MANUFACTURERS OF
Sanitary Appliances.

ESTABLISHED 1876.

SILVER MEDAL AND STAR CERTIFICATE,
Society of Architects, 1887.
SILVER MEDAL, Society of Architects, 1886.
BRONZE MEDAL, Inventions Exhibition, S. Kensington, 1885.
THREE CERTIFICATES OF MERIT, Sanitary Institute
of Great Britain, 1885.

ABRIDGED NETT PRICE LIST
OF OUR SPECIALITIES:

Plumbers' Brasswork.	Water Waste Preventors.
Pedestal Closets.	Stoneware Drain Pipes.
Cast-Iron Soil Pipes.	Rain-Water Pipes.

APRIL, 1905.

HUMPHERSON & CO., 188a, Fulham Road, S.W.

The "Triune" Enamelled Iron Pedestal Closet.
(Used in Cell W.C.'s)

	£	s.	d.
Made in Strong Cast Iron, Basin and Trap Porcelain Enamelled Inside, with loose Galvanized Iron Shield. Trap fitted with large Ventilating Socket, price	2	7	6
Cutting Shield for Soil Pipe	0	1	0
2¼-in. Special Brass Bend for Vent Pipe	0	3	6
1½-in. ,, ,, Union for Inlet	0	1	9

The No. 2 "Beaufort" Pedestal Closet
(Used in Officers and Married Quarters W.C's.)

	£	s.	d.
Made in thick Fireclay with open Flushing Rim to Basin, Highly Glazed Surface and large Ventilation Socket on Trap. Price with either S or P Trap and Vent Socket	1	1	0
Special Pattern Galvanized Iron Seat Brackets, per pair	0	6	0
Polished Teak Seats made in double thickness, with Brass Screws and Special made Heavy Brass Hinges	0	18	6
Polished Teak Paper Boxes	0	6	0
2-in. Brass Bends for Vent Pipes	0	2	6
2-in. Brass Spigots ,, ,,	0	1	6

The No. 2 "Beaufort" Pedestal Closet with Fixed Seat.
(Used in Men's W.C's.)

	£	s.	d.
Made in thick Fireclay with Open Rim Flushing Basin, highly Glazed Surface, and Fitted with Shaped Wood Seat in One Piece	1	6	0

Our 1905 'Abridged Nett Price List' and on page 1 – we can see that the Officers and Married Quarters had rather superior WC's – to the 'Men's WC's'. Note: The multitude of typefaces (fonts) used!

Mark you, they had quite a seat! 'Polished teak made in double thickness, with brass screws and especially heavy brass hinges.' But, I wonder why Officers had to have 'double thickness' and why *special* heavy hinges?

The seat was £0.18.0 (£0.92p). I note that the 'polished teak paper boxes' for the officers WCs were 6 shillings (£0.30p) each – but sadly the men's WCs did not seem to have a paper box specified.

From older employees of the company, I gathered that our activities in World War I were not confined to the supply of wooden products. Our sanitary fittings were in great demand – especially the Beaufort WC. Several times I have heard the story that St. James's Park – adjacent to Buckingham Palace – was turned into an Army training camp. Apparently, the park's lake was drained and boarded over with huts then built on the top. Sidney Humpherson assured me that Humpherson & Co. supplied much of the sanitary fittings for the camp.

Looking back, there was of course, only a short time between the end of World War I in 1918 – *'the war to end all wars'* – and the start of World War II in 1939. Once again, Humpherson found itself a role. This time, it was a combination of its skills in dealing with both metal and wood. They obtained a contract to produce telephone wire drums for the Royal Corps of Signals. They were made in thousands for use in most theatres of war.

This is the standard army telephone wire drums still used by the British Army – even after the advent and increased use of wireless and wireless telephones.

Corporal Waters of the Royal Corps of Signals carrying a telephone wire drum across Caen Bridge soon after 'D-Day'. He maintained vital communications in the face of heavy enemy fire for which he was awarded the Military Medal.

As the war went on, there was an increased use of wireless and wireless telephone handsets. However, there is a picture in the Royal Corps of Signals Museum at Blandford of drums still in use in 1944. It depicts Corporal Waters of the regiment, laying telephone wire from a drum – *just after 'D-Day'* – across the Caen Bridge in the face of enemy fire, for which he was awarded the Military Medal.

Again, the back workshops were adapted for continual production of drums and a number of drilling machines were installed in the area at the rear of the old trade counter. They were made in the United States by the 'Atlas Tool Company' – possibly supplied under the 'Lease-Lend' agreement?

Remarkably Charlie Keen was still there deeply involved, supervising production and I understood he was eighty by the end of the war.

I am pleased to report that Humpherson & Co. played a part – *albeit a small part* in the war effort – in both World War I and World War II.

Chapter 13

Alfred Humpherson

Alfred was a stern man but he was following his own Victorian upbringing and certainly had a very strict father in Edward Humpherson. I think he also suffered from being a younger son, with two outstanding older brothers: William (who became successful in his own business Hexter – Humpherson & Co. in Newton Abbot in Devon) and Frederick, who were brilliant in so many fields. However, he clearly adored his daughter Edith, my mother, and that warmth extended to her sons.

We know Alfred was apprenticed as a plumber to Thomas Crapper but we have no record of the dates, with only his name written on the side of Frederick's apprenticeship papers. The top page of parchment we found in the safe probably referred to his apprenticeship to Crapper. Unfortunately, it was badly affected by the damp and disintegrated as we picked it up. Certainly he could not have been with that company for a prolonged period as he was working for his brother Frederick in the 1880s.

It is important to understand the roles undertaken by Humphersons, as it so rapidly developed. According to the 1887 catalogue the company traded as – *'Manufacturers and Patentees'* – *'Brass founders'* and *'Builders'* and *'Plumbers'*. I cannot explain the building function, except that Edward owned a building company in the Kings Road Chelsea until his death. It is possible that Frederick owned part of the building company and found the building facility helpful on some plumbing contracts.

Frederick, like Thomas Crapper, had realised the need for his new plumbing products to be properly installed

This normally stern looking man would always soften towards mother and her sons. The picture was surely intended just for mother?

by trained men hence the specialist sections. Indeed, it was to that side of Crapper's firm that Frederick was apprenticed in 1871.

Most of the Humphersons work was aimed at larger contracts. Much of this was concerned with the installation of the company's own designed products in hotels and new buildings. However, the most successful contract work was with prisons and police stations. Further evidence of this kind of specialisation appears in the 1903 catalogue showing details of the many fittings we created exclusively for installation in military establishments, including barracks and married quarters.

I believe Alfred worked on many of these contracts as a manager. However, on the formation of the Limited Liability Company in January 1919, he was made a Director, alongside his brother Frederick, at a salary of £4.10.0 per week. Two members of staff are mentioned in the first Minutes of the newly formed company. They were William Hedgecock and Leo Vincent both described as foreman. However, 'Bill' Hedgecock had a salary set at £4.10.0 a week the same as Alfred. Leo Vincent however, had a salary set at *'a foreman's union rate plus 1 penny per hour'!* Frederick made both of these gentlemen shareholders.

I know from my mother, that Alfred resented William Hedgecock occupying the adjacent office to Frederick, whilst his was tucked away at a back corner of the warehouse – behind the sheet lead storage! When Frederick died later in 1919, I believe Alfred was truly astonished to find himself virtually sole beneficiary of his brother's estate and no-doubt soon took his rightful place in the offices.

Certainly, having spent all his working life running contracts he was possibly ill prepared to run a thriving and quite dynamic business. Although Alfred was described in the share register as a 'Sanitary Engineer' I think he was initially out of his depth in his new role as the owner of the business.

One should remember that Alfred was nearly sixty, when he quite unexpectedly found himself as managing director of Humphersons in 1919. I feel his performance must be judged accordingly. Fortunately, Alfred had Leo Vincent and 'Bill' Hedgecock to support him from the outset and profits were made most years up to 1929, when the effects of the world slump began to bite.

Hedgecock and Vincent became shareholders in 1919, but I do not know whether that was by gift or purchase. However, I suspect it was a gift from Frederick Humpherson. Leo Vincent was a superb craftsman with lead. Firstly he was site foreman, and then took managerial roles in the company. We have a lead joint that he designed amongst our memorabilia. William Hedgecock was a sanitary engineer and became a leading designer for large-scale plumbing contracts. He was a director of the company until his death in 1944 – that is a mark of his importance to Alfred.

Alfred and his wife Jane had four children: Maude who died in 1911, Sidney, Ernest and my mother Edith. The two boys were trained as plumbers at Humphersons but Ernest was always a difficult son for my grandfather to handle. He had a very rebellious and quarrelsome nature.

When the General Strike started in 1926, Ernest called a meeting of all the tradesmen working for Humphersons and he persuaded them to come out on strike in sympathy with the trade union involved – *against his father!* Grandfather was furious and never forgave him. My grandmother Jane died the following year. It marked the end of her continued protection of Ernest and meant, that at long last, grandfather could soon get rid of his troublesome son.

The company employed my uncle Sidney Humpherson as soon as he left school. He is later described in the Share Register as a 'Sanitary Engineer' but in truth he was a skilled plumber and was never given the opportunity to gain managerial experience. I found him rather dull.

The loss of the police station and prison work in 1926, severely affected the company and it was followed by the 1929 worldwide depression that wiped out many businesses. From the early thirties onwards, the company was mostly kept going by injections of cash by Alfred – by way of loans.

The great contract days had gone, and by the time World War II started in 1939, the firm was down to accepting minor repairs or 'jobbing' work as plumbers. Over these years, the sales or 'builder's merchant' side struggled to keep going – being largely neglected by Alfred who plainly did not understand it. Nevertheless, that division had contributed cash into the company all the time, by selling fittings to local plumbers and builders.

It would also be wrong to ignore Alfred's own talents. Whilst not as spectacular as Frederick's they were considerable. Firstly, one must accept that he was a master plumber, a true craftsman and earlier he obviously ran important contracts to Frederick's satisfaction.

Alfred made many things on the lathes in his private workshop. These included ivory cigarette holders for him and as gifts for friends. The holders were machined from off-cuts of the ivory used to make our 'Superior' ivory WC chain pulls, and for ivory levers for our luxury tap range. Incidentally, the bath and basin in his bathroom had mixers controlled with ivory handled lever taps.

One of his great joys was his 'Bullnose Morris Coupé' that he purchased around 1928. He had not driven before but the car was delivered to Holmes Place and the salesman took him to Richmond Park to show him the essential points of driving. I know he was taken round the Park once and then took over himself. Four circuits of the Park followed this and then he drove home!

This picture of a 1928 Bullnose Morris Cowley Tourer is exactly as I remember Alfred's car. It is the same dark blue with strapped on spare tyre, a petrol can for emergencies and thermostat on top of the radiator.

He paid the salesman and drove regularly until petrol rationing forced him to put the car up on blocks – for the duration. He died in 1945 just before the end of the war in Europe and father sold the car for £10 in May 1945. The buyer pumped up the tyres, put petrol in the carburettor and it ran perfectly.

Alfred would sometimes call at 33 Clonmel Road, Fulham in West London where we lived until 1929 and he could easily be persuaded to take us for a spin in his Morris coupé. Ron being the eldest sat next to grandfather and Trevor and I were in the so-called 'Dicky seat' – created when the boot was lifted up. Quite comfortable but a trifle draughty!

Alfred in his beloved Bullnose Morris 2 seater coupé. My brothers and I would ride in the 'dickey' seat in the rear – along with the picnic, tools and spares. Incidentally, he usually drove wearing his Homburg hat – and always when driving without the hood. One might wonder how it stayed on but he seldom exceeded 30mph.

Every time we met grandfather he gave each of us a 'half crown' – that was two shillings and six pence – or one 8th of a Pound. Seeing a working man in the twenties was lucky to be earning £3.10.0 a week, it was very generous. My father left us 1 penny each on Saturdays as our pocket money for a week so you can see how welcome grandfather's visits were! The half crown was equal to 30 pennies.

As small children, we quite often went to spend the day at Humphersons. Sometimes mother took us there during school holidays and then went shopping. We always enjoyed the visits. The staff looked after us very well but we were mainly the responsibility of Arthur Meadows, who was then the assistant manager of the trade counter, in the merchant part of the company. We also adored going to the workshops at the rear of the main building shop to spend time with the plumbers and fitters, based on the ground floor.

At tea times, we were treated to quite superb cups of tea. The men boiled the water in a pail over the forge fire, added tea, lots of sugar and condensed milk. This was all brewed together in the same pail – stirred and ladled out. The most junior 'plumber's mate' was sent out to Hemmings the local bakers to buy sticky jam doughnuts for us – it was simply a child's paradise.

Friday was 'Pay Day' so after the whistle had blown indicating close of work for the day, all the men congregated in the area near to the offices. Alfred always paid the men through a small hatchway in the corner of his office. It was difficult to use, both for him handing out the money, and for the recipient. He would call out the employee's name through the little space, and when each man came forward, he handed out his wages in a brown envelope.

Everyone was paid in alphabetical order and on pay-day – that included us waiting for our half crown – under 'P' for Pidgeon. That was fun for us, but why did he force his own son Sidney to wait his turn with the workmen? It was strange to hear him call out 'Humpherson' – then see Sidney step forward to be paid through the hatch.

By the time World War II started, the business had deteriorated to such an extent that Alfred was constantly funding it himself. He told mother that the staff were stealing from him but had no proof. In fact, it was true. After Alfred's death, father and my brother Ronald found that the Company Secretary, was falsifying the cash takings and he was dismissed.

All through the war, grandfather lived alone in his apartment above the offices. The property was large and taller than most local buildings. As a result, its flat roof was a good high 'lookout point' for the newly formed corps of 'Fire Wardens'.

This was a part of the ARP (Air Raid Precautions) organisation and was vital as the Luftwaffe stepped up their quite haphazard dropping of incendiary bombs, small devices 'sown' in hundreds, carpeting homes and offices. They caused untold damage across London and the 'Fire Warden' with his stirrup pump and bucket of water was the first line of defence we had at the time.

Incredibly, at the age of 80 grandfather joined the ARP 'Fire Warden' section and spent many nights on our warehouse roof – pinpointing fires as they started. To get onto the roof, he built a bridge from his flat and I have a clear mental picture of him directing operations.

One incendiary bomb came a little too close and fell on the roof only a few feet away from him. It went straight through the lead and double skin timber of the roof and directly into one of the original Beaufort WC pans. About six had been stored on the racks on the top floor of the warehouse. Here it burned safely, until he put it out with the aid of a stirrup pump. Incidentally, the pan was blackened and after the war we could still see the extent of the flames from the charred roof timbers above. There can be no doubt – that by falling into a Beaufort pan – it prevented the incendiary bomb from burning down the entire building!

This sketch is of a 'Fire warden' part of the Air Raid Precautions' (ARP) organisation that was mostly manned by volunteers. Grandfather was one of the local team and had the advantage of watching from Humpherson's premises – taller than most buildings nearby. Remember, he was over eighty and spent night after night watching and reporting fires caused by German incendiary bombs. As a Fire Warden he would have been supplied with a bucket, a stirrup pump and a shovel. However, he probably did not carry them as his was more of a 'fire spotting' role. Of course, he would have worn a steel helmet and carried the mandatory gas mask.

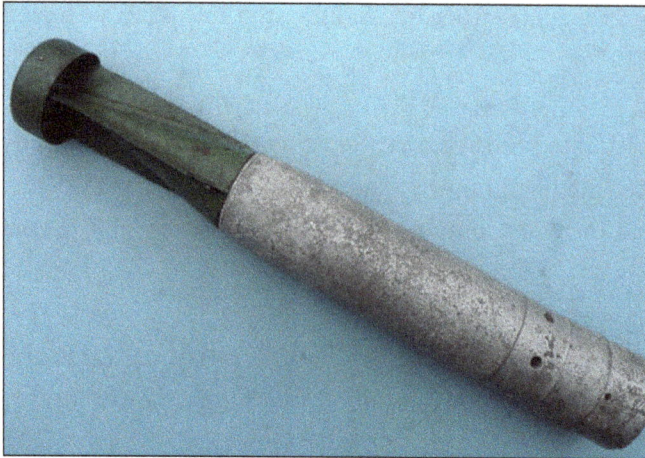

This is the standard German incendiary bomb dropped in the thousands during an air raid. The Fire Wardens job was to find them and try to put them out – if possible – without involving fire engine support. A single aircraft could hold up to 700 of these deadly weapons released in clusters. They each weighed 1kg and were 345 mm long x 50 mm wide. Surprisingly only one landed on our premises but fortunately landed in one of our 'Beaufort' pans. It contained the effect until Alfred could deal with it.

Alfred was on duty when several large bombs exploded nearby. One of these fell diagonally across Fulham Road at the end of Park Walk, alongside the 'Goat in Boots' public house, blowing in its windows. The bomb also blew in the windows of our showrooms, as well as all the windows in his flat above. It caused terrible damage nearby and a number of casualties. An even bigger bomb fell outside St Stephens Hospital some four hundred yards along the Fulham Road. These were quite apart from the many smaller bombs that dropped in the immediate vicinity and all the time – *Alfred Humpherson kept watch!*

His only sport was bowling and he played at Barnes Common Bowls Club in West London. He was a member for many years and I recall going to the club with him several times in his Bullnose Morris Oxford Coupé. We have a picture of him complete with Panama hat, making an energetic delivery of a lignum vitae bowl. Just after he died, mother was given a newspaper clipping from the sports page of one of London's evening papers of the 'Death of the Grand Old Man of Bowls'. He was still playing regularly at over eighty, which was rare in those days. Alfred was buried in April 1945 at Fulham Cemetery, off the Fulham Palace Road, in a grave with his wife Jane and their daughter Maude, who had died back in 1911.

Alfred played bowls regularly at Barnes Common Bowls Club and my brother Ron and I sometimes went there with him in the Morris. Incidentally, you can readily see he was a short and 'stocky' gentleman. He is smoking, now forbidden on the green and the cigarette is in one of his home made ivory holders.

In the 1920s, Alfred had purchased a home for mother and father in Clonmel Road, Fulham and that is where my younger brother Trevor and I were born. When doctors suggested a home outside London would be beneficial for my brother Ron's asthma, he then bought a house for the family in New Malden in Surrey.

This gruff looking man was kindly towards the family and perhaps he kept the 'frown' for his employees? I want to record one other facet of Alfred's kindness. Before World War I – he was the 'Treasurer' of the 'Goat in Boots' Slate Club. In those more poverty stricken days, workers found it difficult to ensure there was enough cash in hand to pay for the Christmas festivities. It was quite common practice to ask a respected local businessman to collect and hold the cash – until Christmas. Alfred was suitable in his own right but no doubt it helped that his brother owned one of the largest firms in the immediate area!

The 'Goat in Boots' is a well-known public house in Fulham Road – diagonally opposite Humpherson & Co. in Holmes Place. Friday afternoon was pay-day and doubt Alfred ensured that a small amount was paid into the 'Slate Club' book – before too much was spent on alcohol!

In 1913, the members of the Slate Club acknowledged his many years as the Club Treasurer and presented him with a gold 'Snake's head' ring with two diamonds as its eyes. It has been handed down through the family and now Laurence wears it at all times. It is a great personal connection to an earlier member of our family. The ring is inscribed inside *From the members of Ye Olde Goat in Boots Slate Club 1913'.*

I earlier mentioned grandfather's habit of giving us 'half a crown' every time he saw us. The last time I saw Alfred was during the war, around October 1944. I was in a secret wireless unit, MI6 (Section VIII) who in 1940 had purchased the stock of new Packard motorcars in the country, from Leonard Williams the UK Packard distributor in Brentford, West London. At the time, the Packard was widely regarded as the finest American motorcar.

I had been working with my boss Dennis Smith, installing our special wireless equipment in motor torpedo boats (MTBs) down in Brixham Harbour, Devon. When the work was completed, we set off early to drive back to our base at Whaddon Hall – some five miles west of Bletchley Park in Buckinghamshire. However, we first dropped Dennis off at his home in Surrey, so he could have a weekend break.

My driver knew London well so we decided to 'divert' a little and pay my grandfather a visit in Fulham Road – before heading north out of London. I well remember it was a Saturday afternoon and the showroom was closed but I knocked at the side door leading to his flat. He came to the door and greeted me most warmly. He took the driver and myself to his dining room and gave us a beer – surely a sign he at last recognised me as being 'grown up'?

As we later stood by the door of the Packard saying our goodbyes, he told me to wait and I saw him go down the stairs leading to the walk-in safe. He came up with a tin cash box and from it quite solemnly handed me a 'half a crown'. (That is £0.12p *or* 12 pennies today). That was exactly the same amount he gave me when I had been a child of three or four years old. Certainly, he made no allowance for my now being 18 years old – in uniform – and obviously in charge of a very expensive Packard motorcar!

I regard Alfred in a kindly light and appreciate all he did for us.

Chapter 14

Edith Adelaide Humpherson

Mother was born, the youngest child of Alfred and Jane Humpherson, at 30, Bovingdon Road, Fulham in West London, on November 21st 1897. The children in order of age were: Maude who died in 1911, Sidney Alfred, Ernest William and then my mother who was christened Edith Adelaide.

Mother told me that although 'Adelaide' was a popular girl's name at the time, hers recorded a family connection with Adelaide, South Australia. I understood they were not Humpherson relatives but from her mother's side – part of the Rodley family.

I have every reason to believe that mother had a happy childhood. At the time, Alfred was working as a site-manager for his brother in his plumbing and bathroom business. His pay was quite good for the industry and as a result, his family were comfortably off, in what we might describe today as 'middle class'. He was strict but basically a good and upright man. She benefited from being the youngest and I think he enjoyed having an exceptionally bright and personable daughter. Throughout her life mother had a 'presence' about her and her personality continued to shine to the end.

My mother Edith A. Pidgeon née Humpherson at 30 Bovingdon Road Fulham, where she was born in 1897. Alongside her is her brother Sidney Humpherson.

Her brother Ernest too was bright, if moody and cantankerous. As a result, mother spent more time with her older brother Sidney, who was more placid, if perhaps a little dull in comparison. However, he was a good amateur footballer and quite a 'ladies man' in his younger days.

Her school days were mostly spent at Peterborough School, just off Peterborough Road Fulham, not far from her home. The school is still there, a solid monument to the Victorians, who spent so much of the wealth they created on infrastructure, schools, town halls, police stations, prisons and the like.

She was a keen tennis player and apparently won prizes at the sport, including a pair of silver topped glass vases at a tennis tournament held at the nearby Hurlingham Club. I still have one of the vases.

After leaving school just before World War I, she tried to join the thriving family business in Holmes Place. However, neither her uncle Frederick, nor her father, would allow a 'woman' to be employed by the company. Unhappy with this attitude towards women, she applied for a position at Harrods in Knightsbridge in its cashiers department – and was accepted. Harrods in those days, clearly had a much more advanced view about the employment of women – than her own family!

Her relationship with my grim faced grandfather was very close. In the difficult days before World War II with first me, then my younger brother Trevor at Caterham School, she sometimes made trips to see him for a cash 'loan' but neither ever expected they would be repaid!

At the suggestion of Lucinda Lambton, I wrote to Mohamed Al-Fayed who was then the owner of Harrods; incredibly they still had her actual files in their archive department. This shows that she applied for the post on 14th January 1913, and started on a 'cash desk' on 27th March 1913. It appears she had to work for a month's 'Probation' presumably without wages? Thereafter, her pay was six shillings per week (£0.30). Her later school dates shown are August 1906 to February 1913 at Peterborough School, near Hurlingham, in Fulham.

Mother had often talked to us of her days at Harrods and of handling gold coins as they came up from the counters – Britain was still on the Gold Standard. The coins were apparently kept in soft leather bags and were heavy to handle.

Mother's enrolling details from Harrods of Knightsbridge. She started there in a 'cash desk' in March 1913. However, she told me she was in the 'accounts office' but they may well have been one and the same thing? I obtained these from Harrods archives after mother died so I was unable to check the point.

From the records, it states that she left *'of her own accord'* and apparently went to a store in Oxford Street. I find it astonishing that Harrods had even kept the visiting card from her new employer – who evidently called at Harrods personally to collect references about her.

In the period we are examining, the theatre was the major source of entertainment and specialist agents sold tickets for the theatre and major shows of all kinds. In those days, the largest 'ticket agent' was Keith Prowse, with District Messengers and Cecil Roy a close second and third. Within the theatre trade they were called 'Theatre libraries'.

At one time my father was working at Cecil Roy's

branch in Knightsbridge close to where Park Tower Hotel stands today. The two are only a few hundred yards away from Harrods where mother then worked. It is just possible that they first met at Harrods or nearby!

Whilst, I do not know for certain how they met, I do know that by the end of the war in 1918, mother was working at Cecil Roy's as a cashier/bookkeeper. Father stayed with that company until the outbreak of war on 3rd September 1939 – when all London theatres were shut down in fear of bombing. As a result, Cecil Roy's also closed so father – for the first time in his life – found himself without a job.

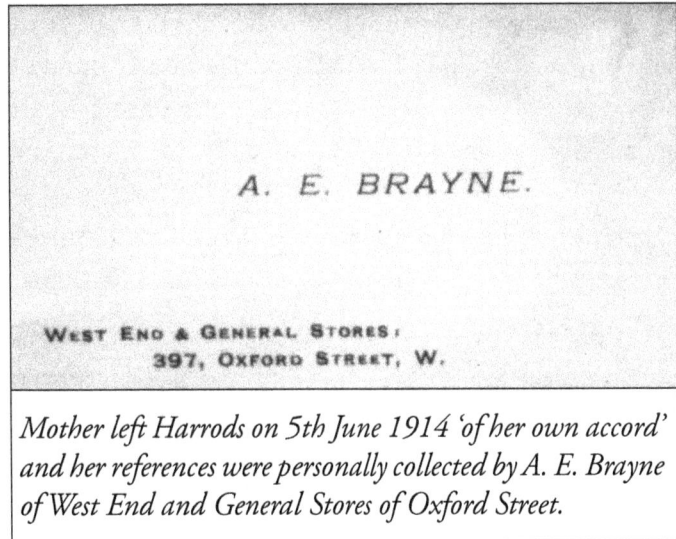

A. E. BRAYNE.

West End & General Stores: 397, Oxford Street, W.

Mother left Harrods on 5th June 1914 'of her own accord' and her references were personally collected by A. E. Brayne of West End and General Stores of Oxford Street.

Fortunately, he had volunteered as an Air Raid Warden back in 1938 and was soon employed full time – albeit at a lower salary than he had previously enjoyed. Mother had joined our 'Air Raid Precautions' (ARP) organisation at the same time but as a volunteer Red Cross Nurse. On the outbreak of war in 1939 she was also offered full time work, in the Red Cross.

She dealt with the casualties following the bombing of Croydon Airfield on 15th August 1940 in a mobile first aid unit – based in a converted single decker bus. We gathered she had a very grim day but she did not talk to us about it. On the Sunday 18th she was off duty, when a much closer air raid took place on nearby Kenley Airfield – with its runway starting less than two miles from our home. We were huddled in the shelter and bombs fell in a field behind our house. Shrapnel damaged the roof of our house – so mother decided we should join my father near his unit in Buckinghamshire.

Though not part of this story, my father had been enrolled into MI6 (Section VIII) in June 1940 and worked at its HQ at Whaddon Hall. That was some five miles west of Bletchley Park, where later mother worked as a Nurse in its clinic. It was whilst she was working at Bletchley Park that her father Alfred Humpherson died in early 1945 and she inherited Humpherson & Co. Limited.

In 1954, I had designed and built two bungalows in Caterham in the Surrey hills. The first was for my wife and young family; the second for mother, father and brother Ronald. Sadly, father died in 1956 and not long afterwards, mother established a weekly habit that seldom varied.

Throughout the following years mother came up from her home in Surrey to London every Wednesday. In the morning, she would shop in Oxford Street and have lunch at Selfridges. Then a taxi took her to Harrods in Brompton Road where she spent the afternoon shopping again, followed by taking tea there. I wonder now, if she was regularly visiting her old places of employment – from all those years ago?

A taxi from Harrods, always from the same door on to the Brompton Road, then brought her to our showroom and offices in Holmes Place. There, she would round off her day with a business discussion with me followed – *at the appropriate time* – by a glass of sherry! Mother's comments during those weekly 'reports' were truly worthwhile for me.

Then I drove her home after she had given my brother and myself a package of Harrod's smoked salmon each and/or other delights from their famous food hall. The timing and routine never varied.

The portrait of mother that hung in my office of the Chairmen of Humpherson & Co. – from its beginning

Mother's unstinting support, and her innate business acumen, were of great benefit to me in the growth of the company.

Chapter 15

My Father and Brother Ronald

Father was born in Battersea in the last years of the splendid and vital Victorian era. After leaving school, his older brother Percy obtained a job 'in theatres' but I do not know in what capacity. However, he later found a job for father as a page boy in a theatre in the West End of London, this gave father his initial taste for the theatrical business that he later came to adore.

His first chance to move up in the World came when he joined Cecil Roy & Co. of 15 Sussex Place, South Kensington, now known as Old Brompton Road. They described themselves as 'High Class Stationers and Printers' but their main business was as a so-called ticket 'Library'. Today we could describe it as a ticket agency.

The owner of Cecil Roy's was Col. Gaskell who, although quite elderly, had had a wartime role in World War I at the Woolwich Arsenal, where they were making munitions. The theatre was the major source of entertainment in those days meaning there would be at least one theatre, even in a small town. For the masses, they flocked every week to their local music

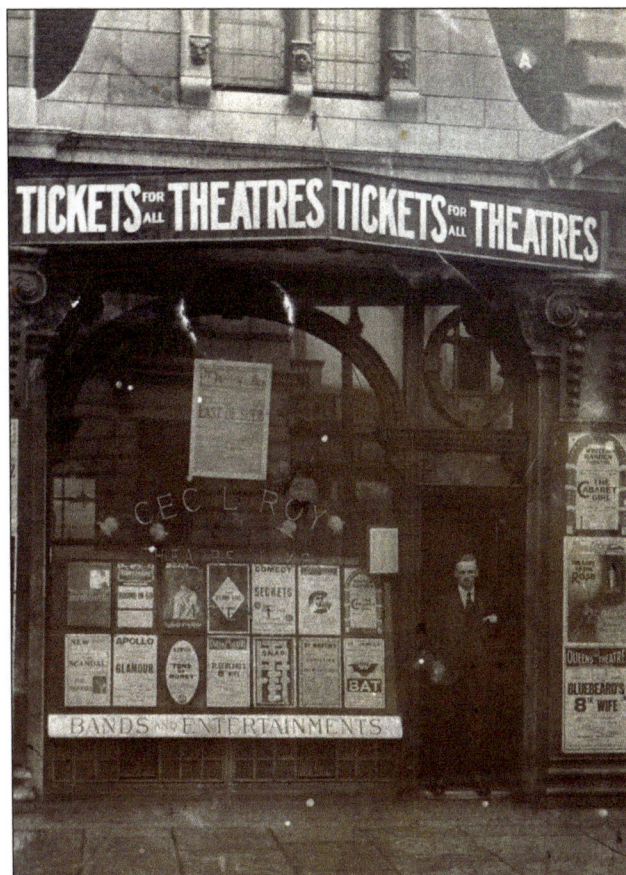

My father outside Cecil Roy's branch in Knightsbridge circa. 1921

hall, and these were more numerous. With most of the older staff in the Services, father was made manager of their Knightsbridge office, close to where Harvey Nicholls are today. Father later went from Knightsbridge to the Head Office in South Kensington and he stayed there until the outbreak of World War II.

In my book 'The Secret Wireless War' I explain how my father came to be recruited into MI6 where he ran the MI6 (Section VIII) Wireless Stores at Whaddon Hall, some five miles west of Bletchley Park for five years, with considerable flair. Towards the end of the war with Germany, most men in the unit were keen to become members of (the unit's peacetime role) the DWS (the Diplomatic Wireless Service, a section of the Foreign Office) or to join GCHQ, then at Eastcote.

However, father wanted nothing better than to return to his beloved theatre business and went back to Cecil Roy in South Kensington. Unfortunately, his time there was cut short by the need to sort out the finances of Humphersons that mother had inherited. He had been Alfred's Executor and his skills at administration – shown by his organisation of the MI6 complex wireless stores – were of great help in sorting out the problems they had discovered.

An employee had regularly been pilfering small amounts from the day's cash takings. When challenged he admitted that it had been going on for years. Grandfather had complained to my mother that he was being robbed during her visits during the war.

Father was also a competent bookkeeper and could add up a page of figures with lightening speed – faster than most people today could tap them into an adding machine! And, remember he had three, sometimes four, columns to cast. Pounds, shillings and pence – and even fractions of pence like ½ penny. We must thank my father for putting the company on an even keel in the earliest days after the war, especially as it was such an alien environment for him – worlds away from the theatre trade where he had spent so much of his life.

My father 1955 – Chairman of Humpherson & Co. Ltd.

In writing this book, I am conscious that I must also give full credit to the contribution made to our success by my older brother Ronald. He had joined Humpherson & Co in late 1945 – well over a year before me. He had taken to the practical side of the business, both during his sessions out with our plumbers and in the shop where he mastered skills connected with the selling of lead sheet and pipe.

Ron had suffered from chronic asthma since he was four and in those days little was known about the illness or how to treat it. Mother took him to a specialist at St Thomas's Hospital in London – often on a weekly basis. As a result, as I grew up Ron was often away in a special home for children with chest complaints. He spent many months in a home in Ventnor on the Isle of Wight and on his second visit there stayed for over a year. Later still, he went to St. Dominic's Home in Godalming in Surrey. With all this upheaval – coupled with the numerous house moves we made due to his health – his education was badly affected.

Not surprisingly when World War II began, he was pronounced unfit for military service at his medical board – as he was still suffering with chronic asthma. Nevertheless, he later played a full part in the local Home Guard in Stony Stratford where we lived during the war.

When father died in 1956 it was agreed that I should take over as managing director and in a few short years we had managed to bring about a considerable rise in our fortunes! Part of that was due to the connections I had made in the industry, both as an expanding company and a member of many organisations connected with the bathroom industry. All this is recorded later. However, none of it would have been possible without my brother Ron acting as my supporter in everything we tackled – giving his depth of practical knowledge and being an utterly reliable lieutenant.

My brother Ronald in 1965

I had a sound foundation to build on, due to the early work of my father and brother Ronald.

Chapter 16

Horse Drawn

Motorised transport became cheap after World War I, directly as a result of thousands of ex-army lorries being dumped onto the market. Gradually, it changed the nature of the traffic as until then, horse drawn vehicles had dominated London streets. Had Frederick Humpherson not died in 1919, I have no doubt he would have soon purchased lorries for use by the company. However, Alfred took a different view of things and decided to keep to his two horse-drawn carts.

If more were needed, they were hired from Burchetts in Old Church Street, Chelsea. Burchetts were basically a furniture removals firm but they had transport for hire as well. I was a member of Chelsea Rotary Club in the 1960s and Ralph Burchett their MD, was a prominent member of the Club.

He told me they had ledgers going back over decades and in earlier years there were frequent entries showing when horse drawn transport had been hired out to Humpherson & Co. In later years, the 1920s and 1930s, it appears we utilised his new fleet of motor lorries for longer runs. Nevertheless, Alfred would still not purchase lorries of his own and continued to use horses for local journeys.

When we were small children in the mid-1930s, there was only one horse left, named Mary, and we were sometimes allowed to go with the driver on local deliveries or collections. I remember the thrill of sitting high up beside the driver who sat in all his glory, blanket across his knees and whip in hand.

Looking back to those pre-World War II days, horses were still much in evidence. All milk deliveries were by horse and cart until well after the war and much of the coal and coke from the local Fulham coke plant used horses, right through until 1949. The greengrocer still called on houses up and down each street – so there were plenty of horse drawn vehicles around. However, apart from milk carts, horses then disappeared quite rapidly around the period around 1949 to 1951. Perhaps it again had something to do with the availability of cheap ex-army vehicles on the market – almost a repeat of the 1919 situation?

When grandfather died in April 1945, the family were still living in a flat in Stony Stratford in north Buckinghamshire, where we had gone to live after father joined MI6 in 1940. I was later in the same unit as my father at Whaddon Hall, the HQ of MI6 (Section VIII), near Bletchley Park. Clearly, the European war was rapidly coming to an end and I was getting ready to be moved out to the Far East, after reaching my 19th birthday in May 1945.

This is Jim Drewitt on Humpherson's delivery cart with 'Mary' outside the Goat in Boots public house – just across the Fulham Road from Holmes Place. It was taken in 1948 just after the war with the pub still boarded up following the German bomb that landed in Fulham Road. The same bomb blew in Humpherson's showroom windows and those of grandfather's flat above – whilst he was in residence!

A cast iron plate was fixed to the cart with the company's name and address. I am not sure if this was a legal requirement but when our lorry arrived the plate was transferred on to it. Perhaps an indication that progress had at last been made?

My father was executor of Alfred's estate and it was split more or less evenly, between mother and the eldest brother, Sidney Humpherson. The other son Ernest Humpherson was not even mentioned in the will. Father had to sort out the estate in London whilst still being involved at Whaddon, some fifty miles north of London. It was a tricky task that I think he managed with great skill.

I went to India in July 1945, and later that year father left the unit and returned to civilian life. In 1946 the family moved to London and took over grandfather's flat in Holmes Place, so that father could keep a close eye on the business. Amongst the many difficult decisions he then made, one was to overturn years of prejudice. He purchased a delivery van, in an attempt to bring the firm more up to date. One of his friends from Whaddon was Major Freddie Pettifer of the Royal Corps of Signals who ran the units considerable fleet of transport. His pride and joy was the large fleet of Packard cars the unit had acquired in 1940, and he had a super drop-head coupé for his own personal use.

I once drove it along the empty runway of the RAF's Horwood airfield at over 100 mph, at the ripe old age of 18. It was rather foolish seeing it was wartime and Horwood was still a training and emergency airfield! Needless to say, Freddie was not told but I did relate the story to him later, when we had become friends in the 1950s.

When father decided to purchase a lorry for the company, the natural person to ask was Freddie Pettifer. He had now left the services and started a garage at Paxton Place off Gypsy Hill, near Crystal Palace. Incidentally, he became the leading Packard repair specialist and had a wonderful stock of spare parts!

The van he purchased was an ex-army Guy 15 cwt open-back truck and it had tyres like a Caterpillar tractor. It was clumsy, hard to steer and difficult to park but when I came home in 1947 there it was – canvas roof, no doors, and a windscreen 12 inches high. But, we still had one horse and it was Mary! The reason for Mary being kept installed in her cosy stables, and the new lorry in the cold outside is difficult to understand – unless you knew my mother. At first, she intended to keep the horse to use alongside the new van but then she became so attached to 'Mary' she was loath to part with her at all. Keeping a horse in London was an expensive business in 1948. We had a driver named Jim Drewitt who cost the then princely sum of £5.00 a week (a London bus

This is the 'beast' I was given to drive! Humpherson's first lorry was an ex-army 15cwt truck made by Guy Motors of Wolverhampton. I know the picture is very poor but it shows my brother Ron at the wheel. He refused to drive it but father was not unduly concerned as I was due home and he thought – certain to join the company. No proper windscreen, a piece of canvas instead of a door and a canvas 'roof'!

This illustration shows the vehicle details that I have described above – including tyres that were more suitable for a farm tractor. It really was difficult to drive in London's traffic and almost uncontrollable on wet roads. Sadly, due to our financial position I had to suffer it for several years delivering and collecting goods – before we could finally afford something better.

In 1951 we could afford to purchase a proper commercial lorry. This is our new Austin 30cwt with the proud driver at the wheel with my brother Ron beside me.

driver earned £4.50 at the time). Mary's feed bill of £3.00 per week, plus straw, and vet's bills. By 1950, the horse and cart were only taken out for a quiet run – as an exercise – twice a week. However, there was one other important task for them. Every two weeks, sometimes less, we accumulated so much manure, that it had to be disposed of – especially during a hot summer. So the cart was loaded up, and Jim drove off down Fulham Road towards Putney, with his steaming load giving off noxious gases as it went on its way.

Jim took the load to Bishops Palace near Putney Bridge, (the home of the Bishop of London) as manure for its gardens. It was only years later that we discovered he was paid £1.50 a load for it. Perhaps Jim saw it as a rightful perk and compensation for the loss of his way of life?

By the early fifties, father was becoming exasperated with the expense and mother finally agreed that Mary could go. I do not recall where the sale of the horse was advertised, but I do remember people coming from Kent and Surrey to see her. Both my parents saw all of the prospective purchasers together and mother quizzed them about their intentions. One she was certain was a horsemeat butcher, so he was promptly seen off. Another, ran a country round as a green grocer but mother wanted to know how many hills there were – he seemed unsure – so he too was sent on his way!

Finally, after many months, mother found a purchaser she felt was genuine and he collected Mary in a horsebox, for the journey to Kent.

Jim Drewitt left a few weeks later after clearing out the stables. I saw him for a number of years afterwards, sadly pushing a broom as a road sweeper in Chelsea. No doubt – as he swept between parked cars – he was dreaming of his halcyon days driving Humpherson's horse and cart.

Thus Humpherson & Co. – in purchasing a lorry – took one more small step to catch up with the Twentieth Century.

Chapter 17

The Healing

Sadly my father had died quite suddenly in April 1956, when he was only 58. I then became managing director of the family business Humpherson & Co. Ltd – just before my 30th birthday.

We had made good strides in rebuilding the company after the war from virtually zero. However, we were still hampered by shortages of bathroom products to sell. At that time, almost everything made by the factories supplying us was swallowed up in the export drive. Supplies for the home market were limited both in quantity and, in looking back, also in design.

In mid-1950s, it became sensible to work more closely with so-called rivals, if only to exchange products that were in short supply. I deliberately set out to court the other local merchants, Green & London of Fulham, Nicholls Brothers and Fraser & Ellis of Chelsea, Froys of Hammersmith for example, and formed links with a number of them. However, in view of all I had been told, I was reluctant to approach Crappers, and they were certainly not on my list.

By this time, I had ensured that our major supplier of sanitary ware was the well-known manufacturer, Twyfords of Hanley, Stoke on Trent. Their London manager was a delightful gentleman, by the name of Don Nalder. He was a good golfer, a bridge, chess and tennis player, as well as being a bowler of considerable skill. I had made the contact directly with their factory via Jimmy Gibson, then a junior in the sales office. He ended up as the sales manager of Twyfords, a good friend and after his retirement, their archivist.

In those days, it was quite usual to adjourn to the nearest pub for a drink at lunchtime. This was a habit at first *just about* tolerated by my father but one he later came to enjoy. I hasten to say this was only allowed on Fridays, but several representatives of our suppliers liked to join us in this pleasant ritual. The public house we used was in Fulham Road, adjoining Humpherson's premises. It was then run by a company with the name of Finch & Co. but widely known, as 'Finches'. It gained a reputation as one of the gathering places of the new 60s 'in-crowd'.

Liz Frink the sculptress was a friend, a regular and seen in there most lunch times. Gilbert Harding of BBC fame was often in the bar, as were Peter Cook of 'Pete and Dud', Mary Quant, financiers, actors and writers. This could be long list as there was usually 'someone of note' present!

Don Nalder was amongst the representatives who joined us on Fridays regularly. However, he had to slip away early because he was already committed to the Crappers lunchtime drinks session – also held on the same day.

When my father died, my brother Ronald and I continued the lunchtime meetings with manufacturers' representatives but in deference to the Thomas Crappers' earlier choice of Fridays, we changed it to Thursdays, so we could always be sure of a good gathering. They were always jolly occasions but there was a serious side that benefited business relationships in many ways. In the earlier days they were certainly a means of helping to ensure the flow of goods in short supply from the various factories whose sales representative had joined us. We frequently had products in stock that were not available elsewhere!

Around 1961, Don Nalder told me that I would be made very welcome – if I cared to go along to the

Sadly there is a MacDonald's on the site of the White Hart public house – opposite Thomas Crapper premises in the Kings Road Chelsea. Of course, it was known only as 'the Post Office' for anyone enquiring about the whereabouts of Robbie Barratt – Managing Director of Thomas Crapper & Co.

Crappers lunchtime 'session' one Friday – held at the White Hart, Kings Road, Chelsea. This public house was on the corner of Kings Road and Royal Avenue and almost opposite the Crappers showrooms. The invitation had come personally from Robbie Barratt, managing director of the company.

There is no doubt that 'Robbie' enjoyed a glass of ale. But, nobody at Crappers ever said they were going across the road to the pub for a drink. They always referred to the White Hart as the 'Post Office'! If anyone asked where Robbie had gone – it was to the 'Post Office'. In due course, that became the White Hart's name in our trade circle.

I well remember my first visit there. I was made most welcome by Robbie who introduced me to many of the senior members of Crappers staff who had joined him in the 'Post Office': Len Orchard, George Clarke, George Brown, amongst others. There were of course, a number of other sales representatives there that I knew as well – indeed it was quite a gathering!

Only a short time later, I received an invitation, via Robbie Barratt, to meet Robert Gillingham Wharam the owner of Crappers. It was suggested we meet at Chelsea Rotary Club, where Robert Wharam was a Past President. In those days, their Tuesday meetings were held at the Rembrandt Hotel, almost opposite

Robert Gillingham Wharam. Past Mayor of Chelsea, President of Chelsea Rotary Club and owner of Thomas Crapper & Co.

the Victoria and Albert Museum, in Brompton Road, Knightsbridge. I can remember the meeting very clearly.

Robert Gillingham Wharam was charming. He talked to me of the past but never about the differences I had been led to believe existed between us! I took him a photocopy of the apprenticeship document for Frederick Humpherson dated 1871. This pleased and excited him. He told me it was the only time he had seen both his father's signature (Robert Marr Wharam) and that of Thomas Crapper, on the same document. Indeed, both signatures were in themselves quite rare.

Around this time, I joined the Chelsea Builders Association, which had been formed during the war to help builders liaise over repairs to building damaged by bombing during the blitz. Merchants, like Nicholls Brothers and Thomas Crapper, were made members to ensure supplies of replacement materials went primarily to essential war repair work. My company became active members and this further cemented the growing friendship between Crappers and us.

I soon joined its committee and later became its President. The President's collar badge depicts Albert Bridge, leading from Chelsea across the Thames to Battersea.

Jane and I at the Chelsea Builders Association annual dinner held at Peter Jones, Sloane Square in Chelsea. I am wearing the collar and badge as its President. The Mayor and Mayoress of Chelsea were always our Guests.

I took a particular liking to George Clarke who was Crapper's sales representative for the Kensington & Chelsea area – that included his calling on us at Humphersons. He became a regular visitor and we liked his pleasant but business-like approach. An excellent example of a company representative – then often known as 'Knights of the Road'. I am pleased to say that George Clarke later joined my company and became a great asset.

One way and another, the staff of Crappers from Robbie Barratt down to the managers became friends. We often socialised with them at functions, like the Christmas luncheon of the Chelsea Builders Association, and its famous annual dinner held in the top floor restaurant of Peter Jones store, in Sloane Square. At both of these events we always had the Mayor of Chelsea as our guest of honour.

Thus, in several ways, I think I healed the rift that had existed between these two old companies for something like seventy years.

Chapter 18

Crappers For Sale

The senior managers and representatives of Thomas Crapper & Co. continued to hold their Friday 'get-together' of trade representatives with some of their customers. Incidentally, this usually started about noon and often lasted until closing time, so a fair amount of alcohol was consumed. In those days of stricter licensing laws closing time was 3 pm – sharp!

In early 1963, as I arrived at one of these enjoyable meetings, Robbie Barratt asked me to step into the other bar for 'a private word'. George Clarke was asked to accompany me. Robbie told me – but I think George already knew – that Robert Wharam was considering disposing of his business Thomas Crapper & Co. Ltd. He suggested that if I was interested in the purchase then I should seek a meeting with Robert Wharam 'fairly quickly'. I should explain that George Clarke was Crapper's 'Star' representative. His territory was the most lucrative area of Kensington and Chelsea that then contained several substantial building and plumbing firms.

Robert Wharam did not visit his business very often but a meeting was arranged about a week later. I remember it well. He told me that he was now 'very tired' and wanted to secure the future of Crappers and his staff, in what he felt were becoming difficult trading times. Developers, who wanted to purchase his warehouse and some adjoining properties, were also approaching him. I truly do not think the money concerned him, but he felt threatened by events.

He gave me an idea about the price in telling me he had been offered *'over £100,000'* for the property alone. That was certainly a great deal of money in 1963 and especially so for our company.

I said I would discuss it with my family and did so at once. We had expanded rather rapidly and were beginning to become quite important again in the bathroom industry. We felt sure it was a good opportunity to expand further but raising the finance required would obviously be a problem.

However, if we could raise the money to purchase the entire business and then sell off the land it might be possible. We had ample space at our Fulham Road premises, and we had already planned new showrooms that could replace those lost in any sale of the Crapper's Kings Road premises. One must remember that there was not a great distance between the two properties. I met with my mother and brother Ronald who were very supportive of the idea. We decided to call it an 'amalgamation' since I felt it would sit better with the staff – rather than a 'take-over'.

A second meeting with Robert Wharam was arranged. Again, I can remember every detail. I had not yet approached our bank, but I knew they thought highly of me at that time and the great property boom in West London had started in Chelsea. I felt sure the property would fetch much more than £100,000 – when sold on.

My offer figure was to be £125,000. I would like to say that it was my starting figure but in truth it was likely to be the absolute maximum we could raise at that time, between our own funds, the Midland Bank and hopefully, the later sale of the properties.

I was unable to seek professional advice about the values from my friends in the Chelsea property market – like Karl Pycraft or Peter Johnson – since that would have led to a wholesale rush of offers. Actually, on the day I met Robert, I had no real idea where the full amount of £125,000 would come from. But that was a problem for later.

I went to Crapper's offices in Kings Road and up to Robert Wharam's office. He started our meeting by asking if I had come to a decision about the purchase and that I should remember that the property was worth over £100,000. I said my offer would exceed that figure – then I started my well-rehearsed bid. However, as I was about to start, he leaned forward and said *'you can't have the Royal Warrants you know!'*. I must have looked puzzled, because it had never crossed my mind to want them as any part of the transaction. Before I could think of a suitable response, Robert told me that the right to display them would cease, if he were no longer a director of the company.

After that unexpected interruption, I started again but before I could actually reach the figure I was offering, he again leaned forward pointing a long bony finger at me – *'Geoffrey, how many of my staff are you going to keep – tell me – how many?'*

This threw me completely. I had rehearsed my speech leading up to the advantages of keeping the two historically linked companies together – in what I was going to describe as an 'amalgamation'– then approach my offer figure. I was certainly not prepared for a staff roll call. Fortunately, I knew all the staff names at that time, except the name of the driver and the two cleaners.

Therefore I started listing the names, beginning with Robbie Barratt and going down to the driver who I said we would employ. *'What about the cleaners?'* he then asked. I replied, that as their work was mostly in the showrooms and those would now be at Fulham Road, they would not be needed. Certainly not both cleaners – full time.

With some earlier small talk, this had taken less than ten minutes and I had still not mentioned our offer figure, except the general phrase that it would exceed the sum he was thinking about. Before I could return to finance he stood up, told me he had a luncheon date and that he would consider my offer. I was left wondering – *what offer?*

Frankly, he seemed out of touch and little interested with material things like property values and the proper price for his company. He was more concerned with the Royal Warrants and the welfare of his beloved staff.

About a week later, he asked to see me again and told me he had decided to sell the business to John Bolding & Sons of Davies Street, Mayfair. I asked why sell to them and not to me? He said *'Because Geoffrey, you do not want to keep on my staff and that is vital to me'*. I replied at once that was not the case as I had offered *everybody* a position in the new enterprise.

'Oh no' he replied, *'You did not want to take on the two cleaning ladies and John Bolding have taken on everyone – including them.'*

I have looked back on those meetings many times. Was I foolish to give an honest answer about the cleaners? How was I to know how important they were to him? What sort of a business might Humpherson and Crappers combined have become? I shall never know.

Soon afterwards, I heard that Boldings paid only £75,000 for the entire enterprise. That sum included the long-established business as a going-concern, its stocks and all the extensive properties in Kings Road Chelsea!

As soon as Boldings signed the agreement, they immediately went on to dismiss a number of staff members. Extraordinarily, Robert Wharam made no stipulation about the continued employment of staff. Perhaps he believed John Boldings verbal undertaking on the matter? However, they then proceeded to

JOHN BOLDING & SONS LIMITED

GROSVENOR WORKS,
DAVIES STREET,
LONDON, W.1.

2nd September, 1963

DEAR SIR OR MADAM,

Acquisition of Thomas Crapper & Company Ltd.

In his report to shareholders at the Annual General Meeting of the Company held on 8th March, 1961, the Chairman informed you that the Company was well placed to take advantage of any favourable trading opportunities which should arise, and that your Directors would not fail to take any action they thought necessary to further strengthen the business.

In this connection arrangements have now been made whereby the Company has acquired the whole of the issued capital of Thomas Crapper & Company Ltd., of Marlboro' Works, 120, King's Road, Chelsea, London, S.W.3. The purchase consideration of £75,000 is to be satisfied wholly in cash, involving temporary bank borrowings of £30,000 pending realisation of investments. In addition £47,956 has been borrowed to repay the loans to Directors and sundry loans as shown in the Accountants' Report overleaf. There are no borrowings for any other purposes. This will result in the acquisition of a second wholly-owned Subsidiary Company as an integral part of the Bolding Group.

Thomas Crapper & Company Ltd. was established in 1848 and over the years has built up a first class reputation as merchants and manufacturers of sanitary equipment. The acquisition therefore represents an expansion of your Company's activities in the same line of business, whereby it is hoped to effect an increase in activity and an overall saving in costs.

The following Accountants' Report has been obtained from Messrs. Painter, Mayne & Walker, the Auditors to Messrs. Thomas Crapper & Company Ltd:—

PAINTER, MAYNE & WALKER,   103, CANNON STREET,
Chartered Accountants.   LONDON, E.C.4.
12th July, 1963.

The Directors,
John Bolding & Sons Ltd.,
Grosvenor Works,
Davies Street,
London, W.1.

GENTLEMEN,

As Auditors of Thomas Crapper & Company Ltd., we have examined the accounts of that company for the ten years ended 31st March, 1963, and report as follows:—

1. PROFITS. The Profits of the Company for the ten years ended 31st March, 1963, arrived at on the basis set out below, were as follows:—

Year ended 31st March.

	£
1954	1,871
1955	2,140
1956	2,324
1957	3,165
1958	2,736
1959	2,523
1960	4,621
1961	4,386
1962	4,660
1963	2,355

(i) The profits before taxation set out above are arrived at:—
(a) after charging all expenses including interest payable, Directors' emoluments, staff bonuses and profit sharing, and depreciation as charged in the accounts;
(b) after making such adjustments as we consider appropriate.

John Bolding & Sons letter to shareholders dated 2nd September 1963, about the purchase of the business of Thomas Crapper & Co. for the sum of £75,000. That sum included its considerable property in Kings Road Chelsea, its stocks and on-going trade. No mention was made of retaining all the staff!

sack the managing director Robbie Barratt, who was just six months short of his 60th anniversary with the firm. Subsequently, Crapper's best salesmen left them and the business declined rapidly. Finally in 1966 they sold the whole Kings Road properties and moved what remained of Crappers to John Bolding's premises in Davies Street, Mayfair.

The story of John Bolding's disgraceful treatment of Crapper's staff rapidly went round the industry. It became a matter of concern to the trade who were, by and large, honourable men. However, Bolding's received their due deserts soon afterwards, as they were declared bankrupt in 1969. The administrators sold off various portions including the non-operative firm of Thomas Crapper & Co.

So it remained a non-trading dormant company until purchased by Simon Kirby, an antique dealer from Stratford-on-Avon, who started up the company some thirty years later in 1999. He commenced trading by offering a selection of reproductions – made by various manufacturers – of the most iconic Crapper products. They were well received by specialist bathroom outlets.

I know Bolding's treatment of Crapper's staff broke Robert Wharam's heart. By now, I was an active member of Chelsea Rotary Club and, from time to time, Robert would attend our Tuesday luncheons as an honoured Past President. He never failed to say to me *'Geoffrey, you really should have bought Crappers'*. I always shrank from giving the right answer to that because he looked so frail.

Robert died soon afterwards – could it have been from a broken heart?

Chapter 19

Flushed With Pride and the Crapper Myth

This chapter really should be in the plural Myths since they are varied and many. This is largely due to the original version of Wallace Reyburn's book 'Flushed with Pride – the Story of Thomas Crapper' and its astonishing impact on the media.

Back in 1967, Wallace Reyburn telephoned me at our Beaufort Works premises in Fulham Road. He told me he was researching Thomas Crapper & Co. and asked if I would meet him. He came along one morning shortly afterwards. He talked about Crapper generally and his having designed the first WC and cistern…etc. I told him very plainly my family's view on the subject.

On 26th June 1967, Reyburn wrote to me to thank me for my help and also for putting him in touch with Harry Barclay the managing director of Twyfords. Barclay had written to him on 22nd June inviting him to visit the factory. The letter was copied to me and both are in Appendix 7.

Some months later, there was a package in the post containing Reyburn's draft book and a letter from his editor/publisher, asking me for my comments. I was incensed by many of the remarks made and replied – trying to have whole sections changed. However, I was told he was an important author and they simply implied that it made good reading! *That is how the Thomas Crapper Myths began.*

Shortly afterwards, I had an irate Reyburn on the telephone telling me I had no right to comment to his editor on his work. Apparently, this had all happened whilst he had been abroad. It did no good to explain he should address his complaint to his editor who sent me the draft – *not to me!*

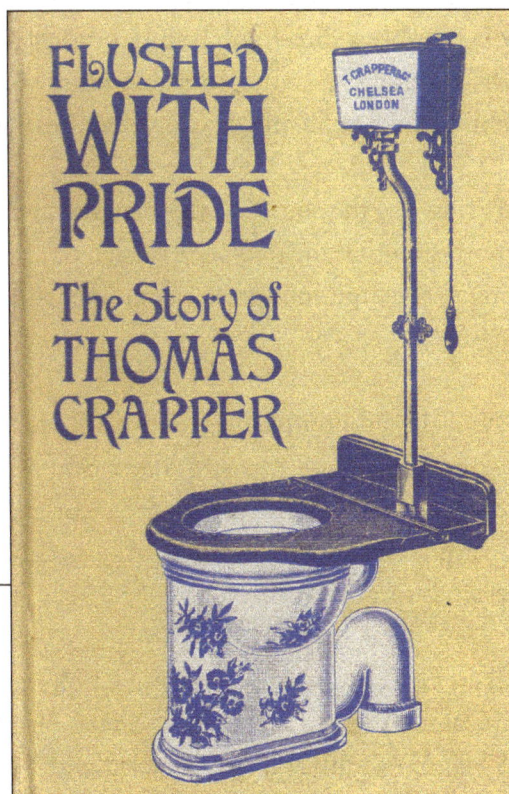

Wallace Reyburn's original book 'Flushed with Pride was first published in 1969. It was the cause of the subsequent debate that has raged ever since. More recent editions have modified some of the original detail but it remains an inaccurate and fanciful record of Thomas Crapper's achievements.

Eventually, I was sent a copy of the final book and found some of my 'corrections' had been accepted or deleted but much of the nonsense remained. Over several later reprints of 'Flushed with Pride' caveats and alterations have appeared – but still leaving the false premise that Thomas Crapper had designed a WC flushing cistern.

The current edition states: *'It would not be absolutely true to say that it was Thomas Crapper who invented the Water Waste Preventer............It was not as clear cut as, say, Diesel inventing the engine which bears his name........More than a few plumbers took up the challenge and just as a hundred years previously the work of James Watt and others had culminated in his producing the 'first effective modern steam engine', so it was that there came into being 'Crapper's valveless Waste Water Preventer. One moveable part only. Certain flush with easy pull. Will flush when only two-thirds full.' In other words he perfected the cistern as loo users throughout Britain know it today.'*

Here we see Crapper's valveless water waste preventer linked with James Watt – the inventor of rotary motion, using steam power. This is worse than impertinent considering that the patent for the water waste preventer in question was registered **not** by Thomas Crapper but designed and registered by Albert Giblin of Fulham in London. He registered it under Patent No. 4990 in 1898 and then sold the patent to Crapper!

On the next page it goes on to say: – *'Pull and Let Go was born'* – implying that it was Crapper's work. This statement ignored the fact that over previous years probably a hundred cisterns – of all kinds – had been launched and all were necessarily fitted with a chain requiring *'Pull and Let Go!'*

Reyburn's book then quoted performance tests carried out on WC pans. These had actually been carried out by George Jennings on his 'Pedestal Vase' WC which was awarded a medal at the Health Exhibition of 1884! It is possibly a direct crib from an earlier book 'Clean and Decent' by Lawrence Wright published in 1960. The same applies to the story about throwing an apprentice's cap into a pan to test if it flushed. Actually it was John Shanks of Shanks & Co. of Barrhead who cried out when the cap disappeared *–it works!*

Leaving out the source of the material and the actual men concerned might easily leave the reader with the impression that the tests were carried out by Crapper. I believe that Reyburn's book, though bringing Thomas Crapper's name into greater prominence, did real harm to his reputation as a designer, manufacturer and engineer.

The 2011 Edition of 'Flushed with Pride' has added a caveat at the foot of page 19 saying that: *'Pat. 4990 was registered to an employee Albert Giblin. It is unknown if he alone developed it or if he submitted it on TC's behalf.......etc...'* That is a totally incorrect scenario and Albert Giblin was certainly not an employee. I am most grateful to Paul Dobson, Albert Giblin's grandson, of Cheshunt in Hertfordshire, for the family and design information that follows.

Albert Giblin was born in 1869 at Chipping Ongar in Essex. By 1881 the family were in Fulham west London and later moved to 20 Studland Street, Hammersmith. It appears he trained to be a plumber with W. N. Froy of Hammersmith. He was married and living at 45 Barclay Road Fulham by 15th March 1897 and from there, he submitted his first design for improvements to flushing cisterns. He obtained Patent No. 6759 for the design.

On 1st March 1898, Albert submitted his second application for improvements to flushing cisterns and was granted Patent No. 4990. He later sold the patent to Thomas Crapper who thereafter incorporated the patent number 4990 onto their flushing cisterns. But clearly it was **not** a Crapper design or patent.

I have added emphasis on passages from a book full of nonsense. On page 59, Wallace Reyburn says: *'The more research I did on Thomas Crapper the more I came to feel he might well be termed the* **Barnes Wallis of the lavatory world**. *Just as way ahead Barnes Wallis was in his time in aircraft design, so too was Crapper in his field of endeavour.'*

There is more, as on page 18 it says: *'As with Stephenson and 'The Rocket', or, say, the 'Wright Brothers with their aeroplane, Crapper did not bring his Water Waste Preventer to perfection until after many a dummy run.'*

The comparison of Thomas Crapper with such giants of invention is silly in itself – but is even worse considering he did not design or patent the Water Waste Preventer anyway!

However, for me personally, the most aggravating section of 'Flushed with Pride' is the beginning of Chapter 15 'Paper Work'. I showed Reyburn the teak toilet-paper boxes being used by our secretaries and typists as envelope holders on their desks. I explained that Charlie Keen our joinery manager had manufactured them in our workshops before World War I.

In the first edition of his book he had twisted that around to say:

'The Humpherson who founded the firm almost a hundred years ago sent his two sons to Crapper's to learn the trade and they always carried a full range of Crapper's products. The present chairman of the company Geoffrey Pidgeon has fine sensitivity about the old days of the loo and when he came across the old Crapper paper boxes he saw to it that they were not only preserved but put to good use.'

Neither the Editor, nor Wallace Reyburn, replied to my angry letter on reading this further distortion of the facts. In the latest print, it still refers to them being 'Crapper paper boxes' and that Geoffrey Pidgeon ensured they were put to good use!

Quite apart from anything else, at no time did Humpherson's need to purchase products from Thomas Crapper & Co. Most certainly we did not, as Reyburn claimed *'...always carried a full range of Crapper products'*. This is yet another complete fabrication.

At the end of Chapter 14 Reyburn also says: *'.....at long last giving credit to Thos. Crapper, the W.C. pioneer.'* We know, of course, that Crapper did not pioneer the WC! There are yet more Crapper myths in Notes: K.

I knew many of the characters associated at the time with this saga. Importantly, these included my mother born in 1897, Robert Gilliam Wharam the owner of Thomas Crapper & Co, Robbie Barratt its MD, John Bolding who purchased Crappers – and so many more of those involved in this story.

Robbie Barratt had joined Thomas Crapper in 1904. By the time of my attempt to purchase the company, we had become friends. I sometimes visited the 'White Hart' (or Post Office?) on Friday lunchtimes and he came to our 'gatherings' on occasions. He was always at the Chelsea Builder's Association annual lunches and sometimes at its 'Ladies Night' dinners at Peter Jones in Sloane Square. The list naturally included the others of Crapper's senior staff, such as George Clarke, Len Markes, George Brown, Len Orchard, Peter Folkard and so on, right the way down to the driver!

My views are well summed up in a Wikipedia article on Thomas Crapper dated 6th May 2009. I quote:

'The story of Thomas Crapper and his achievements has been somewhat confused by Wallace Reyburn's 1969 book Flushed With Pride: The Story of Thomas Crapper – a heavily fictionalized satirical biography in the style of scholarship.'

On reflection, perhaps the book did no good service to Thomas Crapper's image, rather bringing it into ridicule, particularly in the USA, where Reyburn also published **'Bust up – the Uplifting Tale of Otto Titzling and the Development of the Bra!'**.

My quarrel was not (*and never has been*) with Thomas Crapper & Co., nor indeed with Thomas Crapper himself. He was a skilled engineer and ran a successful business with his partner Robert Marr Wharam. My obvious sensitivity centres entirely on Wallace Reyburn's original version of 'Flushed with Pride' because so much of it contains distortions of the facts, which impact on my family history.

I suppose that now that I am 88 this may be a last chance to put matters right.

Chapter 20

Castle Stalker

My solicitors – for much of our business and all family matters – have been Allward & Sons. I have a document from Allwards involving great-uncle Frederick Humpherson that consists of four pages of copper plate writing dated 30th July 1885. On incorporation as a Limited Company in 1919, we find a Resolution in the Minutes dated 21st January, that James Allward of 10 Grays Inn Square be appointed the Company Solicitor.

My first contact with the firm was meeting James son, Frank Allward. I went with my mother and father to see him about the estate of my grandfather Alfred Humpherson in April 1945. My father was Executor of Alfred's Will and there was much to do. Frank's son Stewart Allward was a POW, captured by the Germans in France during the Blitzkrieg in 1940. However, there was good news for the Allward family at the time indicating that Stewart was on the way home, having been released by the Allied armies in the final defeat of Germany.

Stewart later took over and gradually Allward & Sons expanded into a very successful firm. At the same time he had purchased a home in Warlingham in Surrey, where he and his wife Marion raised their family. In the early1960s he began the search for a castle in Scotland that he could restore and make into a home for his retirement – then a long way off. Although at the time there were a number for sale he had specific requirements. It had to be reasonably accessible from his home in Surrey so that he could drive there within a day and that ruled out many of them. Secondly, it had to be sufficiently small and well preserved so that restoration, could be within his limited financial resources. Thirdly, it had to be on the edge of the sea or a loch.

Castle Stalker

After much searching he came across Castle Stalker on Loch Linnhe and thought it might fit his criteria. He and Marion explored the castle and found it had everything they could have hoped for – including a main hall 30 feet long, a dungeon dug 15 feet into solid rock, a winding staircase mainly built into the thickness of the walls, a garderobe, broad battlements, a small square tower on one corner and the remains of a round tower on the opposite corner. However, it had no roof, much of the battlements had crumbled, and it was certainly going to be a challenge to restore it into a family home!

I will pass over the years of work restoring the castle, much of it undertaken personally by Stewart and his family over holidays and even extended weekends. That involved a drive of over 500 miles from his home in Surrey. However, he had discovered a number of friends willing to help in the construction and this is where my brother Ron and I became involved. I will now quote from Stewart's own diaries. The quotation is headed 'Operation Plumbing' and reads as follows:

The scale of the project can be seen from this picture of the scaffolding

"We had now reached the stage in the castle restoration when we could tackle the plumbing. I was friendly with Geoffrey and Ronald Pidgeon who were not only clients, but also friends of mine for many years. Our connection with the family goes back a long way as my grandfather acted for their grandfather. When doing some conveyancing for them recently, I was telling them about the castle and casually mentioned that it would be very helpful if they could come up and do some plumbing for me.

In an unguarded moment, Geoffrey said that he thought this might be possible. Although Geoffrey and Ronald had done plumbing about 25 years ago they are now running a large and successful wholesale plumbers merchant business in London and are far removed from being plumbers themselves. However I followed up their suggestion and to my intense delight, they said that they thought they would be able to come up and help me."

Having suggested we *might* do it Stewart and Marion visited our showrooms in Holmes Place and selected the fittings for the bathroom and toilets to be used in the castle restoration.

At that stage, Ron and I had still not finally committed ourselves to the project, but Stewart's visit and his subsequent order for the plumbing materials, made us feel we should. Having 'Crossed the Rubicon' we suddenly found ourselves very active supporters. Ron had more training as a plumber than me. He had moved into the flat at Holmes Place with my mother and father in late 1945 and worked there primarily, in Humpherson's shop. Nevertheless, he spent some time out with the plumbers that we still employed.

After joining Humpherson & Co., I too had to spend time out with our plumbers. In my case, that was never more than two days a week and usually only one. It was found I was more useful to father in the office so my practical plumbing training lasted for just a few short months. However, in the early 1950s Ron and I spent time together attending Night Classes at Wandsworth Technical College. There we studied plumbing layouts and drawing, plumbing technology, and practical work on welding – the new concept of copper plumbing.

As a result, we felt we could be useful to Stewart, so armed with scale drawings of the intended layouts, we set about seeing what might be required. It was decided to use some of the new materials coming onto the market and the provision of fresh mains water to the castle was the first consideration. We were ahead of the plumbing merchant industry on a number of fronts and we had embraced the new Alkathene pipes for cold water services, as soon as they had become available.

Our slogan 'Humphersons for Plastic Tubes' was simple but brought trade and publicity to our company. Shortly afterwards, we were the first merchant company in the whole UK to stock PVC plastic soil pipes and fittings. The range included 4" pipes for soil stacks and smaller sizes for bath and basin wastes. We had started with a push-fit range called 'Metrex', marketed by Allied Ironfounders, but soon switched to 'Key Terrain' with its solvent welded joints.

We supplied the Alkathene piping to connect the water company's mains to the castle on its island and when we arrived it had already been run out across the loch. So the scene was set for Ron and I to turn our hands to plumbing again! One day in July 1969 Ron, with my middle son Michael, set off very early and drove up to Scotland with a boot full of plumbing fittings and tools. I had an important appointment so had to follow up later by air. My flight was due into Glasgow but on arriving there Ron found it had been diverted to Edinburgh. He then set off to Edinburgh only to find that the flight had reverted to Glasgow – adding miles to his long day spent driving. He had been driving for nine hours covering some 530 miles.

However, we finally met up and I took over the driving from Ron, in increasingly depressing and gloomy weather. I recall driving down Glencoe in heavy rain before reaching Ballachulish, then turning down to Port Appin. There we drove between the platforms in the abandoned railway station and parked up as instructed. We made our way to the edge of the nearby loch and signaled the castle with a torch, waved up and down, again in line with Stewart's instructions. It was now around 10 pm and raining hard so we were relieved to see a light waved in response through the gloom. All this long before mobile telephones!

Some fifteen minutes later we heard a shout and we could just make out Stewart approaching the shore in a rowboat. We loaded our personal gear on board and were rowed to the castle in a swell that caused us all considerable concern!

We stumbled up wet steps in the dark and were met by Marion and quickly got outside a welcome hot mug of tea. Ron and I also enjoyed a nip of the whisky offered to go with it. We were exhausted and that was especially true of Ron who had put in such a long day's driving! We bedded down on mattresses and slept like logs. We awoke to the smell of bacon and Marion gave us a hearty Scottish breakfast before we started work.

The plumbing problems arising in a castle built of hewn rock were soon clear and we had to think our way around them. For example, one could not simply chase out the wall of the castle to conceal pipework as one would with brick. Instead, one had to run pipework along the wall surface having first bolted a plank to the wall, so that the pipes could be clipped on it!

However, first we had to deal with the most difficult task of all – the provision of a soil stack to carry waste from the bath, basins and toilets to the outside. We had seen from the drawings that there was an existing garderobe inside the walls with a 30 foot drop to the ground outside. However, we knew it would not be easy as the hole was narrow at the top, although opening wider at the bottom.

At that time, I represented the National Federation of Builders and Plumbers Merchants on BSI (British Standard Institute) Committee PLC94 – dealing with the creation of standards for plastic plumbing. The other members were representatives of architects and contractors but most were from the manufacturers now handling or making PVC products. One of the largest manufacturers was Key-Terrain part of the Reed Group and their representative on PLC94 was Alastair Davidson who became a good friend. I told him about the Castle Stalker project and he was interested both technically and for possible future publicity. He offered the services of his Scottish representative Bill Robinson for the work on the stack. Early Saturday morning Bill called Stewart from the shore. He was rowed over and it transpired that he had earlier actually worked as a plumber – a real bonus!

We had sent the Key-Terrain PVC pipes and fittings needed for the work, according to the drawings given to me and they were laid out around us. So the work started with the pipe work lowered down the hole inside the wall in short pieces at a time, with more pipe added, as each section's solvent joint dried. Bill Robinson stayed with us overnight instead of going home that day and the team worked until 11 pm on Saturday night. We were up early on Sunday and started work finalising the all-important soil stack.

It had been a difficult task but our 'secret weapon' was Michael, who was slim enough to get inside the bottom of the hole in the wall! He received the sections of pipe as they arrived at the foot of the drop. Finally, on Sunday morning we coupled the obtuse bend at the foot of the stack. Then we added the sections of pipe needed to carry the waste out into the sea. The lunch break – albeit short – was a very welcome relief – we had mastered the biggest problem.

After lunch – and I should add that Marion fed us very well – we started on the next task. It was to provide a water supply for all the outlets throughout the castle. The Alkathene pipe was already inside providing fresh water but it terminated in a simple tap outlet. What was required was a proper water storage facility, feeding the various fittings. We had sent up three 60-gallon plastic water cisterns. These were placed in the roof space and we 'married-up' one to the other. Then we connected the main supply to them via a ballvalve. There was a loud 'Hurrah' when we turned on and the cisterns slowly filled up. Now we had our storage facility from which we could later run our pipes down to the bathroom and toilets. Then we started to run 'down-pipes' from the cisterns in order to connect the fittings, including the bath and basins, that had already been put in place. We only used Alkathene pipe for the cold water main and used copper tube for most of the other pipework since – quite apart from ease of installation – it looked better. The wastes from the basins and bath to the stack, however, were in Key-Terrain PVC. Cold water was run to a copper cylinder we had supplied and the hot water feeds taken from it to the fitments. Electric immersion heaters were used to provide hot water.

It is difficult to explain the pressure we had put ourselves under. Here we were, bathroom merchants trying to install a complete plumbing system from scratch, in a very limited timescale. In addition, it was a most difficult environment – a castle built of stone that did not allow many of the accepted plumbing practices! We continued flat out for the rest of Sunday, again until 11 pm.

Then we started again early on Monday morning after another of Marion's excellent breakfasts. Sadly, we ran out of copper tube and Marion drove down to Oban to see if she could find supplies. Fortunately, no doubt due to her charm and warm personality, she persuaded a local plumber to part with enough for our needs and it was brought back in triumph. One should remember that Castle Stalker is on an island in a sea loch and *every single thing needed* has to be rowed over in a boat!

By Monday night we had worked our way down to the kitchen area. There was only a little more to do, so we continued on. Until in the early hours and working rather too close together, I accidentally hit Ron on the head with my spanner! I decided that was the time to stop but Ron and Michael continued so after a short break, I joined in again. I think Marion finally 'called time' around 3.30 am. But we had finished!

We were up early again on Tuesday morning. We collected our tools together, were rowed over to the mainland to collect our car and started the long journey back to Surrey. We arrived late that evening. Stewart needed our 'plumbing services' again to finish off the connections to the fittings. With a party for his son Ross on the horizon he risked all – and asked me if we could go back to Castle Stalker for a second time? He was delighted when we decided Ron could return to help finish the work. But this time he went up by air to be met by Stewart and Marion.

Over a few days, he commissioned the other toilets and carried out an extensive programme of finishing off the installation of various fitments. His knowledge and practical experience turned out to be of immense help then and again on a later occasion.

The second of these visits was shortly after Ron had married Edna, my secretary. They went up to the castle to complete minor details before the castle had its official opening. This was to take the form of ceilidh. We were invited to attend (dress to be dinner jackets) but we were asked to bring wellingtons for wading out to the rowboat that was to take us across to the island.

Ron, Edna my wife Jane and I stayed at the nearby Ballachulish Hotel and had a taxi drive us down to the beach close to the castle. It was a sight that will remain forever in my memory. There were probably thirty plus people standing near the water. The men attired in dinner jackets, with some in

The great hall of Castle Stalker – it is difficult to believe the building was once an empty shell – just four bare walls with a rowan tree growing in the middle. The windows were non-existent and had to be made individually for each opening.

full Highland evening attire but all of us wearing wellington boots and clutching our shoes. The ladies were dressed – without exception – in long evening dresses and holding them up over their wellington boots.

We were rowed over four or five at a time to be greeted by a piper on the steps up to the castle entrance and what a sight it was inside! Many had already arrived, drinks were being served and there was a roaring fire to greet us!

It was a splendid party, with lots of good food and jolly guests. Then Stewart spoke to the assembled company about the project and how the transformation had come about. Certainly, the local dignitaries must have been amazed to see how the shell of an ancient castle had become a home with all the creature comforts. At the end, Stewart spoke warmly of the many who had contributed to the work. Ron and I were surprised to find us called to the front and presented with a bronze medallion. Mine is much treasured and reads: **'Castle Stalker 1970'** *and on the reverse* **'G. Pidgeon – Beyond the Call of Duty'.**

Stewart and Marion Allward by the fireplace in the great hall.

Michael looking apprehensive as Stewart rows us ashore after our working over the extended weekend. I took the picture so Ron and I must be in the front of the rather small rowing boat – equally concerned!

'The car now waiting at Platform 2 of Port Appin Station' is taking three tired chaps on the 580 mile drive to Purley in Surrey but please wait for the co-driver who is taking the picture!

Chapter 21

Winston Churchill's Bathroom at Hyde Park Gate

In 1962 Mr Churchill was staying in a hotel in Monte Carlo when he had a fall and broke his hip. He was flown home by the RAF and taken to hospital.

He was a difficult patient for the hospital staff and insisted on going home, to 28 Hyde Park Gardens to recuperate. In his condition – he was both injured and overweight – this was going to be a tall order for any household. However, he had set his heart on it and persuaded his doctors, and Mrs Churchill, that it was a practical proposition.

Clearly, one of the major problems was going to be the ability to bathe at home without the facilities afforded in hospital. There was also the need to provide a suitable toilet facility since he abhorred the use of bedpans. This had to be near his bedroom and it was decided to use a room off the main ground floor corridor leading to the lounge. The room was almost opposite his new bedroom, across the corridor, and had a view over Hyde Park Gardens. This was to be The Bathroom. No matter that it had no connections to water services, or the drainage system – *it had been decided!*

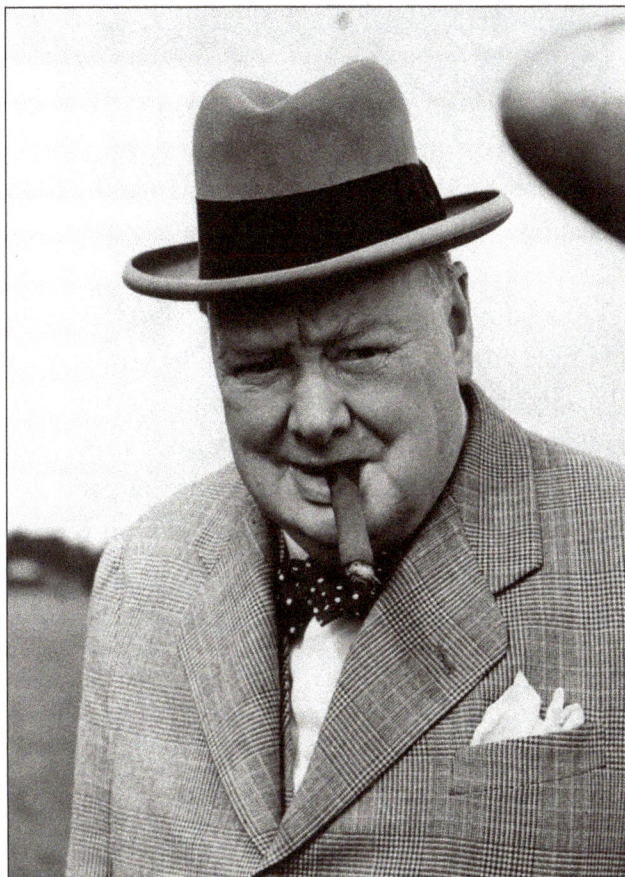

Sir Winston Churchill K.G.

The builder selected was Frederick Parker & Sons of Kensington, who used subcontractors for all their plumbing work. The company was Oatings (owned by two partners Tom *Oates* and David *Hastings*) based in Kinnerton Street, near to Harvey Nicols in Knightsbridge. My firm had long been their main supplier of bathroom and plumbing materials.

I was told by Tom Oates, in the strictest secrecy, of the decision to build a special bathroom for Mr Churchill

28 Hyde Park Gate Kensington home of Sir Winston & Lady Churchill and the Blue Plaque fixed to its wall.

at his home. One of the first problems was the choice of a suitable bath, so I sent them catalogues of the few remaining British cast iron bath manufacturers.

The orthopaedic surgeons attending Mr Churchill selected a short bath (5 feet long overall) so that he would not slide down it – bearing in mind he was below average height but very stocky. The Bilston Foundry near Birmingham was the manufacturer of the bath chosen but the factory had closed for its two weeks summer holiday! Fortunately, I recalled the name of its managing director, so after finally tracking him down at his home, I explained the urgent need for this particular bath and the secrecy surrounding the order. I could not have wished for greater cooperation. He contacted the works manager who opened up the factory and found that they had one of the chosen baths in the warehouse. However, Churchill's surgeons had decided it should be fitted with a hinged transverse grip across the bath, not standard stock. Normally, the selected type of grip was fitted to order.

That necessitated finding a specialist member of staff to drill the edge of the bath to fit the massive hinge for the cross-bath grip. Again, they found the right workman, fetched *him* back from holiday, and the bath was drilled and the grip fitted.

That now left the problem of getting the bath to my warehouse in London. A driver was found who had not gone away for his holiday, and so this precious bath was delivered to our warehouse in Tadema Road, Chelsea, amidst the greatest secrecy.

All the bathroom fittings chosen were gradually gathered together in a quiet corner of our warehouse then delivered to Churchill's home at 28 Hyde Park Gate. This delivery was just before the weekend that was followed by the August Bank Holiday Monday!

Normally, we closed for the long Bank Holiday weekend at noon on Saturday. However, knowing the determination of everyone concerned to complete the work at the earliest possible time, my late brother Ron and

I decided to keep our showrooms and stores open over the entire holiday weekend – just in case anything was required on site. Actually we played cards and I think over the weekend I ended up owing Ron thousands of pounds. Good job it was only to pass the time!

At that time, we had one of the largest stocks of plumbing materials in West London – quite apart from our stocks of bathroom equipment. It seemed to us that the men would certainly need *something* over such a long period. When the business closed on the Saturday we stayed in the office until late evening. Then back early on Sunday until late and we carried out the same routine on the Bank Holiday Monday.

Each day, I went to the house in Hyde Park Gate to check on progress. I was astonished to see the number of workmen that could be packed into one relatively small room – and all hard at work. Every building trade was represented there, working side by side (an unusual sight in those Union dominated and strike ridden days). The electrician was helping the plumber, the plasterer assisting the carpenter everyone 'mucking-in'.

By the Tuesday morning considerable progress had been made. It was decided to fit the bath lower than normal to aid access and the only way was to cut into the floor joists. This was done, without planning permission from the local authority – then The Royal Borough of Kensington. It was agreed that the joists should be cut, plans drawn up, then permission sought to do the work *afterwards*. Truly, that was a unique situation. Indeed, the whole building operation was carried out without any formal sanction, which was then sought – *after the event!*

Later in the week, the new apple-green carpet was laid and the bathroom looked almost complete. The bath was in the centre of the room facing a washbasin that had no less than five taps. The hot and cold water was duplicated (I know not why) and there was a drinking tap connected to the mains supply.

Behind the bath were the WC and a bidet. Unfortunately, these had to be raised up and sited on a dais because otherwise it was impossible to connect them to the outgoing drainage. Because of Winston Churchill's weakness, we supplied a frame to fit around the WC to assist in its use and it had two side arms each with a teak pad. Anyone using it would certainly look as if they were sitting on a throne!

By the Thursday morning the bathroom was complete and almost ready for the great man to use. On making one of my now twice daily visits, I met Mrs Churchill who called me over to the WC. She pressed on a corner of the cistern lid and then showed that it was clearly rocking – indeed she pressed it hard several times just to demonstrate the point.

'Mr Pidgeon' she said *'Mr Churchill won't like that – please do something about it before he comes home.'*

What could I say, except something like *'Of course Mrs Churchill'* without any real hope of success!

At that time, the problem of ill-fitting WC cistern lids was common amongst all our sanitary ware manufacturers. At Twyfords, they employed two lady pensioners, working to one side of the production line, whose

Lady Clementine Churchill.

sole task was to match up cistern shells with lids that did not rock unduly! Having found a 'pair' they numbered the lid and the cistern, then tied the two together.

The WC suite I supplied was a Twyfords Model No. 2774 and we had 57 of them in stock in our Battersea warehouse at the time. I remember the number distinctly because of the Heinz advert about 57 Varieties!

At the warehouse Ron and I cut the lids from the cisterns and I put all 57 into the car and took them to the bathroom in Hyde Park Gate. I spread the lids over the new apple green carpet, then carefully tried them out in turn on the installed cistern. Sadly, in spite of my efforts, not one of them was materially better than the original one selected by the ladies, back at Twyford's factory!

Various tradesmen were finishing off the room, and a plumber's mate (*apprentice*), was giving a final polish to the taps on the washbasin. As he worked, he was chewing gum and I asked him for some pieces of his Wrigley's Spearmint gum. I have always disliked gum but I chewed until it was really soft and then stuck a small piece down on the corner of the cistern. I then firmly pressed the lid down on to it. I was fortunate: Mrs Churchill came in a moment or two later – looked across the mass of lids and asked if I had found one to fit properly? With my fingers crossed, I said I had been lucky to find a better fit amongst the lids in our warehouse and would she like to try it, which she did. To my great relief she exclaimed:

'Ah good! Mr Churchill *will be* pleased' – What more could I ask?

Chapter 22

Humpherson and Howson

In the 143 years since my family entered the bathroom market we have dealt with many sanitary ware manufacturers, at home and abroad. Baths, taps, iron goods, all come from a variety of sources but the ware fitted in a bathroom (washbasins, WCs and bidets) should come from a single pottery company. The simple reason is that the colour of their pottery is distinctive, even white varies depending upon the clay mix, the firing temperature and so on. Therefore, one should not sell a WC from one company to be fitted alongside a washbasin and pedestal from another. That is especially true of coloured ware.

Looking back, we have handled sanitary ware from all the leading potteries, as well as many that no longer exist. There were many amalgamations in the period just before World War II, and others have taken place subsequently.

In the 1930s we purchased sanitary ware from firms like Outrams, Sharpe Bros, Johnson Bros of Hanley, Robert Brown of Ferguslie in Paisley, Alfred Johnson & Co. of Queenbrough in Kent, Twyfords of Hanley Stoke on Trent, Edward Johns and Ideal Standard amongst others. However, we also imported sanitary ware in the 1920/30s, for example from Keramag in Germany.

It is interesting to note that in the late 1800s German cities suffered from poor sanitation and sewer systems – at least as bad as those in Britain. In the 1890s a number of English potteries recognised the sales opportunities arising there. To avoid the high import duties, firms like Twyfords, Alfred Johnson and his cousins the Johnson Brothers all set up factories in Germany.

After World War II our purchasing power was negligible and I bought sanitary ware from wherever I could find it. I remember the huge delight when Alfred Johnson's sent us 24 (!) washbasins packed in straw in wire cages – each cage charged at £5 returnable. Earlier I explained how we later grew to be a substantial account for the major manufacturers like Armitage-Shanks, Twyfords and Ideal Standard. However, I had always kept in touch with Howson & Sons – a smaller pottery in Hanley, Stoke-on-Trent. It had been formed in 1865 by George Howson and traded in his name until 1879, when it became Howson & Sons.

Howson had also supplied W. N. Froy of Hammersmith and on Froy's demise we took over two ranges that had been reserved for them previously. In conjunction with Laurence, we made some minor alterations to the designs that did not require over-expensive changes to the moulds at the factory. We then launched both

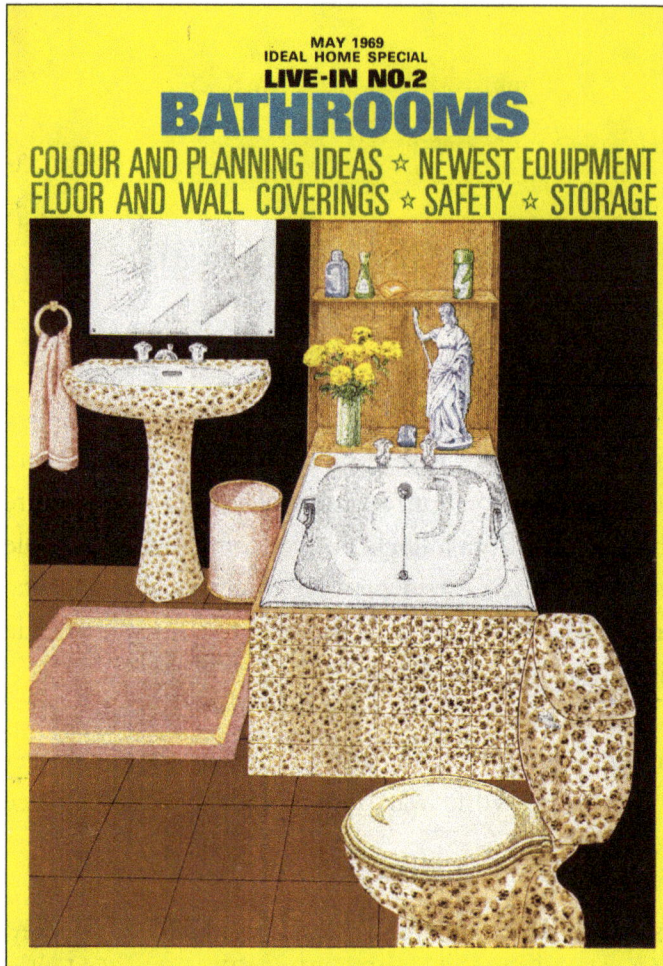

You may now look askance at Tabasco decorated ware but at the time it was a radical departure from the plain colours being offered. Every home interest magazine featured it and the Ideal Home Magazine is typical. Howson's factory could not keep up with our demand made more difficult after I allowed Armitage-Shanks to add it to their own ranges!

ranges; one with the larger size basins known as 'Condor' and the other 'Aztec'.

I had always dealt personally with Richard Howson and was sorry to learn he had decided to move to Australia. However, before leaving, he came to see me with an idea he thought would interest a leading specialist firm like Humpherson & Co. He had found a light brown transfer that could be fired on to the surface of sanitary fittings.

He brought with him examples of it fired onto 6"x 6" tiles of different colours. This technique seemed to work well with a number of the colours and as Richard offered it exclusively to us, we quickly decided to take it into our range. We ordered a selection of washbasins and WCs from the Condor and Aztec ranges in white and a small hand basin in several colours. All were to be fired with the new design that we decided to call 'Tabasco' – being a region of Mexico connected with Aztecs.

We quickly took 'Tabasco' into our main product range and it was an immediate success. I should add that this was a period when pottery manufacturers were offering their fittings in white and a number of colours but Howson & Sons had no less than fifteen colours available.

Tony Parkes became the new Managing Director of Howsons and I quickly formed a good relationship with him. In our showrooms we created a display of small hand basins in each of their fifteen colours and all decorated with Tabasco. The remarkable thing about the transfer is that the effect was quite different on each colour when fired. We even sold several complete bathroom suites in Tabasco decorated on black!

One leading fruit merchant from London's Covent Garden was so pleased with his resulting *personal* bathroom in Tabasco on black, that I received a crate of apples delivered by taxi to show his appreciation!

I should add that Howson & Sons in Stoke-on-Trent was a division of Shanks & Co. of Barrhead in Glasgow. Therefore, when Shanks merged with Armitage to form Armitage-Shanks, Armitage had almost unwittingly acquired Howson & Sons.

Armitage-Shanks started to receive enquires for Tabasco and approached me to know if they could use the transfer on their fittings under the same name – subject to them paying us a small commission for each piece made. It is amusing to note that Armitage were thus paying us commission for a product being made at Howson & Sons that was actually part of their own organisation!

In the next chapter I explain how I became the UK merchant industry's representative on the Ministry of Works Metrication Board, under the chairmanship of Herbert Cruickshank. One of the concepts being preached at the time was 'Dimensional Coordination' whereby one might plan in increments of 100mm (10cms). I could see the advantages of this in the bathroom industry – where such a vast range of seemingly random sizes existed – leading to difficulty in planning.

Dimensional Co-ordination for the Bathroom

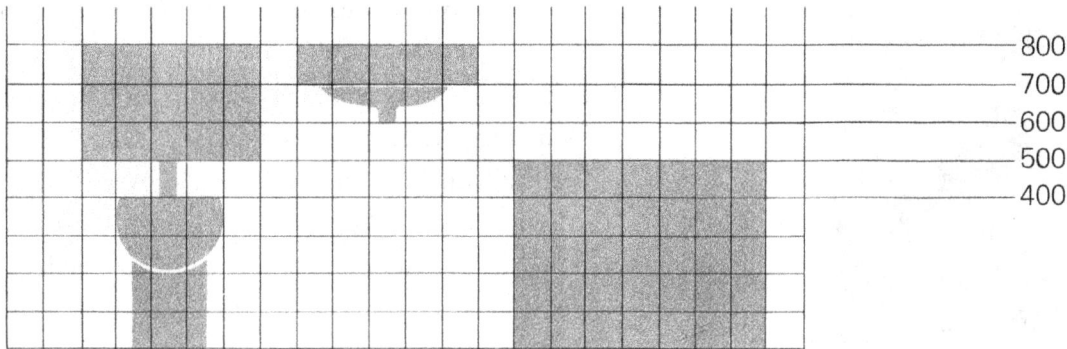

800
700
600
500
400

The bathroom is an assembly of dimensionally co-ordinated components and fixings sized to BS 4011. These components can be located within a 100 mm grid taking into account the actual space to be achieved. (As in BS 1192 : 1969 metric units Building Drawing Practice.) The necessary degree of tolerance has been allowed for in their design and manufacture.

The wall finishes - whether tiles or other materials - will be within the controlling lines on the boundaries of zones, as defined in BS 4330, i.e. within the thickness of the wall or partitions.

The designer is able to allocate space for components on grid drawings in the knowledge that it can be reproduced on site. When tiles are used components can be lined up on the grout line which should correspond to the grid lines.

Tolerances 'Metriware' vitreous china and 'Vogue' baths are designed and manufactured to allow +0 mm -5 mm and +0 mm -10 mm respectively on overall dimensions, i.e. they will fit within the basic space allocated to each component sized in accordance with BS 4011.

Ordering

Coding for 'Metriware'

The first group of numbers refer to type or an assembly such as a complete closet suite, the second to colour and the third to special features - in the case of washbasins - to taphole positions.
Example 1. (02) 400 mm x 300 mm handrinse washbasin, (100) in white, (F) with one central taphole, is described as MW 02-100-F.
Example 2. A low level washdown suite in primrose with a black seat and cover, P trap pan, will be specified as MW 71-105 comprising MW 41-105 cistern MW 42 fittings, MW 61-105 P trap, MW 58-110 seat.

Handing of Baths and Panels

When standing in front of the bath and about to step into it if the waste hole is on your left hand side then this is a left hand bath.

When standing in front of the bath and about to step into it if the end panel is on your left hand side then this is described as a left hand end panel.

This is a portion of our sales leaflet briefly describing the outline principle of dimensional co-ordination. As a result of the Building Metrication Board's work the building industry was beginning to plan in multiples of 100mm wherever possible, and products were developed to meet the demand.

It occurred to me that I could design a range of fittings on that basis. If one was to adhere strictly to the multiple of the 100mm then we had to have sanitary fittings, baths basins and tiles that stayed within those parameters. Sanitary ware was traditionally offered for sale to ± 2% tolerance – the British Standard. I wanted to work to +0% -2% and asked Twyfords if they could produce pottery to that tolerance? I chose Twyfords as I expected a big demand and they had the potential capacity.

I had a meeting with the Twyfords Board at their Hanley offices, and having discussed it with their experts they said – it was simply not possible to produce pottery to those tolerances on a commercial basis. I then returned to my friends at Howsons who, after only a day to consider the matter, agreed it could be done. I gave the factory our sketches for each piece. Only a few weeks later, I was looking at trial pieces that conformed to the concept in every way. So I decided to go ahead and produce the range and then seek to have a bath made on the same grid basis.

One of our first showroom displays to demonstrate Metriware at its simplest. The 1700 x 700 mm baths were made by Vogue – especially for our show. They subsequently became the norm for baths in production today, all based on the 100mm multiple – 1500 x 700, 1600 x 700, 1700 x 700, 1700 x 750 and 1800 x 800mm.

Britain's most popular bath size, and indeed the British Standard was 5'6" (or 1676mm). Glynwed, by now the largest bath company in Britain, agreed to my suggestion that these now be 1700 x 700mm. For the launch of our new range – by now called 'Metriware' – Glynwed took a standard 5'6" cast iron bath and cut it into four parts then joined it up with fibreglass to make the Metriware dimensions. When it had been sprayed it was impossible to distinguish it from a standard cast iron bath – unless you happened to tap the fibreglass section! I note with some pleasure that 1700 x 700 became the European standard.

The launch of Metriware took place in our showrooms with many of the architectural and builder's merchant press present, along with representatives of several Home magazines and daily papers. Besides Herbert Cruickshank, there were senior officials of the Ministry of Works, from the RIBA (Royal Institute of British Architects), the Chairman of Glynwed, Kenneth Stott Chairman of Armitage-Shanks, and a host of other dignitaries.

The result was amazing, with good editorial in the press. Soon after the launch we received orders from private customers and builders – as well as enquiries from architects and developers. We thought it was a very positive and exciting start for our new product.

That year Kenneth Stott was also the Chairman of the British Sanitaryware Manufacturers Association (BSMA) and took the chair at their annual meeting held at Rhyl in North Wales. Strong criticism arose from other manufacturers present. They complained that working to the close tolerances needed in Metriware was not a viable proposition for them. Apparently, Kenneth Stott bowed to the general condemnation of Metriware at the Rhyl Meeting, *known to be one of his products*, and he agreed to refer back to his Board.

The other manufacturers were concerned that if the concept caught on, they would have to devise their own versions of Metriware. That would mean revising the existing very wide tolerances they enjoyed – under existing

We had many distinguished guests at the launch of Metriware held at our showrooms in Holmes Place. They included a number of leading architects, officials from the Ministry of Works, media and trade press. On the left to is Herbert Cruickshank: Chairman of the Metrication Board for the Building Industry at the Ministry of Works – Joint Managing Director and Deputy Chairman of the Bovis Group. The author is in the middle. To the right is Kenneth Stott, Chairman of Armitage-Shanks – whose group included Howsons of Stoke-on-Trent.

British Standards. We already knew from Twyfords that they did not think Metriware was commercially viable – but that was based on out-dated practices. Yet Howson & Sons managed to produce all the range to my tolerances without waste of any kind!

A couple of months later, Tony Parkes asked to see me on an urgent matter. He came the next day and told me that Kenneth Stott had decided to cease production of Metriware and close down Howson & Sons. That meant not only the loss of Metriware but also all the other exclusive fittings they made for us like the Aztec and Condor ranges, plus ware decorated with Tabasco.

However, Tony Parkes already had a plan in mind and decided to set up his own business, to be called 'Balterley' after his village on the Cheshire – Staffordshire border. He had one partner coming from Armitage-Shanks and asked if I would invest in the company and make up a Board of three, with a view to produce all the existing Howson ranges. With so much going on and our expansion requiring all the capital I could raise, I regretted I could not join them.

The new company had to start with limited finance and one of the highest costs is making production moulds.

At the launch Michael – though having newly joined Humphersons – engages knowingly with senior Armitage-Shanks staff on the Metriware principle.

Tony Parkes argued with Armitage-Shanks that the working moulds for the Aztec and Condor ranges, made before the merger, actually belonged to Humphersons – so with my permission he started business with those and a few other models. The company became Balterley Bathrooms and after a few upheavals over the intervening years, the name still exists today.

The loss of Metriware was a personal blow to me but the loss of a willing partner at Howson's – being financed by Armitage-Shanks – meant that, reluctantly, I had to give it up. With architects already specifying Metriware for their contracts it was a double blow. Nevertheless, I took some pleasure in the change to modular fittings in the kitchen industry. Until this time, our popular kitchen sink and unit sizes were 42" x 21" (1066 x 533mm) and 63" x 21" (1602 x 533mm) but Will Wrighton decided to manufacture a 'Metric' kitchen range.

It was called 'Wrighton Californian 2 Metric Kitchens' and this brand new modular range was launched in our showrooms in Fulham Road. Will Wrighton, and his sons Keith and Alan were present. Although at first it was a rather hybrid range – it gave me some satisfaction.

Johnson Bros. the world's largest manufacturer of wall tiles stopped making its best-selling 4 ¼" x 4 ¼" tiles and, instead, made 100 x 100mm tiles. That and the new 1700 x 700mm baths were some consolation!

Chapter 23

Our Growth

The First World War came to an end in November 1918 and Frederick Humpherson died shortly afterwards, in 1919. Following that dreadful war, the 1920s are sometimes described as the 'Roaring Twenties' but the concept did not apply to many British families faced with the country's severe financial problems. Indeed, there was an almost continued economic depression over the period, with much unemployment, exacerbated by the General Strike of 1926.

Nevertheless, there were some good years for the firm in the 1920s but the depression did have a marked effect. In the more difficult years, my grandfather Alfred Humpherson funded the business, as necessary, from his own resources. When he died in April 1945, mother and her brother Sidney Humpherson jointly inherited the business, but my family had to wait until they could move from Stony Stratford (near Bletchley Park) to take control and run it. In late 1945 they moved to London, into the apartment above the showrooms in Holmes Place. They soon found that the Company Secretary was 'involved in irregular conduct' with the finances of the merchant (sales) portion of the business and he was dismissed.

In Chapter 15, I recounted how my father left his beloved theatre ticket business in 1946 to 'sort out' the finances, and to plan the future of the company. When I came home from Singapore in 1947 it quickly became clear that the business was still not viable. It was being held together by its low overheads, mother's continued financial support and the low wages my parents paid themselves – *and me.* My starting salary at Humpherson & Co was about half that I was receiving from DWS (by then a division of the Foreign Office) in Singapore, where I also enjoyed no income tax and living 'all found!'.

As the company accounts did not differentiate between its plumbing operations and the merchant trade, it was difficult to judge the viability of the business. Our accountants, Lord, Foster & Co. had suggested separating the two parts to father in a letter dated September 1945, and I gather he had long tried to persuade grandfather to do the same. We attempted to apportion costs equably and that indicated the losses came from the operational side. Nevertheless, before making the decision to close the long-established 'plumbing works' we formed them into two totally separate companies, each being its own cost centre. It rapidly confirmed that we should be concentrating on the merchant trade. So in May 1947 we closed down the plumbing contract business that had started in the early 1870s and disposed of its few assets.

When I joined the company in 1947, father put me to work in the office. I think it was because I had taught myself to touch-type whilst we had marked time in Calcutta, a situation caused by the sudden end of the war after the dropping of the atomic bombs. At the same time, I was *the* lorry driver, *the* draughtsman, whilst studying the merchant trade. I soon realised that the wholesale trade aspect was the way forward for us – not plumbing. None of the family, father, Ronald or myself, had any in-depth knowledge of the plumbing contract business. To begin with things were tough – as most manufacturers were concentrating on exports and that left little for the home market. It was doubly hard, since I had to find my way in an industry new to me, and to try make a mark.

Once a week I drove the company's ex-army lorry – *without side windows or heating and with tyres like a tractor* – to an area of London just south of the Thames called the Borough. There were many manufacturers with London warehouses and/or distributors, handling bathroom products of all kinds. These included Peglers brasswork (taps and fittings from Doncaster), John Webb from Birmingham, Sperryn gas fittings, Bissekers, and Weatherston & Kell.

The Alfred Johnson pottery at Queenborough in Kent also had a London warehouse, so sometimes I obtained washbasins and WC pans from them. The giant American company Crane Limited were in Leman Street in the City, where I could sometimes find steel tube and fittings – and so it went on. If I was lucky I came back with my little lorry quite loaded. This was only possible because, instead of telephoning to ask if there was anything available, I was right there in their warehouse – with order pad ready. Sometimes, I could actually see the goods I wanted. That made it hard for them to refuse a persuasive young man – dressed in a flying jacket!

If I was delivering anywhere in the area of Pimlico, I never failed to look in on Belco Limited, major importers of Grohe taps being made in its factory in South Africa. I was embarrassed at a trade luncheon at the Dorchester some years later when Belco's MD Sidney Popper made a speech about salesmanship, in which he referred to me. He related how I called at least once a week, dressed in a flying jacket to see if there was anything I could purchase. If successful, I changed into a suit jacket to deliver them to a buyer!

When father died in 1956, the business deficit had turned round into a slight profit. The company became a leader in many spheres and it is right that I show how it happened from those small beginnings. Our salaries were kept limited and closing the loss-making plumbing department helped, along with the cash flow generated by the sales of materials to the plumbing trade.

I will try to explain how we developed from our low turnover in 1956, into a quite important company, with our share of good and bad times along the way. The first year after I came home, I recall the stock value being under £4000 – and some of that was old material that should have been thrown away!

We purchased the shares when they became available from the only two outside shareholders, William Hedgecock and Leo Vincent. Fortunately, my uncle Sidney Humpherson did not want to purchase any of them so they were then put in Ron's and my names. Thus mother's side of the family became the majority shareholders.

By 1950, I was already controlling our shop selling prices and choice of suppliers, instead of Arthur Meadows by now the shop manager who was buying from the most convenient source. That was often other local merchants or wholesalers, rather than the manufacturer. I stopped it by seeking out the actual manufacturers. However, we were still small fry compared to everyone around us in West London, so I had to make our mark in several ways.

In those early days, we were one of the few firms in West London where you could often find cast iron baths for sale. That was due to a friendly connection with the manager of the British Bath Company factory at Greenford. I did not wait like others to be allocated baths for eventual delivery to their warehouse. Instead, I drove my lorry to the factory on Saturday mornings, when no deliveries were being made, but the plant was still in production.

I managed to pack between twelve and fourteen 5'6" baths onto my lorry – many still warm after enamelling. Each bath weighed in at 2.5 cwt ('Cwt' is a 'hundred weight' in the UK that is 112 lbs) – so my little lorry intended for carrying a maximum load of 15cwt, was carrying up 1.5 UK tons. No wonder I could usually smell rubber burning on my rear tyres, scrapping against the mudguards!

Most manufacturers I contacted in the early days had never heard of us. However, on occasions, some ancient soul in their sales office remembered us from Humpherson's more affluent days. So my approach was (a) to source my chosen products only from the actual manufacturer; (b) to present them in the best possible way in our showrooms, though the funds for that were very limited at the time; (c) to promote the company within our limited budget.

I had thought it essential to learn about the industry around us – so early on we began to attend meetings of the West London Builder's Merchants Association (WLBMA). It had been formed in the early 1900s and there were 58 members of all sizes, spreading out from Chelsea to Feltham and Kingston. One must realize that many merchant firms had started in prime sites – town centres, rail yards, and select high street locations. Sadly, their very position made them a first-class target for developers in the 1970s, leading eventually to the demise of the Association. Indeed, by 1979 there were only three of the members left on their original sites!

In 1959, my brother Ron, a guest from Crane Limited and I attended the Association's AGM and Dinner at a restaurant in Osterley, West London. The restaurant was so packed that we almost had to take it in turns to eat! I complained at the next monthly meeting and found myself (a) on the Committee; (b) told to organise the next AGM and Dinner; (c) asked if I would be the next Secretary?

I was then expected to attend the National Association of Builder's and Plumber's Merchants' (NFBPM) meetings, held at Holborn in London. Knowing of my interest in the use of plastic in plumbing, I was then asked to represent the NFBPM on BSI Committee PLC94 – dealing with plastic soil pipes, rainwater goods and the like. Then I attended all the BSI Committees dealing with taps, baths and sanitary ware.

Before long, I was receiving the papers on 22 BSI (British Standards Institute) Committees to monitor. I

then became Chairman of the BSI Committee dealing with Perspex (acrylic) baths. Later, I lead the BSI Delegation to European Standards on Spatial Planning for the Bathroom, held in Paris.

By 1963, I was Chairman of the West London Builder's Merchants Association. I had long since transferred its Annual Dinner to the Rembrandt Hotel in Knightsbridge and my chosen Guest of Honour that year was Jack Hay – Chairman of Twyfords Limited – then the UK's leading manufacturer of sanitary ware.

In 1963, I was Chairman of the West London Builder's Association. It then had 58 independent members with their own premises.

Much of this arose simply because I complained about being crushed at dinner!

Menu

Saumon Fumé

—

Consommé Mikado

—

Tournedos de Boeuf Sauté Chasseur

Brocolli au Beurre

Pommes Parmentier

—

Baba au Rhum

—

Croute Diane

—

Café

Toasts

HER MAJESTY THE QUEEN

Proposed by - - - - - The Chairman

THE WEST LONDON BUILDERS' MERCHANTS' ASSOCIATON and its CHAIRMAN

Proposed by - - - - J. R. T. HAY, Esq.
Chairman and Managing Director, Twyfords Ltd.

Response by - - - - G. PIDGEON, Esq.
Chairman, West London Builders' Merchants' Association

THE GUESTS

Proposed by - - - - L. W. GIBBS, Esq.
Treasurer, West London Builders' Merchants' Association

Response by - - - - G. WHEELER, Esq.
President, National Federation of Builders' and Plumbers' Merchants

—

TOAST MASTER
Mr. Leslie Jones

ARTISTS
Barrie Manning presents
"Champagne"

R. H. Leach - Pianist

The West London Builder's Association Menu and Toasts at the Hotel Rembrandt on Monday 8th April 1963. My guest was 'Jack' Hay, Chairman and Managing Director of Twyfords. It cost in the region of £5.50 per head for the 300 + attending. Note: the price included a six-course menu, the services of a Toast Master, a pianist and the 'Champagne' troupe of eight dancers. The whole card is naturally printed in Humpherson's green!

When my father died in 1956, over one third of our turnover was dangerously with one company – Heat & Air Systems – based in the offices above Victoria Coach Station. I had walked into their offices on my first day out as the firm's representative and handed one of my brand new cards to the receptionist. A few minutes afterwards a man, who I learned later was a director Lieut. Col McFarlane OBE, walked in to collect some papers and wanted to know if he could help. I had seen pictures of engineering plant on the walls so I told him we sold pipes and fittings. He asked if I could find sixteen 3" gunmetal gate valves quickly. I immediately said yes, though I never seen gate valves even approaching that size!

My ex-Army lorry was parked outside and I drove to Borough High Street where the London offices of a number of brass foundries were based. I picked up six from John Webb & Co., a few from Peglers and the rest from Cranes in Leman Street. I telephoned Col. McFarlane and told him they would be delivered the next day. I arrived with them in my van and, after several trips carrying them to their top floor offices, laid them out in reception.

He was very pleased and over the following years, we supplied his firm with valves and fittings on a number of major contracts. They installed degreasing, plating and/or spray plants, for the likes of Ford Motors at Dagenham, Vauxhall Motors at Luton; the Rover car plant; Rolls Royce in Glasgow; Crompton Parkinson in Doncaster and many others, including military installations. There were contracts abroad like an abattoir in Karachi and a refrigeration plant in Singapore. We supplied all the tubes and fittings on these and many other Heat & Air contracts (See Appendix 8).

Our largest contract for Heat & Air Systems in the UK was for the London Transport Bus Depot at Aldenham where they stripped, degreased and re-sprayed double decker buses. On this contract, we supplied all the pipe work needed, ¼" valves for compressed air lines, ½" for paint lines, and numerous cast iron flanged valves right up to 8" in size, that each weighed 85 kgs.

The London Transport bus depot at Aldenham was one of our largest UK contracts for Heat & Air Systems. Here, double decker buses were 'taken apart' and the body cleaned and re-sprayed using valves and pipe work supplied by Humphersons. It was officially opened in 1956.

Ready to be delivered. The largest valves we supplied on the Aldenham contract were 8" flanged cast iron – each weighing 85 kg. The scale can be judged by the ½" domestic valve alongside them. Though clearly not 'bathrooms' fittings – Heat & Airs' contracts helped bring the company back into profitability – thus enabling us to then fully return to the family's true line of business.

We were the first company in London and the South of England to embrace acrylic baths, first sold under the ICI registered name of 'Perspex'. I later became Chairman of the BSI (British Standard Institute) Committee drawing up a British Standard for this new entry on the bathroom market.

There is no doubt that our real growth and profitability began with the Heat and Air contracts but I did not see 'pipes and fittings' as our main way forward. I knew that our future lay in promoting kitchens and bathrooms. So we then concentrated a large portion of the growing profits into improving the premises and showrooms, whilst I sought out new products to put on display. When I say 'new products', we were the first bathroom showroom in London and indeed southern England, to have Perspex (acrylic) baths on display!

Our lead in the acrylic bath market led to a surprising incident in 1969. Three senior members of Ideal Standard's sales team asked to see me one day – it was all rather 'cloak and dagger!'. I think it included Dennis Ball their sales director. I was asked if I would meet a number of Ideal Standard directors and talk to them about acrylic baths. It was made clear that the meeting was to be kept secret although I had no problem in that direction. They asked if it could be held on the coming Saturday morning.

On the due day, two large limousines pulled into Holmes Place just below my office window. About nine or ten gentlemen alighted and came up to my office where I had arranged for coffee and biscuits to be served. It turned out the 'delegation' included the President and CEO of American Standard Corporation and the President and/or CEO of all the company's plants – worldwide!

I explained the virtues of acrylic baths that had already become apparent from our sales. I described the difference in the manufacturing process as compared with cast iron, the handling, the lower price and the importance of instructions to plumbers – all used to installing cast iron baths. I had seen several bath plants and knew they were hot, noisy, required considerable space, a large labour force and were very capital intensive. I compared that to the vastly different almost 'clinical' working conditions in the first acrylic bath plant I had visited.

The upshot was that the 'delegation' went from London to the Ideal Standard factory in Hull for a meeting of international chief executives. At the meeting, they decided to gradually phase out the manufacture of cast iron baths and introduce those made of acrylic. I was later thanked by Mr Nicholson, the UK Managing Director and had a letter from the President of American Standard.

A word is necessary about our 'displays'. As soon as we could afford it, I ensured that instead of fittings being shown within four foot high surrounds, I would make a bathroom display look like a *real* bathroom, complete with tiled walls, flooring, towels and soap. The aim was that customers would see the fittings in a proper setting. We later did something very similar with kitchens displays.

With improved displays and interesting products, I set out to woo the press and was successful in those early days. Good fortune shined upon us when Peta Fordham of the Guardian spotted us when passing by. Under the heading 'New Lines', she wrote:

"Tucked away behind the Fulham Road is an old-established builder's merchant shop, which is to be highly commended to anyone within its reach, since you will here obtain skilful and willing advice and help about anything within its range. This is Humphersons': The address is 188a Fulham Road, SW10. If you are meditating a personal call, (which you might well do, for the sake of the intelligently displayed showrooms) be warned before you start that it is behind the main road, not on it.

The presiding genius, Mr Pidgeon, is an enthusiast with a very hard head indeed. He is a member of the relevant British Standards Committee and he winkles out nonsense from what is new with a shrewd judgement from both sides of the counter as it were…."

Peta Fordham became well known for her book on 'The Robbers tale – the Real Story of the Great Train Robbery' that was a best seller. Her insight into the trial of the Train Robbers was said to arise from her lawyer husband's involvement in the case.

Arising from my knowledge of the potential market for plastic rainwater and soil pipes, I asked permission of the Royal Borough of Kensington & Chelsea to replace the soil stacks to our offices in Beaufort Works with the new plastic pipe and fittings. After giving a *written personal* guarantee to remove it if problems arose, the stack was built with much publicity. It was the first

Humphersons built the first plastic soil stack erected on UK domestic property to its offices in Holmes Place. I knew plastic was the way forward from my earlier work as a member of British Standard Committee PLC94 – where I represented – the NFBPM (the National Federation of Builders' and Plumber's Merchants).

plastic soil stack erected for use in the UK, with the exception of a sample 'display' stack at the Sanitary Institute.

We purchased stocks of the 'Metrex' Plastic range of pipes and fittings from Allied Ironfounders – again the first in the country to do so. Later we took in Key-Terrain fittings when its factory started down in Kent as they were actually manufacturing the fittings and used solvent weld joints which I considered were superior to 'push-fit'.

In 1967, our eldest son Laurence joined us – the first of the fifth generation. With his keen interest, and ability in art, he immediately became our kitchen designer. He really was thrown into the job – but as I believe him now to be the leading kitchen designer in the UK – you will see how much progress he has made. When he joined us, we only had Daintymaid and Leisure kitchens on display but we quickly added English Rose, Kandya, Hygena and Wrighton.

Later, we had a visit from a Jan Stoltz, sent on by Harrods, to ask if we would be interested in becoming a dealer for his parent company Stickling Küchen from Germany, manufacturers of Nobilia kitchens. The first German kitchen imported into Britain was Poggenpohl, then being sold by Heals of Tottenham Court Road, so we introduced the second! That was a very successful trading link and under Laurence we set about appointing Nobilia showroom dealers across the country. Laurence reminds me that his first kitchen sale exceeding £1000 was of Nobilia – to Sam Wannamaker. It was cause for us to open a bottle of Champagne in my office to celebrate breaking the 'One-thousand Pound' barrier!

Our progress seemed to attract those watching our growing importance. Ken Griffin had earlier joined us from the giant 'Mercian' Builder's Merchant Group, where he ran their London outlet in Chelsea. Along with architect clients, he also brought all the Woolworth stores' trade with him. That included sanitary ware and the purpose made sink units for their burgeoning delicatessen counters. He was very successful in growing business for us but sadly died before seeing the fruits of his labour.

Nigel Froy came to us in late 1968. He had been a director of a large family business W. N. Froy – builders' merchants of Hammersmith. On its closure he became a director of Finch-Froy, based across London in Barking. He had an good knowledge of the sanitary trade and he was later appointed as Sales Director. His major contribution to us was in reorganising the business into more specific tasks. We had grown too fast with most people multi-tasking but that could not continue with such rapid expansion. In June 1970, his uncle Ronnie Froy joined us (again from Finch-Froy), and he headed up our fast expanding contract business in hotels and housing developments.

In the early 1970s, the Government became aware of the shortage of hotel rooms in the country and offered incentives for the construction of hotels – on a room basis. However, the largest area of growth was already in supplying the hotel trade.

Humphersons had always supplied hotels in the Kensington/Chelsea area until World War II – when most of them were put to a military use – of one kind or another. At the end of my first year, I well remember an incident at The Glendower Hotel at South Kensington. The owner Mr Schmidt, asked us to quote to replace the baths in some six bathrooms undergoing refurbishment. I went on site and found they were 6ft baths that were especially difficult to obtain. Nevertheless I quoted him. He accepted my price – on the condition that I take away the existing baths when delivering the new ones. I agreed in writing as instructed, only to find out to my horror that the baths were fireclay – and weighed upwards of 650 lbs each. It was a costly mistake – especially as I had to help break them up with a sledge hammer, carry the pieces down the back stairs, then drive them to a dump in my ex-army lorry!

The first hotel of any size I handled was the Park Tower Hotel in Knightsbridge. It was originally a joint venture between Capital & Counties Properties and Canadian Pacific. Capital & Counties had extensive properties across the Knightsbridge area and had long been a customer of mine. Because of the multi-faceted construction, the rooms tapered towards the centre, making the layout of the rooms more difficult. I attended several joint meetings with the architect Richard Siefert of Siefert & Partners, with the developers and major contractors. Siefert was regarded as one of the leading British architects of the time. Some of these meetings became quite heated – especially when it was even *hinted* that the rising costs *might* lay with his overall design. To sit next to him at a meeting, when he was in full-flow, made me quake at times.

Above: The Sheraton Park Towers Hotel, Knightsbridge.
Below: Richard Seifert – of Seifert & Partners the architects responsible for the Park Towers Hotel.

I mention it to demonstrate that we were seldom simply the chosen supplier to an architect's specification but frequently involved in the design as in this case. I remember there was later a discussion about the 'Room Price' likely to be necessary. There was a gasp when the developers said they would probably have to charge rooms at £16 per night. I attended a similar meeting about the Intercontinental Hotel, with Bechtel the consultants and the client. There it was suggested that the 'Room Price' might have to be as much as £25 per night. Times have changed since.

I again refer to Appendix 8 that includes a list of the many hotels we supplied. It was part of an indoctrination brochure for new staff. It shows *7500 hotel bathrooms* delivered over a short period and did not take into account smaller hotel contracts. These bathrooms had recently been delivered or about to be sent to site. It did not include our contracts of the past or possible future contracts. The larger pottery manufacturers granted us special terms – to ensure their products were used in a number of these substantial and prestigious contracts.

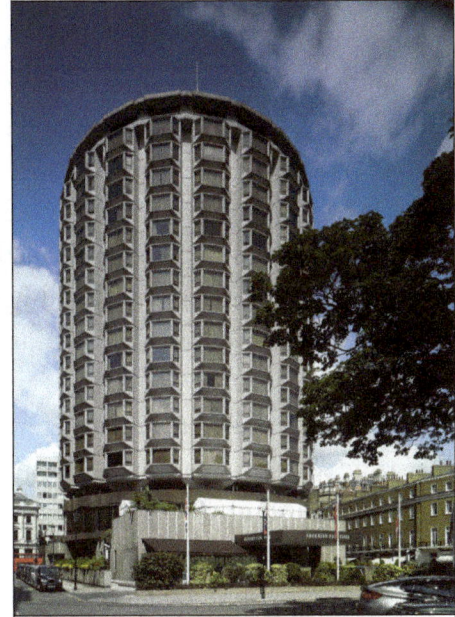

I should add that the competition was very keen and we barely made a profit out of the work – usually depending on 'extras' of all kinds where we imposed a reasonable return of profit. A good example was the Intercontinental Hotels' 'London Park Lane' where I showed the architect and contractors from Bechtel around the showroom. They chose chrome fittings with onyx heads for the shower, basin and bidet. That consisted of five heads for the bath/shower, two for the washbasin and two for the bidet – a total of nine per bathroom. I should add that the heads were 'push-fit' and easy to remove.

Soon after the hotel opened, the onyx heads were disappearing at a great rate – probably taken to be used as elegant paper weights! However, we were soon supplying them replacements one hundred at a time. I joked afterwards that we made more money from the 'extras' than from the supply of the bath, basin, bidet and fittings to its 450 bathrooms!

Ewe Hannek a representative for Neff was sent to us by 'Will' Wrighton (Chairman of Wrighton Kitchens) to see if we would like to handle Neff products. Ewe and Laurence discussed terms and Laurence was very impressed – in the days when hand-held calculators were rare – that Ewe worked out terms on a slide rule. As a result of their 'slide rule' negotiation, ours was the first order placed for Neff ovens in the UK.

There was a rapidly growing interest in us in the media. A visit by Monica Tyson Editor of Ideal Homes Magazine seemed to put a seal of approval on us! We were frequently in the Home Journals and the 'Woman' or 'Home' pages in the leading newspapers. We were fresh and full of new ideas leading to interest and visits from most of the 'Glossy Magazines' staff, upwards to their editors. We were not the largest merchant but clearly the most interesting to the media. I have cuttings about our showrooms from most of the known magazines and newspapers.

Anne Edwards wrote about us in the Sunday Express and I see from a cutting dated May 28th 1967 that we would deliver a complete coloured bathroom suite, bath, low level WC with seat, washbasin all complete with taps – *anywhere in England and Wales*, for £34.7.6p (£34.35p). I have articles by Unity Hall in the Sun, Sheila Black in the Financial Times amongst many others.

Over a short space of time articles about us appeared in most of the Daily Papers and Home Magazines by such as Jacqueline Inchbald, Barty Phillips, Lucia van de Post, Elizabeth Benn, Pamela Dixon in She Magazine, Victoria Reilly in The Sunday Telegraph, Vivien Duret in the Observer and Mary Kennedy in Ideal Homes Magazine. That is apart from constant attention from the Trade Press.

The 'Home Page' in the Daily Telegraph featured Alice Hope, the doyen of such reporters, and she wrote several articles about us. We had acquired 186 Fulham Road which gave us a frontage onto that important thoroughfare and the basement went as far as under the adjacent shop No: 188. I decided to utilise the space with a long held wish to show aids for the disabled. At the time, there were few such aids available and those that did exist, tended to be very expensive.

For example, I showed how an ordinary bath grab rail could be used to aid those having difficulty lowering and raising oneself from the toilet. Indeed there was a multitude of quite simple aids for the shower or bath. I called it 'For the young and not so young' and word soon spread about it. I found myself giving talks to Councils including a gathering of delegates from all 32 London Boroughs attending London's first 'Safety in the Home' exhibition at Chiswick Town Hall. This was followed by radio chat shows on BBC Radio Oxford, BBC Radio Suffolk and others.

I wrote a paper entitled 'Safety in the Bathroom' and extracts of it appeared in many journals including that of The Royal Society for the Prevention of Accidents (RoSPA). Unfortunately, Alice Hope reported that Geoffrey Pidgeon was ready to help with advice to anybody who asked. We had many callers, which is what I expected, but we also had hundreds of letters explaining their problems and asking for my help. It was quite impossible to deal with them all but some of them were very sad. A letter from a partially blind and disabled lady especially distressed me. With apparently nobody to help her, she had to sit on the edge of the bath and throw a jug full of water over each half of her body at a time. It seems archaic and we should be grateful for the help now available to people with her difficulties from the NHS.

Our son Michael joined us in 1969. After a short introductory period in various departments to learn about the products we handled, he had a spell in our Tadema Road warehouse just off Lots Road in Chelsea. After our successful move to Holman Road in Battersea that he helped organise, Michael started in the Holman Road telephone sales office in Battersea, then moved to its trade counter, later managing the Holman Road warehouse and transport. After a period at Farmer Bros, he was put in charge of the seven branches of a builders merchant group called Standard Wallpaper Company that we merged with in 1976, then eventually purchased. As a result, Michael had a most comprehensive grounding in the builder's merchant industry, as well as in our own specialised field of bathrooms.

By now already a Freeman of the City of London, I next became a Founder Member of the Worshipful Company of Builder's Merchants of the City of London. I was later a Founder Member and Fellow of the Institute of Builder's Merchants (FIBM).

My interest in education started with marking exam papers for students who had taken the postal course arranged by the National Federation of Builders and Plumbers Merchants (NFBPM). I handled the papers concerned with plumbing and heating materials. I marked them whilst at home and I must admit some were very amusing. My favourite was one students answer to 'What material is used in the manufacture of cold water storage cisterns?' The student listed steel, lead, brass, iron, copper and (running out of metals) he added bricks and glass – amongst those I can remember from an even longer list. I marked it well – since it showed imagination!

Realising the need for staff education led me to arrange the first night-school for Builders' Merchants in the West London area. Students attended two nights a week in the winter: one at Hammersmith College of Art and Building dealing with the technical side and the second at West London College of Commerce. Some twenty-five students started the course and all but one completed it, no doubt due to the financial incentives offered by their company for a full attendance record. Our company offered a prize for the highest marks in the final exams and we were a little embarrassed to find our own John Whayman the winner!

Somewhere in all this, we acquired the bathroom division of Morgan's of Hounslow from my friend Len Morgan. In the late 1960s he wanted to concentrate on his success with the rapidly expanding heating market selling boilers and radiators. His bathroom division was based in extensive property alongside the Thames in Staines and had on going trade including supplying toilet fixtures to Heathrow airport!

We later bought the Staines freehold property and that turned out to be very profitable. We owned the company stock, took over existing contracts, and then later sold the property to developers. The sale proceeds covered substantially more than we paid for the on going company, its assets and the land in the first place.

In the late 1960s we purchased the long established company Farmer Bros. & Company Limited. After passing through several hands it is still in business in the Fulham Road, Chelsea.

We had also purchased the old-established ironmonger company – Farmer Bros & Co. Limited. They were just along the Fulham Road between Holmes Place and Beaufort Street. We sold the shops and property on the north side of the road to local developers. That covered the purchase costs and left us with a profitable business on the south side of the road. Also, due to the nature of the tax-efficient deal with its directors, we also had considerable cash in hand. I am glad to see that after passing through several hands, it is once again a thriving business.

In early 1973 we sold Holmes Place for a number of reasons. Firstly, we had outgrown the office space available. Secondly, our showroom expansion was hampered because it was limited to the area in what was previously warehouse space. However, this all coincided with a letter from the London County Council (LCC) stating that they shortly intended to compulsorily purchase our new warehouse accommodation, in nearby Tadema Road in Chelsea. The reason given was that it would lie in the path of the planned 'West Cross Route' – an ambitious road scheme that never saw the light of day. Importantly, the LCC letter promised full compensation for the costs of the move elsewhere.

We were very fortunate in finding a substantial property in Holman Road Battersea that had just been vacated by Carsons Limited, a leading paint company. We could have moved in straight away as most of the high-grade offices were excellent for our purpose and would accommodate our planned expansion. The loading bay, warehouse and the rest of the property were complete without requiring much attention. However, as we intended to move Humpherson's trade counter there as well, some work was essential. We employed Richard Daniels Associates as our architects and they produced a splendid frontage to the building and included the trade counter just inside it.

The site included the long leasehold of a series building which had previously been stables – underneath some dilapidated flats called 'Lombard Dwellings' (and they certainly lived up to the name). This area was entered via Lombard Road and we also cut into the stable yard from the main warehouse. Overall, the properties gave us upwards of 36,000 square feet of offices, showrooms and warehouse.

Following the beneficial sale of Holmes Place, we were in the fortunate position of being able to buy the main freehold property outright, do all the alterations, and still have funds left over. We made the move after careful planning, both by the sales office and warehouse managers, in the hope that sales would not be too seriously affected.

We had taken great care to notify everyone of our move – in a series of announcements. We pointed out that we were only a short distance from Beaufort Street in Chelsea, over Battersea Bridge

Carsons Headquarters building in Battersea purchased to replace our overstretched offices and showrooms in Fulham Road and our warehouse depot in Tadema Road Chelsea. It was big enough to also absorb the offices of the Standard Wallpaper in the merger with that company.

on the way to York Road. Ley Kenyon a friend and well-known Chelsea artist, produced a Christmas Card for 1973, announcing that 'Humpherson's New Showrooms are Open' with details of the products available on the inside.

We called our new headquarters 'Beaufort House' continuing the long connection with Beaufort Street just across the Thames in Chelsea.

Unfortunately, our move coincided with nearby Albert Bridge being closed for repair putting great strain and traffic jams onto the adjacent Battersea Bridge. Customers were frustrated and sales suffered badly in those six months or so. We did all we could with press adverts and promotions but sales were inevitably down and they stayed down until well after the bridge reopened.

Fortunately, soon after Albert Bridge opened up again the traffic flowed in the area and things slowly came back to normal. We used warehouse space on the first floor as showrooms and combined with

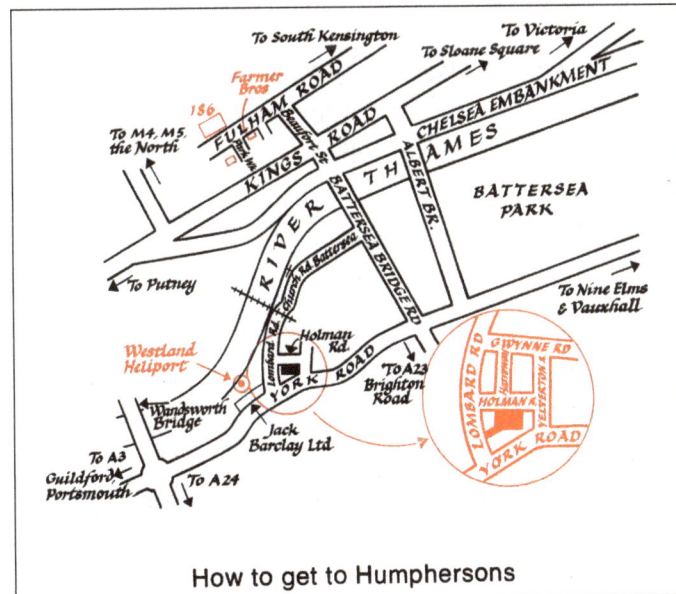

How to get to Humphersons

The map inside the 'We are on the move' notice sent to everyone we could think of – customers, suppliers and press alike. It shows how really close we still were to our previous area of operation. The '186' in Fulham Road refers to the shop in front of Holmes Place. We had used it as a bathroom boutique and the basement below as the widely reported 'Safety in the Bathroom' display.

the drawing offices, measured in the region of 7,500 sq. ft., Humpherson's showroom was soon regarded as the best in the London. Again, we drew the attention of the press, as being in the very forefront of the industry, displaying the very latest and best of bathroom and kitchen products. We proudly announced we had 65 displays of bathrooms and kitchen equipment in the new showrooms – then the largest and most up-to-date anywhere.

Whilst sales of our bathroom fittings grew fast, our major growth was in kitchen furniture and equipment – largely led by Laurence. We had the largest stocks of Wrighton kitchen furniture anywhere in the UK. We were the first showrooms to display Gaggenau kitchen appliances, major stockists of Neff and Bosch and much else besides – including our own 'Flaxman' range of stainless steel sink tops to Metric dimensions.

The Bulthaup factory in Aich in Lower Bavaria. I recall how Laurence and I were impressed by factory and especially its hi-store – the first we had seen.

There is little doubt that Bulthaup is the leading kitchen manufacturer in Germany and many would say – in the world. Having his product already shown across Europe, its CEO Gerd Bulthaup (son of the founder) decided the time was to seek a partner in Britain. He arrived with a list of contacts but his first call happened to be to Humpherson's showrooms in Holman Road, Battersea. Seeing the quality of our displays – and after listening to Laurence explaining our design ethos – he tore up the list and appointed Humpherson & Co his sole distributor for Great Britain.

So Bulthaup was added to our impressive list of kitchen manufacturers! We had Hygena (then regarded as a high quality range) Kandya, Wrighton and ABC Cuisine from France – amongst others.

In 1976, we merged with the Standard Wallpaper Company with its HQ in Chiswick. In spite of its name, it was a true builder's merchant company, covering all aspects of the industry. Our group already included Farmer Bros. the well-known hardware and ironmonger store in Chelsea, so it did not seem too great a step. Besides their merchant depots, they had several quite prestigious outlets in Twickenham and Chiswick that I saw as areas for growth in our specialised area of top-end kitchens and bathrooms.

Our core business at Humphersons continued to grow and Laurence added Italian sanitary ware from Cidneo – a pottery based in Brescia in northern Italy. Their designs were modern and struck a fresh note into bathroom fittings. So far as I am aware, the only other Italian ware being sold into the UK at the time was Cesame – made in Sicily. Having started to purchase from Italy, we added Teorema taps to our ranges. Their offices were again in Brescia but their factory was in Lumezzane some miles north of the town – in an area we found was full of tap manufacturers – rather like Birmingham in our earlier days!

Shortly afterwards we were offered the products of Salvarni – a very large Italian kitchen manufacturer based in Parma. Laurence and I were flown to see the factory but it was closed due to one of those frequent strikes that so crippled Italian industry at the time. However, the communist-led strikers opened the gates for us so that we could see the plant – a very hard headed decision, perhaps based on their hopes for a successful outcome to their strike! To use the word 'vast' to describe kitchen furniture factory may seem somewhat of an exaggeration. However, it was the only one I had seen where they took in trees at one end and turned out completed kitchens at the other. Inside, managers drove around in small Fiat cars and scooters with bicycles used by the staff to reach the toilets. They even made their own laminates 'Formica' and only the few metal parts needed were manufactured off site. I had never seen or heard of anything like it before.

Nevertheless, for sheer efficiency, I saw nothing approaching the Bulthaup plant at Aich near Munich. Laurence and I had visited the factory before taking on the range. We were deeply impressed by the factory; the attitude of the work force; the design team and the products on display. Coupled with the knowledge and understanding of the kitchen market, shown by Gerd Bulthaup its MD, we knew this was going to be a great success for us.

It might cross your mind to wonder where we were going to show all these kitchen and bathroom product ranges we had acquired?

Around this time we negotiated the purchase of the 'Norway Food Centre' – a double fronted shop on the high pavement on the north side of Brompton Road, a few hundred yards west of Harrods. The shops were deep and its basement matched – meaning that we could fit a large number of displays into the premises. We fitted in about twelve bathrooms, mostly downstairs and around fifteen fully fitted kitchens on the ground floor. In those, at least five had all the appliances connected so we could demonstrate them. Ovens, washing machines, dishwashers and microwave ovens – all working!

The standard of shop fitting was exemplary and the centre of the drawing office had a full height hexagonal glass-fronted cage containing two parrots known as 'Brahms' and 'Liszt'! All in all it was a quite stunning display and I have seen nothing to match its quality – before or since.

Of course, the opening party had to match the showrooms! As they arrived, each of our hundred or so guests was given a copy of the newly launched book 'Temples of Convenience' by Lucinda Lambton. The guests included *'Everybody who was anybody'* in the 'Glossy Magazines' – as well as the Editors of the Woman's Page of the press. Lucia van de Post told me it was one of best-attended launches she had seen. We had Brian Binns – winner of the Sunday Times 'Cook of the Year' award – cook several dishes including my favourite 'Humpherson's Fish Pie' made with Harrod's Lobsters. I should say it *was* my favourite – until I saw the bill!

Around the same time, we had stripped out the top floor of the Standard Wallpaper showrooms in Chiswick High Road. We refitted them with Wrighton kitchens and a selection of our newly acquired ranges including Salvarani kitchens and Cidneo bathroom fittings from Italy. The ground floor space was cleared of some of the existing 'builder's merchant' products and the several bathroom and kitchen ranges displayed in the windows. It was a good showroom in a prime area.

We also utilised the other substantial 'Standard Wallpaper' showroom – in Heath Road Twickenham. It had a rather grand wide staircase in oak, leading directly from the twin front doors up to the first floor, again giving space for numerous displays. Here we installed kitchens by Bulthaup, the French company ABC Cuisine and Wrighton. Again, several kitchens were fully functional. By this time, we were also the agents for Cesame sanitary ware from Catania in Sicily. That too was put on display but in the right hand ground floor window, visible from the street.

Making display kitchens fully functional was a major step forward. Depending on the size of the showroom, I believe we had between three and six kitchens with sink, refrigerator, washing machine, dishwasher, hob, and oven and microwave – all working. My late wife Jane was very much in demand by branch managers – all keen to have her demonstrate the fittings. Best of all, was the smell of her cooking wafting round the showrooms. It was very beneficial to sales!

Another opportunity now arose and it seemed simply too good to pass up. We were offered the chance to create a Humpherson kitchen and bathroom showroom in a substantial part of the lower ground floor of Heals of Tottenham Court Road. Heals is certainly London's most famous name for furniture and they clearly felt our approach was compatible with their design philosophy. We had to contract for a period and 'rental' was on a commission applied to the sales generated.

In spite of our considerable financial commitments at the time, we went ahead. Again, Laurence and his team created a quite stunning exhibition, of all that was good in the kitchen and bathroom industry of the period. By this time, manufacturers were asking us to take their brands into our showrooms. Apart from a fine display of bathroom fittings, we included the latest Bulthaup and Wrighton kitchen fitments and a new comer to us – Siematic Kitchens offered by Siematic UK. Ultimately, this latter relationship was to lead to the family losing ownership of the business.

At the same time, we had some sixty-five displays of kitchens and bathrooms at our Holman Road showrooms, so we were able to give extensive coverage to all our manufacturing partners. Although I have mentioned many new products, we were still a substantial account for Armitage-Shanks and Ideal-Standard. In addition, we were an important to Delta, the manufacturer of most of our taps, especially our exclusive 'Beauline' range. Much of these products were being used in our contract trade – hotels, developments and the like – that had grown over the past few years.

However, the country's overall economic position was rapidly worsening. The earlier miners' strikes, the 'three day week' and power cuts were just a few of the elements that put trading in the UK under such a strain.

This all combined to create 'The End of an Era'.

Chapter 24

The End of an Era

In looking back now over the sixty-seven years since I started work at Humphersons, I realise how turbulent some of them have been. The expression 'ups and downs' comes readily to mind and perhaps some of the 'downs' – have been rather deeper than I might have wished!

We had taken great care to notify everyone of our move to Battersea in a series of announcements. In these, we pointed out that we were only a short distance from Beaufort Street in Chelsea, then over Battersea Bridge, leading to Holman Road. Unfortunately, our move coincided with nearby Albert Bridge being closed for urgent repair, putting great strain – and traffic jams – onto Battersea Bridge. Customers were frustrated and sales suffered in those first six months or so. We did all we could with advertising and promotions but sales were inevitably down, and stayed down.

Then to add to our problems, a series of Miner's strikes over the period brought us another major problem. In view of the lack of coal at electricity power stations, the Government declared industry should run on the basis of a 3-day week. With effect from 1st January to 7th March 1974 users of electricity were allowed to be operational only three days a week! To make matters worse, we were also forbidden to work longer on those days in order to try to catch up!

The government declared this crippling blow should commence just as we moved. One of the two bridges leading from our old premises, over the Thames, closed AND a three day week – how could we run a business under those circumstances?

The strikes crippled many industries and made our own projected growth difficult. At the same time, we faced inflation and a soaring bank rate. The worldwide prices for raw materials were caught up in the inflation spiral and we were adjusting prices for some products on a daily basis. This particularly affected copper, a major component in the production of taps. At one stage, we often received two price increases from our copper tube suppliers in the same day!

Now our new catalogues only showed codes instead of prices. As a result, we could issue new price lists inexpensively and regularly to keep our customers informed. This high rate of inflation was particularly difficult with the larger contracts we were handling, where developers required a fixed price.

Strikes seemed to be almost constant in various industries – including the motor industry – but the biggest effect was felt from the mines being closed on numerous occasions. Looking back, the Seventies was a period of unrest politically and in the workplace. The final straw was the 'Winter of Discontent' over 1978/9 with all the hardship and misery it created.

In parallel with all this woe, the inflation rate had peaked at an incredible 26.9% in the 12 months to August 1975. Compare that with 2014, with inflation presently running at around 2%!

At times in 1979, the Bank of England Base Rate was 17% and the interest on our bank overdraft was calculated at Base Rate plus 3%. However, during the latter 1970s, we were trying to trade with a Bank Rate of between 14% and 16% – to which you must *add* our overdraft facility costs of base rate + 3%. Before making a profit, we had to pay **between 17% and 19% interest** on our borrowing. It made trading difficult and our ambitions to expand virtually impossible. To survive, we had to take some drastic financial steps, including making some valuable staff redundant. I was sorry to lose their contribution.

In late 1976 we had merged with the Standard Wallpaper Co. Ltd., (SWC) based in Chiswick but with some ten branches spread over outer west London. They had branches across the area, in Hounslow, Southall, Ealing, Twickenham, Acton, Feltham as well as two outlets in Chiswick. In addition, the group included a tiling firm and a successful electrical wholesale outlet 'Stanwall Electric.' In particular their branches in Heath Road Twickenham and Chiswick High Road were substantial, built to a high standard and with clearly suitable showrooms for our growing portfolio of quality kitchens and bathrooms. At the same time, I thought our lower cost ranges could do well in the new outlets.

It was clear from Standard Wallpaper's accounts that they were broadly suffering, like us, from the economic situation. However, the accounts did not – *could not* – show the shifting pattern of trade in the Builder's Merchant industry. Sales in the wholesale paint and wallpaper business, the heart of their trade, was slowly passing to the new 'Sheds' that were appearing. These were being supplied by manufacturers in bulk – particularly by paint manufacturers – on very competitive terms and we could not match their selling prices. Apart from anything else, these outlets were selling to the public at our trade prices or below. Then they added tools, wallpaper and everything needed by the emerging breed of handyman appearing in the new DIY do-it-yourself era.

I personally had every reason to believe this merger would benefit us. However, sadly in our due diligence, I soon found their underlying financial position was worse than that shown in their accounts. It did not help that the owners were friends and gave me assurances regarding their various shortcomings. In the end, we did merge with them but I quickly discovered how serious their cash position had become. Extraordinarily, we both used the same city firm of solicitors. The partners concerned assured me they would be even 'tougher' in their approach to each other than outside solicitors would. On reflection, I am sure that was not the case and our position during the merger negotiations was not fully secured.

Having merged, and after discovering these failings, my family purchased a controlling interest in the company.

We promptly began to sell off one or two of their bigger loss-making branches. These were handling the 'Heavy Goods' like bricks, sand and cement and occupied substantial sites very suitable for developers. As a result, I obtained considerable sums for them one by one – creating cash – which more or less matched their trading losses. However, any surplus was being absorbed by the expansion of Humpherson's showrooms – so it was difficult for us to juggle the two!

We had merged the two companies to form SWC-Humpherson with merged trading accounts. With hindsight, I had foolishly put us back into the same position I found on joining Humphersons all those years earlier (Appendix 9). Then, we had not been able to judge from *combined* accounts, which was the bigger loss maker. Sales or plumbing contracting? Now I found it just as difficult to establish (with such a variety of outlets) the loss makers – other than from departmental management figures.

Our situation with the Midland Bank gradually became quite delicate. A finance manager was appointed to oversee the company and he required me to personally explain our trading position – usually with only a day or two days notice.

Whilst happily lecturing us, Midland Bank had become embroiled with a costly purchase of a majority share in the Crocker National Bank of California. It later proved disastrous for them and was one of the reasons for HSBC (Hong Kong & Shanghai Banking Corporation) acquiring a 14.9% stake in Midland in 1987, and then finally taking them over entirely.

Back in 1968, the Midland had granted us an overdraft facility, on the basis of a floating charge on all our assets, including the premises. However, they also required the continuance of an existing 'Joint and Several Guarantee' by my brother Ron and myself. With the firm's properties valued at considerably more than the overdraft – and rising faster than inflation at the time – we were not *unduly* concerned. In all the acquisitions and mergers in which I was involved, I always tried to secure the property to our name by ensuring we held a freehold on their property or a long lease.

Through all this upheaval, it was necessary to bring the Midland Bank along with us and I kept them well informed of our actions. I was also very fortunate in befriending Herbert Cruickshank CBE, Joint Chairman and Group Managing Director of Bovis Holdings Ltd. Bovis were one of the country's leading building companies, covering everything from the housing market to major industrial contracts at home and abroad. In addition, they had shipping interests, and indeed, a global presence.

I first met Herbert when I was appointed to represent the National Federation of Builder's and Plumbers Merchants (NFBPM) on the Ministry of Works Metrication Board. He was its Chairman and the Board consisted of leading figures from all the professional bodies including architects, builders, surveyors and so on. A very powerful body!

I should add that Herbert – by then a widower – became a close friend and came to our home for dinner after his weekly visit to my office. It was of great assistance that Herbert agreed to accompany me in talks with the

Midland Bank. He was well known in the City and they listened carefully and politely to his comments about our objectives, our strengths and the way forward.

One of Herbert's friends was a partner in Armitage-Norton, a firm of accountants in the City of London. We were very fortunate that its senior partner Allan Davis – later to become Sir Allan Davis and Lord Mayor of London – agreed to become a director of our controlling body Humpherson Holdings Limited.

We had managed our continued expansion through the recessions of the mid-70s caused by amongst other things, the earlier oil crisis of 1973. That was later followed by the deep recession of 1980. Then, I am led to believe, UK company earnings went on to drop 35% and unemployment rose 124% from 5.3% to 11.9% within a couple of years. Fortunately, we had earlier been buffered by the profit arising from the sale of Holmes Place and the sale of the Standard Wallpaper Company loss-making depots to developers.

Our Heals operation was successful and one of its best-selling ranges was Siematic Kitchens a popular brand at that time. With the expressed aim of facilitating the growth of our business together, in a toughing economic climate, the owners of Siematic UK had offered us a long line of credit. Using this generous credit line, we naturally and predictably became much more committed to their brand. Shortly afterwards, they expressed an interest in taking a major stake in the company.

I will not relate the details of how this two-pronged approach created such difficulties for the company. Our only way out was to raise a considerable sum in most difficult trading times – or acquiesce to the proposal.

In spite of the efforts by Allan Davis, the Midland Bank refused to help us. One often hears the notion that banks are 'Fair Weather Friends' but that was truly their position towards us. My great-grandfather Edward Humpherson had opened an account at their Onslow Square Branch in South Kensington in 1874. It was then a branch of the London Joint Stock Bank, acquired by the Midland Bank in 1917. We were still banking in that same branch in 1981 – over one hundred years later.

Several Midland Bank managers at the Onslow Square Branch, from Cliff Steele, 'Chick' Evans onwards, had described me, as a 'golden client' but it meant nothing when we *really* needed help. The Midland clearly had its own problems at the time, so our needs to save our long established company, were tiny compared with the difficulties they were facing.

Suffice it to say, they would not budge and a Board Meeting was held in August 1981 where we handed over our company to the new owners.

**Even then, in an attempt to salvage something from the wreck,
I insisted that all the Humpherson Memorabilia – so important to the family –
should belong to me and I collected it two weeks later.**

Chapter 25

Onwards

I felt completely exhausted by the negotiations that led downwards to the collapse of the company. I had worked so hard for years rebuilding it towards its former glory, and these few weeks had been a nightmare for me. Finally, it was humiliating to walk away from the boardroom table in my office, leaving the new owners seated around it. Perhaps the hardest thing for me to swallow was the simple way in which the business was acquired!

There followed a few days at home going over the dramatic changes to my life. I had to accept responsibility for mistakes I had made along the way and that was difficult. I was especially angry with myself not spotting the menace waiting in the wings. However, I made up my mind to take a short break to plan my future.

Just by chance that very week Purley Bury a local tennis and bowls club, were canvassing for new members so Jane and I joined. Neither of us had played lawn bowls before but we made most welcome and were soon enjoying our first lessons. The club also had a tennis section, and both having played tennis we quickly felt at home there.

After five weeks enforced rest, I was already anxious to see if I could start afresh in the industry I had come to know so well. I knew that 'Cersaie' was the biggest bathroom and tile exhibition in Italy and discovered this annual event was about to be held in Bologna. Jane knew I wanted to see the exhibition so we flew to Milan and took a train down to Bologna.

I spoke not a word of Italian but the information desk at Bologna station advised us that there were no hotel rooms available in the town, nor for miles around. Some visitors to Cersaie were based in Florence and they knew of one party who travelled back and forth daily all the way from Milan. However, they took pity on us and found a room for us in Ferrara – *only* fifty kilometres away!

We took a taxi to the Cersaie exhibition grounds and deposited our cases in the left luggage office. The exhibition was housed in numerous buildings covering many acres, so it was difficult to know where to start. However, we had recently imported fittings from several Italian companies, so I sought them out from the plan in the exhibition brochure.

The first stand I found was Teorema, a large tap manufacturer based in Brescia whose fittings we had recently imported. Next, we found the Cidneo displays from a pottery firm making stylish ranges of sanitary ware; again we had previously handled Cidneo in a minor way. We were made most welcome on the stands and encouraged to import their products, in the event we should start again. Furthermore, I was gratified to learn that other manufacturers had heard of the Humpherson history and were keen to supply us.

Cersaie was a total surprise. The sheer variety of wares and the Italian design flair caught my eye as I was so used to the comparatively dull products from British manufacturers! That evening as it was closing for the day, we took a taxi to our hotel in Ferrara. It was close to the station and then called the Hotel de Ville. We went for a walk and chose a restaurant from the many in the area. Later, we sat in the hotel's lounge bar and I asked Jane if we could start up a bathroom business again. She knew I was excited by what I had seen at Cersaie and keen to start again, even from scratch. To my surprise, she immediately agreed, providing we only had _one_ shop instead of fifteen or so!

We then spent another three days at the exhibition meeting manufacturers and selecting products that I would like to include in our brand new enterprise!

Back home I instructed estate agents to look for a property in three very specific areas where I wanted my _one_ shop to be located. They were in Wimbledon Village, parts of Pimlico or in Richmond. Whilst this search was going on, I flew to Paris to visit 'Batimat' the long-established Building Exhibition that drew an international range of manufacturers. I met some of those we had had discussions with in Bologna and was happy to confirm we were planning to start a completely new business. I spent two days there and came away even more convinced there were great opportunities waiting for us.

Incidentally, I had not yet formed a company, nor chosen a name. I went into the local shops in Purley and found a printer who could provide business cards whilst I waited. It was my personal introduction to computer printing methods and I was astonished to see the variety of fonts he offered. I had chosen the name 'Bogart Bathrooms' and added our home address and telephone number. My new business card was very helpful at Batimat. The resulting card is illustrated.

During the property search, I was extremely fortunate to find a double fronted shop with its lease for sale in Kew Road Richmond. It was over 100 feet deep with a basement under the first 40 feet. Its first floor was partially used as offices but I suspected the second floor offices were being used without planning permission. So far as finance was concerned, we had savings and so purchased its lease without delay. Having driven over

```
        Geoffrey Pidgeon


B O G A R T     B A T H R O O M S

86, Riddlesdown Road,     Purley,
Surrey, CR2 1DD.

Telephone:            01-660-4415
```

Having decided to go to Batimat in Paris I realised I needed a business card to use.

Why Bogart? The night before going to the local printer – we had watched Casablanca on the TV on one of a series of classic films being shown. The name seemed so obvious and caught attention on the various stands!

from Purley to Richmond a few times, we found the journey tiring. So we decided to sell our home and convert the first and second floors into a flat. The sale of our house went through quite quickly. Coupled with our savings and proceeds from the sale of the house, we now had plentiful funds for our new enterprise. Some may think Jane's acquiescence to my plans – selling the family home and starting again at 55 astonishing – but they did not know Jane!

We called our new company 'Original Bathrooms' and decided to ensure the products and displays would be to the high standard set during the family's earlier trading.

I found that Laurence had rapidly become disenchanted with the new owners of Humphersons and was forming his own company 'Alternative Plans' – a very descriptive title! As soon as Michael heard of my plans to start up again he too left Humphersons to join me. Shortly afterwards John did the same. That meant none of the family that gave spirit and substance to the name 'Humpherson' were with the new owners. They merely owned a name – 'SWC Humpherson Holdings Limited' – (Standard Wallpaper Company Humpherson Holdings).

With the input of Michael and Johns' skills, the new business was a success from its start in 1982. The concept of high-end products, set in well-designed and fully detailed displays, quickly paid off.

I was increasingly aware of the need for 'period' fittings especially in Richmond with many Victorian, even Georgian houses. I remembered the Neo-Classic range by Ideal-Standard: who in the immediate post war period potteries were using their pre-war moulds, rather than embark on the cost of new designs! Thus there were many washbasins, pedestals and WC pans with a cut corner that was so typical of the 1920s and 30s periods. Many ranges come to mind. The 'Pyramid' range by Alfred Johnson of Queenborough in Kent, Shanks of Barrhead, Wildblood and Taylor all had such classic ranges. Actually, most potteries had something like it but quickly more modem ranges have superseded the style, by that time regarded as 'old fashioned'!

In the spring of 1982, with Michael supervising the work on the showrooms, Jane and I visited Milan in March. This time to 'Mostra Convegno' – a kitchen and bathroom industry exhibition held in the city. We met considerable enthusiasm for our project and the problem became one of selection from a wide potential portfolio. Whilst at the exhibition, I met Oscar Colli Editor-in Chief of 'Il Bagno Oggi e Domani', the world's leading bathroom journal. We have shared many a pleasant evening together over the years and I hold him in high regard.

My major find at the Mostra Convegno was on the 'Sbordoni' stand where I came face to face with a genuine Neo-Classic range. It had apparently been in continuous production since 1918 and was extensively used in Italian railway stations! I was introduced to Marco Sbordoni who told me a finance group now controlled his company. Its representative was Signor Jaccovachi who had responsibility for Sbordoni and he happened to be on the stand that day. I explained the niche I saw for Neo-Classica in the UK market but insisted that it had to be made exclusive to my company. They debated the matter and said they would give me an answer at the end of the fair. To my delight they agreed and I placed an initial order for several pallet loads. It became a success for both companies.

John Hart of C. P. Hart later contacted me wanting to purchase Neo-Classica. He was not impressed with my offer of a further 15% off trade prices so invited me to lunch with him and his son Gregg. We agreed better terms – especially as he paid for an excellent lunch in Pimlico!

This will give you some idea of our rapid growth with Sbordoni's products. Only a short time after we had started, two 40ft containers full mostly of Neo-Classica, drew up outside the showrooms in Kew Road instead of our warehouse, and pointing the wrong way. Redirecting two such monsters meant they had to drive all the way to the Chiswick roundabout to turn round.

Other merchants wanted our exclusive ranges. The only way to deal with the increasing demand was to form a distribution company and so 'Original Bathrooms Distributors' came into being. Eventually it covered virtually all the UK from Inverurie north of Aberdeen in Scotland down to Cornwall – but deliveries to both areas were limited to once a fortnight.

By this time, we were the sole UK distributor for a number of Italian manufacturers including 'Montini' cast iron baths made in their factory in Treviso. These came in 20-ton loads direct to our new modern warehouse in Isleworth. Perhaps the biggest coup was to obtain the rights to handle Cesame sanitary ware right across the UK! They were then Italy's third largest pottery in vitreous china and second largest, when taking fireclay fittings like sinks into account.

I found this classic art-deco basin on the Sbordoni stand. I knew it was exactly what I was looking for as our 'key' into the UK market.

Neo-Classica was an instant success with cut corners to the pedestal coupled with an anti-splash roll under the leading edge.

It turned out to be hugely popular – with the range appealing to the rapidly emerging market for 'period' ware.

There were still mistakes made along the way!

Bernard Smith was an old friend and sales director of the famous foundry – Carron of Falkirk in Scotland. They had cast the 'Carronade' guns for HMS Victory used at the Battle of Trafalgar. They made post boxes for The Royal Mail, red telephone boxes for the Post Office, as well as a wide selection of cast iron baths.

Carron built a new plant to manufacture stainless steel products and made Humpherson's 'Flaxman' range of stainless steel sink tops for us to metric dimensions. A super company sadly declared insolvent in 1982, after two centuries of trading. Bernard then became a freelance agent with wide connections across the sanitary world, due to his work with European Standards – especially with baths. He lived in nearby Twickenham and often called in to see us in our new premises. Amongst others firms, he became the UK agent for the Spanish firm Roca. Knowing of my wish for exclusive products and our ability to set up distribution, he offered us Roca for the UK market.

At the time, I knew little about Roca except that they were very large and covered the entire sanitary field from sanitary ware and taps to baths. We ordered about three pallets of mixed basins, WCs and bidets as samples and selected one range to make into a display. Our collective view was that it was fairly 'ordinary' a view we did not change when it later sold extensively across the whole country. So I have mixed views whether this was mistake at that time – or not!

The next major offer we received was from Vitra sanitary ware from Turkey. I do not recall how that came about unless it arose at an exhibition. I had samples sent over and we planned to include a small display on our stand at the forthcoming exhibition at NEC. However, its arrival coincided with a visit from Richard Wildblood who by now was running a small plant for bathroom accessories. He looked at the samples and declared it had *'kiln disease that would take two years to clear'* and he *'would not touch it with a barge pole!'*

Richard Wildblood had been a director of the Wildblood and Taylor pottery in Longton (one of the six towns forming Stoke-on-Trent) before the factory was sold to Shires Limited. At the time I was not sure what *'kiln disease'* was but with less than two weeks to prepare the exhibition, I accepted Richard's advice. Jealous of our reputation, we sold off the samples and subsequently watched as Vitra sales climbed upwards and upwards – *year after year!*

In 1969 I wrote a paper entitled 'Britain's water policy analysed' giving my views on the way in which our existing bye-laws and traditions, were holding back the use of new ideas and products. It was published in a number of trade journals. Ideal Homes printed it in full and it appeared in the media. Its main focus was on the continued use of a 'low-pressure' system feeding our taps – resulting from our domestic cold water being stored in the loft, or within the flat.

I pointed out that most of Europe and much of the world, allowed water to come direct from the mains, thus giving greater pressure at the point of discharge. I urged that the high-pressure system be introduced in all new buildings.

Arising from that, I found myself involved in the drive to allow the use of the 'Valve' to flush WC pans, instead of the now outdated and wasteful syphon. Clearly, this directly opposed to the syphon flushing cisterns that had dominated the industry since Victorian times. It might have seemed curious for me – a descendent of Frederick Humpherson – to be pressing for a return to the valve he helped to eliminate but I knew there were many benefits including a substantial saving in water – and thus energy. Those in favour of the valve succeeded in the end. (See Note H).

Another claim for our company – as one of the early importers of sanitary ware from Italy – is our insistence on them making a fully back-to-wall closet. It took many visits to factories drawings and arguments but now one wonders what all the fuss was about – with every pottery making them.

Over the following years, Original Bathrooms and Original Bathrooms Distributors grew and had a presence at all the important exhibitions. Several major distributors of UK sanitary ware later approached us with offers to take over our customers, and more importantly our portfolio. In the end we sold the distribution company and its exclusive ranges, profitably to H&S of Long Eaton. They had a nationwide network but were keen to obtain our 'top end' ranges. On completion of the sale, I took several of their directors on a tour of the various factories in Italy. The way was then clear for them to make a success of their purchase. They had the finance and a large fleet of lorries giving a daily delivery over most of the country.

Sadly, they started out by dismissing our team of ten agent representatives. They then put in their people, familiar with the more mundane products from British manufacturers. They were clearly out of their depth with these specialised ranges that we normally sold through the growing number of bathroom showrooms. H&S representatives were more used to selling to Builders' Merchants and the 'Sheds'. In a short time their new enterprise began to fail. They dropped most of the products and finally this special unit they created around our fittings closed.

Naturally, we had agreed not to purchase any more from the suppliers handed over to H&S but the manufacturers concerned started to complain about fewer purchases by H&S that then ceased altogether. All of them asked us to take up the UK distribution of their products again, so we formed Beaufort Bathroom Distributors (BBD), and sales soon exceeded our earlier turnover!

To begin with we tried to limit our sales area but we were soon delivering again up in Scotland and down in Cornwall. From time to time, I went out with our agents to visit customers. I went down to Devon and across South Wales, at other times to Suffolk and Norfolk. I particularly enjoyed my visits to Scotland in the company of our agents there – the Crombie brothers based in Glasgow.

We were again taking space at exhibitions and Cesame in particular were keen to establish a greater cover in the UK. On several occasions, they mounted our display themselves bearing all the costs. One of these, at the NEC in Birmingham, covered over 90 sq. metres. The stand was designed in Italy, sent over complete with all the products and an Italian team of fitters

The stand itself created quite a stir, quite apart from the design and quality of the fittings on display. I noticed a number of British sanitary ware manufacturers look closely at our stand as they nonchalantly ambled round but actually they were scrutinising their competitors! For example, I saw Tim Bennett, then Sales Director of Armitage-Shanks, wandering close to our displays with fellow directors, so I invited them onto the stand. Tim told me they were very impressed and later enjoyed pieces of Parmesan cheese and the Italian red wine we were offering visitors!

Cesame were not alone in participating in various exhibitions. Indeed, most of our Italian suppliers offered assistance of one kind or another. I went to the ISH fair in Frankfurt, sometimes with Jane, and on two occasions with Laurence. Whilst he was operating entirely separately, he did purchase some of his bathroom fittings from us, naturally at advantageous terms!

At one ISH fair we saw a stand belonging to an Italian pottery I had not heard of before. It was called Flaminia Ceramica. They featured new basin ranges named 'Aquagrande' and 'Twinset' as well as a WC called 'Link'. I thought the designs were brilliant and forming a distinct trend. The designers of 'Aquagrande' and 'Twinset' were a man and wife team – Ludovica and Roberto Palomba. Travelling to all the trade fairs in both Germany and Italy over a number of years, I formed the opinion that Italian designers of sanitary ware were the pacesetters in the bathroom industry. Of the many designers I met, or whose products I saw on display, I felt Ludovica and Roberto Palomba – now known as 'Palomba Serafini Associati' were outstanding.

Likewise, I would choose Fantini as the most notable tap manufacturers of the period. Under Daniela Fantini, the company has always been design leaders of the industry. I would select Sfera and Stilo as examples of their outstanding design ethos. (See Appendix 10).

Amongst the many designers I have met over the years none have the ability to master products – in so many fields – as Ludovica and Roberto Palomba.

However, I am naturally interested in their sanitary ware and Flamina were fortunate to ask them to produce new designs for them.

This picture was taken recently in Laurence's new showrooms where he is featuring the Elmar kitchen range from Italy – designed by this brilliant team again demonstrating their versatility.

The author is seated in front of this nice couple and hopes he has not spoiled the picture!

Perhaps I should say something about my wish to have products on an exclusive basis. I felt that any bathroom shop promoting our products needed protection from other showrooms selling the same range. There had to be a good return for any showroom prepared to display our fittings properly. That can only happen if it is the *sole* outlet for our products in the town. In large cities like Edinburgh for example, we appointed two dealers. However, that would only be done on advice from our local agents, knowing the people concerned, and that they would not cut prices

For years, I had tried to persuade British makers to do something similar, thus ensuring loyalty and good promotion of their sanitary ware. They could go on selling the ordinary fittings to all and sundry through their wholesale outlets but their high-end market products needed outlets with flair and loyalty. That was only possible by a two way understanding.

Ideal-Standard, so often the industry leaders, had done something like it earlier with their 'Penthouse' range of bathroom fittings. They only sold it through showrooms they thought would display it properly and provide a design service. Later they formed specialised outlets under the name 'Sottini' to handle such product

The years went by and the bathroom industry enjoyed ever increasing growth. Nonetheless, the trade had gradually moved from being a part of the traditional Builders' or Plumbers' merchant, to the specialised bathroom outlets that sprang up in every town. A typical Builder's merchant opening a bathroom showroom promoted staff from within – whereas the specialist sought people with design flair from art colleges, interior design firms and the like.

A friend had a substantial chain of merchant outlets. He asked me to visit his largest store, which he believed he had brought in line with the new style of showrooms. But to start with, very few of the displays were full room settings; most of the displays were within 4ft high walls, which he had heard me preach against at the NFBPM Conference at Gleneagles. One display had no less than nine price and trade stickers on the bath alone. My late friend, whose company is still trading, told me he had taken my advice and sought outside staff to man the showrooms. However, he complained to me that one new young lady from a design college – first of all turned up in jeans *and* addressed him by his Christian name!

So our business continued to flourish along these lines during most years. Then in 2005, two brothers Giuseppe and Pietro Corbisiero, confirmed their interest in purchasing Original Bathrooms as a going concern.

Their expressed aim was to use the firm as the pattern for other 'Original Bathroom' outlets run on the same lines. The transaction would leave Michael and John as Directors running the show and provide us with an additional retirement package. It was finalised in 2006 when Jane and I both reached 80. So I was no longer in the industry I had joined some 59 years earlier. I had seen its trade change dramatically and our fortunes fluctuate over that time.

However, our three sons continue to sell bathrooms 143 years after their great-great uncle Frederick Humpherson started working for Thomas Crapper in 1871.

Chapter 26

My Family Today

I thought it might be painful to relate the demise and sale of the Humpherson Group. Of course, the immediate days following were uncomfortable for me. We had taken this company from being a small size Plumber's Merchant to the most prestigious bathroom and kitchen firm in London – helped in no small measure by our three sons as they joined me in turn.

I have recorded the years that followed, when we formed Original Bathrooms, and the events leading up to 2006, when I retired. However, I have kept a close interest in the industry in addition to writing, firstly about my wartime work in MI6 (Section VIII) in 'The Secret Wireless War' and now this book telling of my family's five generations in the bathroom industry.

It is not for me to tell the story of our three sons' involvement in the bathroom and kitchen industry. No doubt they will one day want to tell their own stories and version of events. However, they played a significant part in the earlier story before my retirement. I acknowledge their input and the great support they gave to its growth – each in their own way. I must in particular refer to Laurence, who helped turn our small kitchen department into a number of truly major kitchen showrooms of national statue.

Laurence still has substantial interests in kitchen companies in West London. I do commend his initiative in recently launching out on his own, with a completely new enterprise. It is based in Fulham High Street some five hundred yards north of Putney Bridge and called *Laurence Pidgeon - Kitchens and bathrooms – "The Essence of Good Design"*. He is a member of the Royal Society and I believe he is the country's leading kitchen designer.

Michael and John have great depth of knowledge about plumbing and spatial requirements – essential to those involved in bathroom design. They have few superiors in the field.

In the eight years since the sale, the new owners of Original Bathrooms have not thus far applied themselves to expansion – as we expected after the sale. Michael remains there, filling their need for someone who actually *understands* not only design, but also the technical side of the bathroom industry.

Sadly, John was forced to leave the company in 2011. In line with the family's tradition he immediately started again. He has formed 'AJP Bathrooms' with his wife Aneeta the 'A' in the title! In the sale to Davroc, I retained the right to all the memorabilia and collected it two weeks after John left. Some of it is on display in his already successful showrooms in Kingston.

For my part, I continue to write about my wartime work connected with Bletchley Park. Several times a year I send out a Newsletter to the few old colleagues around, their descendants and historians.

However, this book has been a long time in the making and I owe a debt of gratitude to the many who have helped – particularly my patient wife Jane – who acted as initial editor through the long journey. Perhaps the family are all in her debt since she supported me in the decision to start yet another business, whenever the need arose! Sadly, she died suddenly in January this year so I was determined to complete the book and it is, of course, dedicated to her.

**Although this book is finished – no doubt I shall find
another worthy subject to write about!**

Geoffrey Pidgeon
Richmond Surrey
October 2014

Appendix 1

My Family's Five Generations in the Bathroom Industry

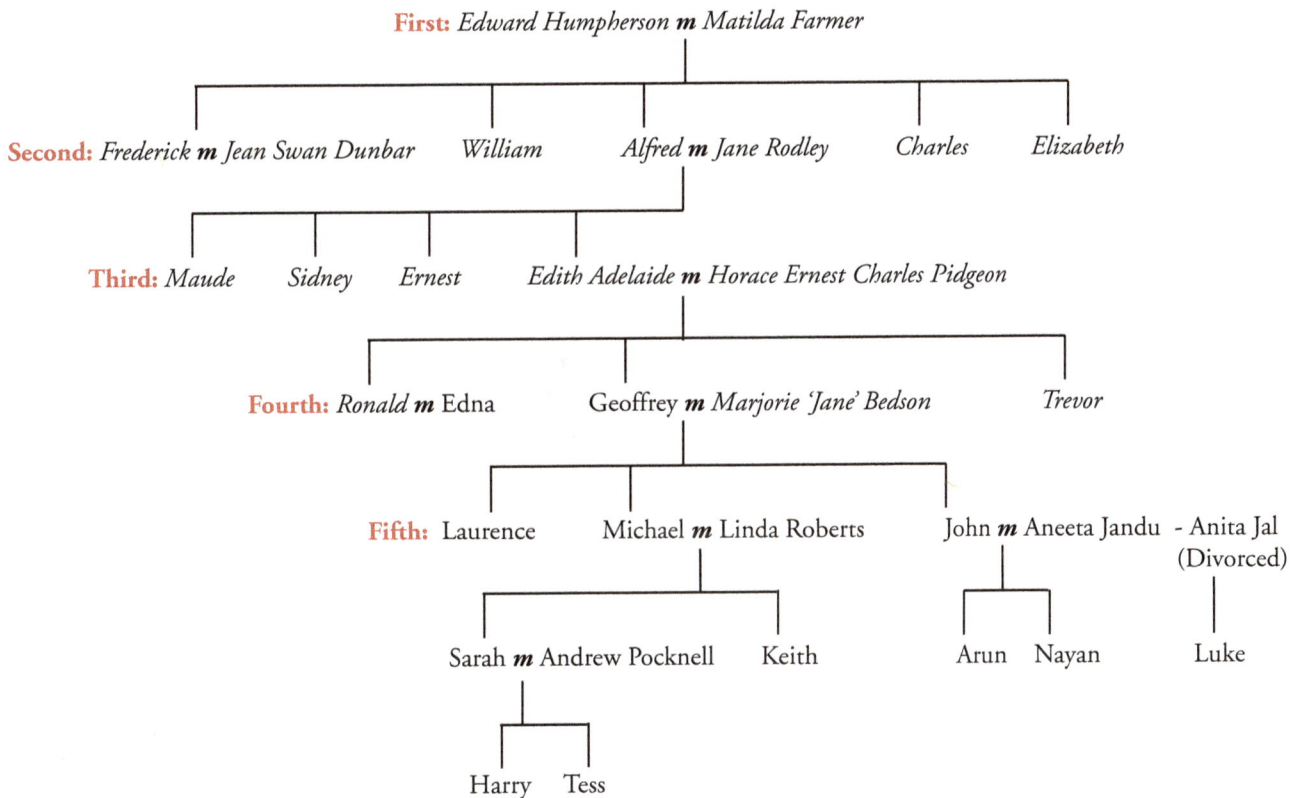

First: *Edward Humpherson **m** Matilda Farmer*

Second: *Frederick **m** Jean Swan Dunbar*   *William*   *Alfred **m** Jane Rodley*   *Charles*   *Elizabeth*

Third: *Maude*   *Sidney*   *Ernest*   *Edith Adelaide **m** Horace Ernest Charles Pidgeon*

Fourth: *Ronald **m** Edna*   Geoffrey **m** *Marjorie 'Jane' Bedson*   *Trevor*

Fifth: Laurence   Michael **m** Linda Roberts   John **m** Aneeta Jandu - Anita Jal (Divorced)

Sarah **m** Andrew Pocknell   Keith   Arun   Nayan   Luke

Harry   Tess

Legend: I have not attempted to show marriages or to follow any descendants, unless they are part of our five-generation story and the deceased are shown in Italics.

Appendix 2

Frederick Humpherson's Apprenticeship Indentures

Frederick Humpherson was seventeen when he was apprenticed to Thomas Crapper the owner of Thomas Crapper & Co. in April 1871. Note, he is bound to the man and not to the company. The responsibility therefore, lies with Thomas Crapper to ensure he is properly trained in the craft. An Indenture at the time, reflected a binding contract between a 'Master' in this case, Thomas Crapper and an 'indentured servant' – Frederick Humpherson. Both had responsibilities one to the other!

The first picture (overleaf) is of the actual Indenture document on parchment – still in my possession. It is signed first by Frederick Humpherson, then Thomas Crapper and finally by my great-grandfather Edward Humpherson. The witness to the signatures is Robert Marr Wharam, Thomas Crapper's partner, who also looked after the finances.

I appreciate the original parchment indenture is difficult to read. It is remarkable however, it has survived at all after the adverse treatment it received, especially spending many years in a damp cellar. That is not the way to store parchment! The term parchment refers to any animal skin, particularly goat, sheep, or cow, that has been scraped or dried under tension. I am guilty of spilling tea on my desk when examining it closely – hence the damage to Edward's signature.

Therefore, I made a typewritten version of the Indenture but so did my good friend Ken Grabowski in Chicago and it is his reproduced opposite the original.

The practice of taking an apprenticeship has not died down, indeed it is probably more common today than for many years. However, some are more formal than others. Laurence was apprenticed to me through the Chamberlain's Court of the City of London to learn the plumber's merchant trade. It was for a period of four years and dated 16th October 1967. Again, in keeping with the past I am described as the 'Master' but now Laurence is described more simply as 'The Apprentice' and not the 'indentured servant' – as in the case of Frederick Humpherson.

On the completion of his apprenticeship Laurence became a Freeman of the City of London and used it to be inducted into the Worshipful Company of Builders' Merchants of the City of London 'By Servitude'. I am a Founder Member of the Company and at one time its 'Clerk'!

This Indenture WITNESSETH, That *Frederick Humpherson of 45 Marlborough Rd in the parish of St Luke Chelsea. Middlesex, son of Edward Humpherson of the above address* —

doth put himself APPRENTICE to *Thos Crapper. Plumber &c of 52 Marlborough Rd in the parish of St Luke, Chelsea, Middlesex* to learn his art, and with him (after the manner of an Apprentice) to serve from the *Eight day of April. One thousand eight hundred & Seventy One* unto the full end and term of — *Four* — years from thence next following to be fully complete and ended: during which term the said Apprentice his Master faithfully shall serve, his secrets keep, his lawful commands everywhere gladly do. Shall do no damage to his said Master nor see to be done of others, but to the best of his power shall let or forthwith give warning to his said Master of the same. Shall not waste the goods of his said Master nor lend them unlawfully to any. Shall not do any act whereby his said Master may have any loss with his own goods or others during the said term without the licence of his said Master. Shall neither buy nor sell, nor absent himself from his said Master's service ~~by day or night~~ unlawfully, but in all things, as a faithful Apprentice, shall behave himself towards his said Master and all his during the said term. And the said *Thos Crapper in Consideration of the services so to be rendered by the said apprentice, shall, to the best of his knowledge and skill teach or cause to be taught*

his said Apprentice in the art of *a Plumber* which he useth, by the best means that he can, shall teach and instruct, or cause to be taught and instructed, ~~finding unto the said Apprentice sufficient meat, drink,~~ *Paying to the said Apprentice* ~~lodging and all other necessaries during the said term~~ *the following weekly wages. viz.*

For the First year of such Term the sum of Ten shillings Pr Week

For the Second Year thereof " " " Twelve " "

For the Third " " " " Fourteen " "

For the Fourth " " " " Sixteen " "

And for the true performance of all and every the said covenants and agreements, either of the said parties bindeth himself unto the other by these presents

In Witness whereof the parties above named to these Indentures interchangeably have put their hands and seals the *Eight* day of *April* in the year of our Lord One thousand eight hundred and seventy *One*

It is hereby further agreed that the working hours shall commence at 6 a.m. and end at 5.30 P.m. allowing Half Hour for breakfast. & One Hour for dinner and the said Apprentice shall at the request of his said Master. work

Signed, Sealed and Delivered by the above-named *overtime, in any case of emergency, to be paid at the rate of Wages he is then in receipt of and that any loss of time from illness shall be deducted in like manner and should the said apprentice absent himself from his employer unlawfully then the said Thos Crapper shall be at liberty to deduct from the said apprentices' money the sum of Five shillings per day or a proportionate amount for time lost —*

Parties

in the presence of *Robt McWaram*

Frederick Humpherson

Thos Crapper

Edward Humpherson

This Indenture WITNESSETH, *That Frederick Humpherson*
of 45 Marlborough Rd. in the parish of St. Luke
Chelsea, Middlesex, son of Edward Humpherson
of the above address –

doth put himself APPRENTICE to *Thos. Crapper - Plumber*
of 52 Marlborough Rd in the parish of St. Luke, Chelsea, Middlesex
to learn his art, and with him (after the manner of an Apprentice) to serve from the *Eight day of*
April, One thousand eight hundred & Seventy One
unto the full end and term of – *Four* – years from thence next following
to be fully complete and ended: during which term the said Apprentice his Master faithfully shall
serve, his secrets keep, his lawful commands everywhere gladly do. Shall do no damage to his said Master
nor see to be done of others, but to the best of his power shall let or forthwith give warning to his said Master
of the same. Shall not waste the goods of his said Master nor lend them unlawfully to any. Shall not
do any act whereby his said Master may have any loss with his own goods or others during the said
term without the licence of his said Master. Shall neither buy nor sell, nor absent himself from his said
Master's service *by day* or night unlawfully, but in all things, as a faithful Apprentice, shall behave himself
towards his said Master and all his during the said term. And the said *Thos. Crapper*
in consideration of the services so to be tendered by the said
apprentice, shall, to the best of his knowledge and skill
teach or cause to be taught
his said Apprentice in the art of *a Plumber*
which he useth, by the best means that he can, shall teach and instruct, or cause to be taught and instructed,
finding unto the said Apprentice sufficient meat, drink, *Paying to the said Apprentice*
lodging and all other necessaries during the said term *the following weekly wages, viz.*
For the First Year of such Term the sum of Ten *shillings per Week*
For the Second Year thereof " " " Twelve " " "
For the Third " " " " " Fourteen" " "
For the Fourth " " " " " Sixteen " " "

And for the true performance of all and every the said covenants and agreements, either of the said parties bindeth
himself unto the other by these presents.

In Witness whereof the parties above to these Indentures interchangeably have put their hands and seals the
_____ Eight _____ day of *April* in the year of our Lord One thousand eight hundred and
seventy One *It is hereby further agreed that the working hours shall*
commence at 6 a.m. and end at 5.30 p.m. allowing
a Half Hour for breakfast & One Hour for dinner, and the said
Signed, Sealed and Delivered by the above-named *Apprentice, shall at the request of this said Master, work*
overtime, in any case of emergency, to be paid at the rate
_____ Parties _____ *of Wages he is then in receipt of, and that any loss of time*
from illness shall be deducted in like manner, and
in the presence of *Robt. M. Wharam* *should the said apprentice absent himself from his*
employer unlawfully then the said Thos. Crapper shall be
at liberty to deduct from the said apprentice money
the sum of five shillings per day or a proportionate
amount for time lost.

Frederick Humpherson
Thos. Crapper
Edward Humpherson

Text of apprenticeship indenture of Frederick Humpherson to Thomas Crapper. Note the
many restrictions on Frederick, especially the loss (and the amount!) of wages in case of
illness or unlawful manner. Ouch! A few of those and one could easily find oneself
quickly in untenable debt.

Usually entrance to a City Livery Company is by **Redemption** – which means you have two Sponsors who are already members and you then pay a fee. Secondly, by **Patrimony** which is open to any child of a Freeman of the company, on reaching the age of 21. Thirdly, and undoubtedly the rarest is by **Servitude** as an apprentice to the craft involved. It used to the traditional way of entering a company. It is still valid today and was how Laurence became a Freeman of the Worshipful Company of Builders' Merchants.

Coat of Arms of the Worshipful Company of Builders' Merchants

Appendix 3

1871 Census for Parish of St. Luke, Chelsea

The 1871 National Census (above and reproduced larger overleaf) showing details for Marlborough Road in the Parish of St. Luke Chelsea. Number 45 is the home of Edward Humpherson, his wife Matilda and their six children. The relationship age and occupation is shown alongside.

Edward:	Head	age 40	Carpenter	My great-grandfather
Matilda:	Wife	age 36		
Frederick:	Son	age 17	Plumber's apprentice	My great-uncle
William:	Son	age 14	Zinc Worker's Mate	
Alfred:	Son	age 9	Scholar	My grandfather
Charles:	Son	age 7	(no details but surely scholar ?)	
Elizabeth:	Daughter	age 3.		

Edward's family living in No. 45 is on the opposite side of Marlborough Road Chelsea from Thomas Crapper & Co. Marlboro Works. That was at No's 50, 52 and 54.

Frederick and later Alfred were apprenticed to Thomas Crapper – across the road.

1871 Census for Parish of St. Luke, Chelsea

Appendix 4

Frederick Humpherson's Examination Results

Frederick Humpherson's examination results in the Science and Art Department Her Majesty's most Honourable Privy Council for Education.

We know nothing about Frederick's early education and one might assume it was at a local school belonging to the LSB (London School Board). However, the LSB was not formed until 1870 so he more likely to attend one or other of the schools in the Marlborough Road area of Chelsea. In those days children left school at 14. Frederick did not join Thomas Crapper until he was 17 so one wonders where he studied in the three intervening years? Clearly, because of the range and nature of the subjects, he must have continued his studies up to 1871, when he started working full time for Crapper.

I have a leather bound book, containing 23 original Examination Certificates for Frederick Humpherson. It has '**Certificates FH**' in gold block on the cover and spine – so presumably he assembled it. A full size copy follows and is a certificate for '**Second Class in the Elementary Stage in Inorganic Chemistry**' and the examination was held on 4th May 1871. Curiously, on April 8th nearly a month earlier, he had signed papers as an apprentice to Thomas Crapper! He must have been given time off by Thomas Crapper to take this examination. Being such a relatively obscure subject, it surely demonstrates that he had continued his schooling?

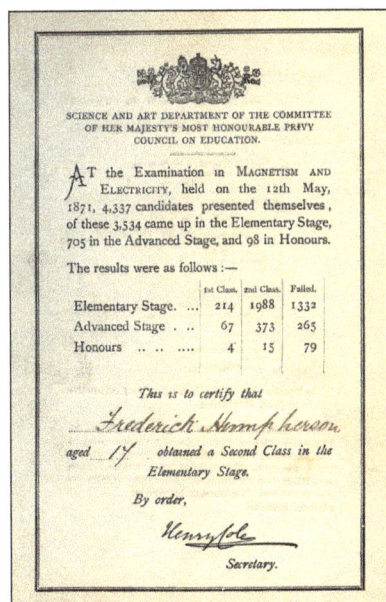

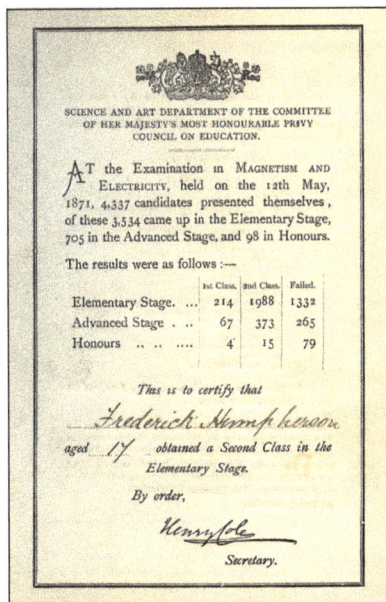

One should note that each year the examinations were taken on three consecutive days.

The certificates cover a wide variety of subjects from Inorganic Chemistry / Acoustics Light and Heat / Magnetism and Electricity / Theoretical Mechanics / Metallurgy / Practical Plane and Solid Geometry / Physical Geography / Machine Construction and Drawing / Geology / Vegetable Anatomy and Physiology / Building Construction / Applied Mechanics.

Frederick passed these important examinations, at Elementary, Second or First class levels, between the ages of 17 to 21. It is a remarkable and scholarly achievement considering that otherwise, he was working daily from 6.30 am to 5.30 pm! It also indicates a very receptive and intelligent individual - as well as a hardy one!

Frederick's last series of examinations began on 24th April 1875 (above). The second was on 1st May 1875 the subject being Building Construction, in which he obtained a First Class in the Elementary Stage. The last was on 11th May 1875 for Applied Mechanics in which he obtained a Second Class in the Elementary Stage. I note he obtained several First Class results in the Advanced Stage – for example for Magnetism and Electricity on 2nd May 1872.

SCIENCE AND ART DEPARTMENT OF THE COMMITTEE OF HER MAJESTY'S MOST HONOURABLE PRIVY COUNCIL ON EDUCATION.

AT the Examination in MAGNETISM AND ELECTRICITY, held on the 12th May, 1871, 4,337 candidates presented themselves, of these 3,534 came up in the Elementary Stage, 705 in the Advanced Stage, and 98 in Honours.

The results were as follows :—

	1st Class.	2nd Class.	Failed.
Elementary Stage. ...	214	1988	1332
Advanced Stage . ..	67	373	265
Honours	4	15	79

This is to certify that

Frederick Humpherson

aged *17* obtained a Second Class in the Elementary Stage.

By order,

Henry Cole

Secretary.

Appendix 5

The Story of the 'Beaufort' WC

The story of the 'Beaufort' WC design and press comments at the time.

HUMPHERSON'S
IMPROVED
FLUSH-DOWN CLOSET.
THE "BEAUFORT."

Awarded

Certificate

of Merit

by the

Sanitary

Institute

of Great

Britain.

In Three Qualities, and may be used with either Lead or Earthenware
Trap.

THE ADVANTAGES ARE AS FOLLOWS:

A Free Flushing Basin, specially constructed so that the Flush
is concentrated at the spot where the Basin is usually
corroded. The dip of the basin entering the water ensures the
thorough Cleansing of Trap at each discharge. Having a narrow
flushing rim great force is given to the flush. Specially
adapted for our Syphon Cistern.

PRICES (with Traps).

Cane and White Basin Cane Trap	6/6
Cane and White Basin, Cane and White Trap	7/6
All White Earthenware Basin and Trap...	13/-
Blue Printed Earthenware Basin and Trap	14/-
BASINS only—Cane and White Basin	4/9
All White	9/6
Blue Printed	10/6

Lead P Traps, fitted with Receiver, for above Basins, 12/- extra.
When ordering please state if S or P Trap is required.

HUMPHERSON & CO.,
297, FULHAM ROAD, LONDON, S.W.

16

The first illustration of Humpherson's improved '**Flush-down**' closet is in an un-dated catalogue believed to be late 1880s or early 1890s. It was called 'The 'Beaufort' and is illustrated below. Its advantages included: 'A free flushing basin, specially constructed so that the flush in concentrated at the spot where the basin is usually corroded'……*'Having a narrow flushing rim great force is given to the flush.'*

This first 'Beaufort' was useful in that the trap was separate and therefore could be swivelled (within certain limits) making it suitable for confined spaces. The Sanitary Institute of Great Britain awarded it a 'Certificate of Merit' in 1885.

However, Frederick followed that success by producing the one piece '**Beaufort Pedestal Closet**'– the WC as we know it today. As you will have read in Chapter 7 even the mighty Twyfords acknowledged that: '….. *just as Thomas William [Twyford] had perfected the 'Unitas' a completely new type hove into view, when Humpherson's of Chelsea introduced the 'Beaufort' – as far as we know, the first wash-down WC.'*

This might be a good moment to mention the advantages of the **wash-*down*** over the **wash-*out*** closet that held sway over two or three decades, until Frederick Humpherson produced the wash-down. A **wash-*out*** closet, as the name suggests, means that the 'contents' of the bowl lay in a shallow tray of water, perhaps an inch or so deep awaiting a flush from the cistern to wash it out – hence 'Wash-out'! However, although the flush may empty the tray – it loses most of its force in doing so – thus the 'contents' might well remain visible in the trap. Another problem with the design was that the shallow depth of water could evaporate somewhat during summer – requiring a 'pre-use' flush! We might well feel such fittings repugnant but they were in general use for decades. All the merchant catalogues of the period include them. Thomas Crapper's catalogue of 1888 was no exception.

On reflection, few of us would like to go back to that form of WC pan. Frederick Humpherson's Beaufort wash-down WCs gradually eliminated it, as more and more manufacturers turned to making them. Twyfords, then one of our largest sanitary ware potteries, had taken up the Humpherson's wash-down closet design as we have seen, just before the turn of the century.

38 THOMAS CRAPPER & CO.,

"Wash-out" Closet.

(NEW PATTERN)

No. 94

No. 94. ... Cane colour outside, white inside, ... 12/6
„ 95. ... White outside and inside 14/6
If printed inside, extra 3/-

Marlboro' Works, Chelsea, S.W.

This page from Frederick Humpherson's catalogue proudly proclaimed he had the 'Original Pedestal Wash-Down Closet'. Above the closet, he shows his 1885 Patent No. 2492 Water waste Preventer that won him a Bronze Medal at the 1885 International Inventions Exhibition held in South Kensington.

The first comments below come from: **'The Sanitary Record', A Monthly Journal of Public Health** *and* **The progress of Sanitary Science. Edited by Ernest Hart**

July 1185 – June 1886. Volume VII. New Series. The Sanitary Record 7: 509 (April 15, 1886).

THE

"Beaufort" Pedestal Closet.
STRONG. CHEAP. RELIABLE.
COMBINING
WATER CLOSET, URINAL, AND SLOP CLOSET.

The Original Pedestal Wash-Down Closet.

The Original Pedestal Wash-Down Closet.

HUMPHERSON'S PATENT SYPHON CISTERN

Complete as shown with white basin and trap, polished
mahogany seat, white paper box, 2 gall. galvanised
syphon cistern, galvanised brackets, ivory pull and
brass chain £3 15 0
Galvanized Seat Brackets, 8/6 extra.

HUMPHERSON & CO.,
Patentees and Manufacturers of Sanitary Appliances,
297, FULHAM ROAD, LONDON, S.W.
7

'Amongst household sanitary appliances the exhibit of Messrs Humpherson & Co. Limited in King's Road, Chelsea, is worthy of attention. We have had occasion to speak favourably of the productions of this firm on former occasions in connection with their siphon-cistern and water-waste preventer, improved pipe joint, and Beaufort and other closets. These are all shown in different qualifies on the present occasion.

The 'Beaufort' is exhibited in the approved form of a combination-closet, combining water-closet, urinal, and slop-closet, enclosed in an ornamental ceramic casing. Some excellent specimens of wrought and cast lead work are shown, including rainwater heads, square piping, and a fine dome-like finial of large dimensions. These are also on view some good examples of steam and water cocks and valves.'

The further comments below are from: **'The Builder 52: 447 (March 19, 1887)'.**

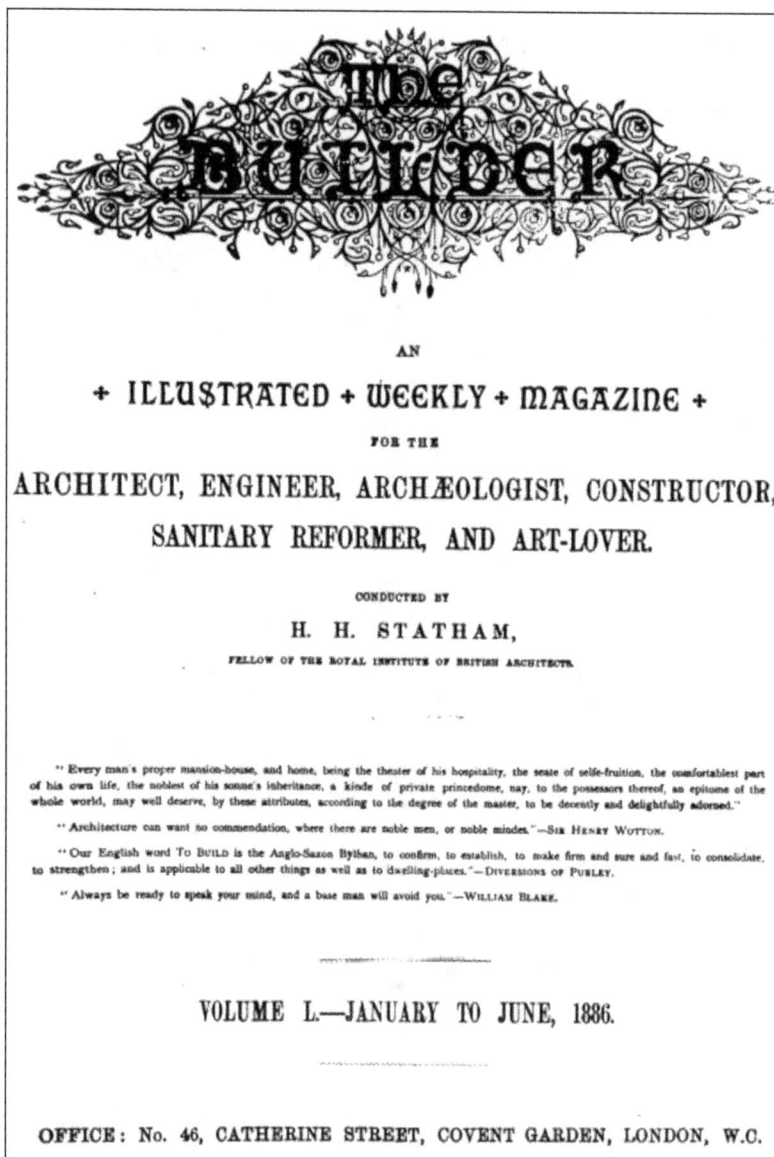

The Builder

AN

+ ILLUSTRATED + WEEKLY + MAGAZINE +

FOR THE

ARCHITECT, ENGINEER, ARCHÆOLOGIST, CONSTRUCTOR, SANITARY REFORMER, AND ART-LOVER.

CONDUCTED BY

H. H. STATHAM,

FELLOW OF THE ROYAL INSTITUTE OF BRITISH ARCHITECTS.

"Every man's proper mansion-house, and home, being the theater of his hospitality, the seate of selfe-fruition, the comfortablest part of his own life, the noblest of his sonne's inheritance, a kinde of private princedome, nay, to the possessors thereof, an epitome of the whole world, may well deserve, by these attributes, according to the degree of the master, to be decently and delightfully adorned."

"Architecture can want no commendation, where there are noble men, or noble mindes."—SIR HENRY WOTTON.

"Our English word To BUILD is the Anglo-Saxon Byldan, to confirm, to establish, to make firm and sure and fast, to consolidate, to strengthen; and is applicable to all other things as well as to dwelling-places."—DIVERSIONS OF PURLEY.

"Always be ready to speak your mind, and a base man will avoid you."—WILLIAM BLAKE.

VOLUME L.—JANUARY TO JUNE, 1886.

OFFICE: No. 46, CATHERINE STREET, COVENT GARDEN, LONDON, W.C.

'Messrs Humpherson & Co. exhibit another tour de force in lead-working, some plumbers' brasswork of excellent quality and finish, and some good water-closets, including the "Beaufort", which combines in one fixture a WC, urinal, and slop-sink; this closet, like one or two others in the Exhibition, is of the pedestal-type and consists of an improved form of hopper, with a good flush.'

The above is typical of the wide praise for the 'Beaufort' at the time of its launch. However, few knew that it would eventually become the model for all WC pans for generations to come.

Appendix 6

Freehold of Holmes Place

Royal Borough of Kensington & Chelsea – Freehold of Holmes Place.

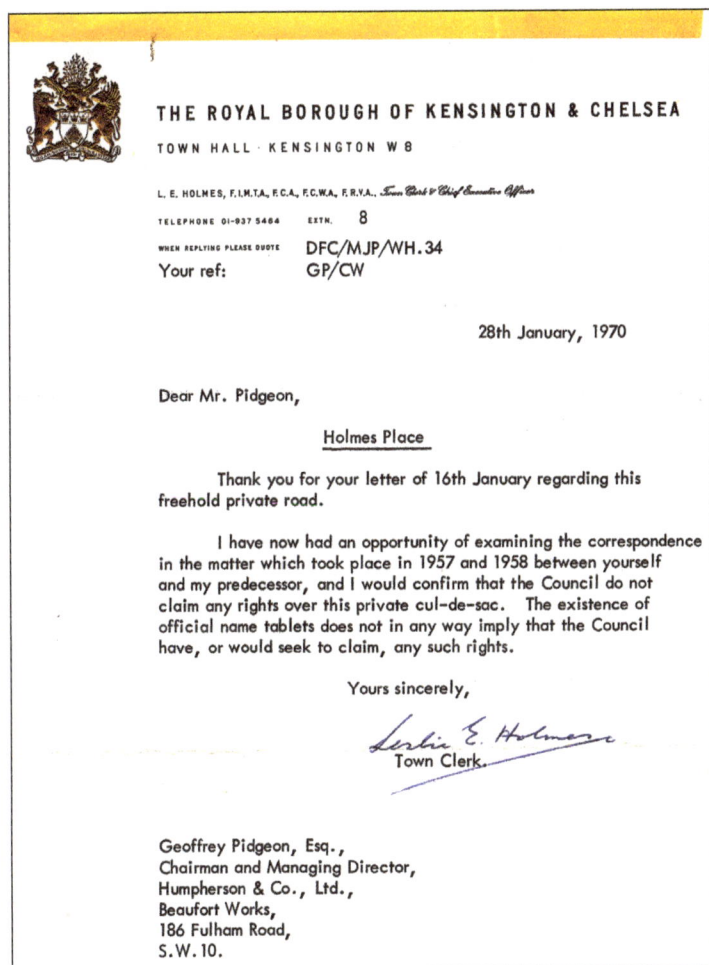

THE ROYAL BOROUGH OF KENSINGTON & CHELSEA

TOWN HALL · KENSINGTON W 8

L. E. HOLMES, F.I.M.T.A., F.C.A., F.C.W.A., F.R.V.A., *Town Clerk & Chief Executive Officer*

TELEPHONE 01-937 5464   EXTN.   8

WHEN REPLYING PLEASE QUOTE   DFC/MJP/WH.34
Your ref: GP/CW

28th January, 1970

Dear Mr. Pidgeon,

Holmes Place

Thank you for your letter of 16th January regarding this freehold private road.

I have now had an opportunity of examining the correspondence in the matter which took place in 1957 and 1958 between yourself and my predecessor, and I would confirm that the Council do not claim any rights over this private cul-de-sac. The existence of official name tablets does not in any way imply that the Council have, or would seek to claim, any such rights.

Yours sincerely,

Leslie E. Holmes
Town Clerk.

Geoffrey Pidgeon, Esq.,
Chairman and Managing Director,
Humpherson & Co., Ltd.,
Beaufort Works,
186 Fulham Road,
S.W.10.

In 1901 Frederick Humpherson purchased three cottages No's 1, 2 & 3 in Holmes Place, a short cul-de-sac off the Fulham Road. It was part of the extensive Gunter Estate then owned by Sir Robert Gunter. Frederick was granted an 80-year lease from 1901 on the cottages and Holmes Place, fixed at £80 per annum. The property included quite extensive gardens behind the cottages. However, the local Gas Company had to light the gas lamp on the sidewall of the road, during the period of the lease.

The King's Arms Public House – widely known simply as 'Finches' – was on the west side of Holmes Place and there was considerable misuse of the right-angled road by its clients, especially on Friday and Saturday nights. Back in 1957, I obtained permission to shut off the road when we were closed. The only proviso was we had to continue to illuminate it. We did this with electric lighting instead of the gas fitting – that had required a Gas Company lighter man at dusk and dawn to turn it on and off.

In 1962 I purchased the Freehold of Beaufort Works. However, there were on going arguments about the Council's street sign on our flank wall – implying that it meant that it was still a public way. I wrote to Mr Leslie Holmes (!) the Town Clerk about the council's 'Holmes Place' sign on 28th January and he replied saying '...*the Council do not claim any rights over this private cul-de-sac.*'

Appendix 7

Wallace Reyburn's Letter

Wallace Reyburn's letter and a response from Twyfords.

On 26th June 1967, Reyburn wrote to me to thank me for my help and also for putting him in touch with Harry Barclay, then Managing Director of Twyfords. Barclay had written to him on 22nd June inviting him to visit the factory. The letters are below.

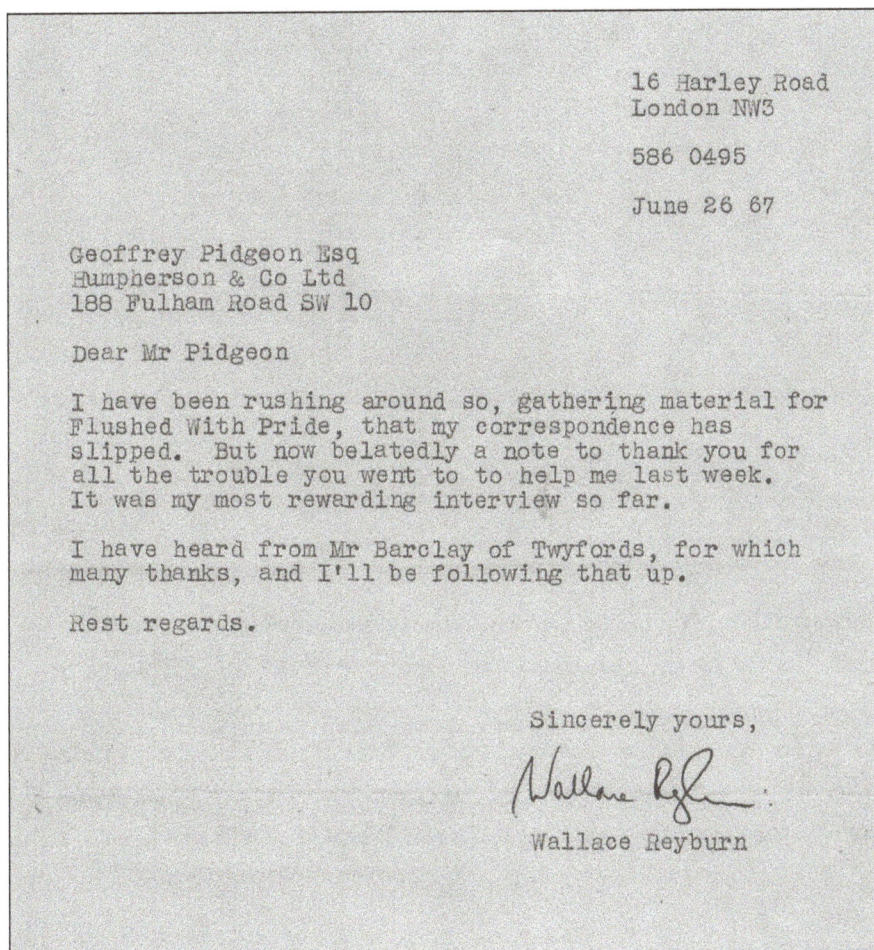

```
                                           16 Harley Road
                                           London NW3

                                           586 0495

                                           June 26 67

Geoffrey Pidgeon Esq
Humpherson & Co Ltd
188 Fulham Road SW 10

Dear Mr Pidgeon

I have been rushing around so, gathering material for
Flushed With Pride, that my correspondence has
slipped.  But now belatedly a note to thank you for
all the trouble you went to to help me last week.
It was my most rewarding interview so far.

I have heard from Mr Barclay of Twyfords, for which
many thanks, and I'll be following that up.

Best regards.


                                           Sincerely yours,

                                           Wallace Reyburn

                                           Wallace Reyburn
```

After I sent Reyburn's draft book back to his editor and commented adversely on it – his later letters were not so polite!

Managing Director's Office

**TWYFORDS LIMITED
STOKE-ON-TRENT**
Telephone: Stoke-on-Trent 23411

22nd June 1967

Wallace Reyburn, Esq.,
16 Harley Road
LONDON NW3

Dear Mr. Reyburn

    Geoffrey Pidgeon of Humphersons has mentioned to me that you
are carrying out some research into the history of the flushing cistern
with a view to writing a book on this subject.

    Since we have been engaged in the manufacture of Ceramic
sanitaryware since the very earliest days, it could well be that some
of our early catalogues could be of interest to you and I would be
pleased to arrange for our technical people to make available to you
any information that would be of interest.

    It would probably be worth your while to visit us so that you can
have the opportunity of seeing what is available and asking questions
and I suggest therefore that you may like to write and suggest one or
two alternative dates if our invitation is of interest to you.

        Yours sincerely

        (H.F.H.Barclay)
        Managing Director

Copy to: Mr. G. Pidgeon of Humpherson & Co., London

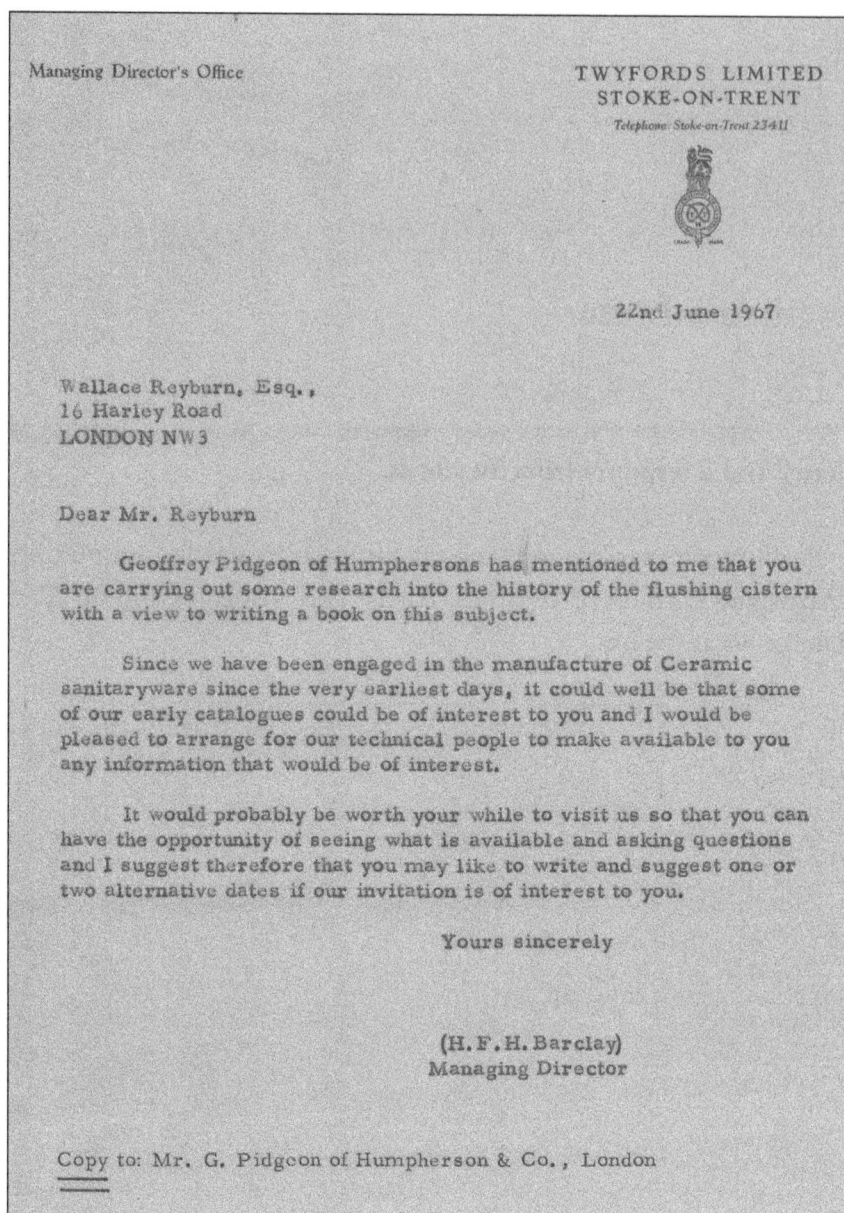

This is signed by Harry Barclay – Managing Director of Twyfords. He later endorsed the **'History of Twyfords 1680 – 1982'** written in 1982 by the historian James Denley – who wrote inter alia:

"…But in 1884, just as Thomas William [Twyford] had perfected the 'Unitas' **a completely new type hove into view, when Humpherson's of Chelsea introduced the 'Beaufort' - as far as we know, the first wash-down WC. The wash-down is the closet that most of us in the Western world are familiar with."**

Appendix 8

Major Contracts and Thousands of Hotel Bathrooms!

Heat & Air Systems

I have explained in Chapter 23 how I started to supply Heat & Air Systems Limited with valves, pipes and fittings for degreasing, plating and/or spray plants, for a number of major companies and contracts in different parts of the world.

Our success was due to our shipping the tubes and fittings as a complete package. Their draughtsmen would have to go to perhaps a dozen different suppliers and then try to coordinate their deliveries within the desired timescale.

Heat & Air contracts involved my brother Ron and myself in considerable work. We had the tube components cut to size to suit the drawings, and that meant knowing the thread length and fitting depth of fittings. We gradually moved away from this rather labour-intensive work back towards my long-term aim for us to concentrate on bathrooms and kitchens.

Bathrooms and kitchens

At first, our funds limited our infant showroom displays but gradually we developed the idea of fully detailed displays of both bathrooms and kitchens. By the early 1960s, they had reached the stage of being worthy of mention in the Home magazines and daily press. We were the sole outlet for Shanks of Barrhead in Glasgow, before their merger with Armitage, so we had their products on display including the Cavendish suite in 'Savannah'. This was the first range of sanitary ware in what I then described, as a 'furnishing colour' and it became very 'Newsworthy'!

Then no doubt the inclusion of major products, like Nobilia kitchens, the interest in our exclusive items like Metriware and Tabasco, added to our appeal. So we slowly grew, but this was speeded up when Ronald Froy joined us, with his extensive architect connections. He brought in numerous enquires but actually turning them into orders was down to our excellent estimating department under Les King.

The following are some of the 7500 hotel bathrooms we supplied over a very short period. Where I am not certain of the number – then that is in Italics. The names are those at the time the list was made, as part of the indoctrination of new Humpherson staff, back in the 1970s. Clearly many hotels have changed their names since – some several times!

Hotel bathrooms

Holiday Inn, Bristol – 300 bathrooms
Holiday Inn, Swiss Cottage – 300 Metriware symphonic WC suites
Essex Centre Hotel, Basildon – 139 bathrooms
Malt Shovel Hotel, Walsall – 106 bathrooms
Centre Hotel, Cardiff – 160 bathrooms
Hayling Island Hotel – 99 bathrooms
Chelsea Hotel (then became Holiday Inn)
Newcastle Centre Hotel – 250 bathrooms
London Tara Hotel Kensington – 850 bathrooms
Caernarvon Hotel, London – 120 bathrooms
Selfridges Hotel – 307 bathrooms
Grampian Hotel, Stevenage – 100 bathrooms
Regent Centre Hotel – 342 bathrooms
Intercontinental Hotel – 450 bathrooms
Kensington Hilton Hotel Holland Park – 396 bathrooms and 315 shower rooms
Park Towers Hotel, Knightsbridge (then the Sheraton Park Towers Hotel) – 300 bathrooms
Hilton Hotel, Stratford upon Avon – 260 bathrooms
West Centre Hotel Fulham – 510 bathrooms
Gloucester Hotel, London – 565 bathrooms
London Airport Hotel (Heathrow Hotel) – 735 bathrooms
Sheraton Hotel, Heathrow – 440 bathrooms
London Embassy Hotel – 200 sets of sanitary ware
Kensington Palace Hotel – 250 bathrooms
And there were others not then listed.

Other important contracts involving sanitary ware:

Gatwick North Terminal Tower
New Stand, Sandown Park
Blue Coat School
Jumbo Jet Hangers, Heathrow
Sun Alliance House, Slough
Ready Mixed Concrete Head Offices, Staines
Gallaghers Offices, Kingsway
Guy's Hospital extensions
Metal Box Company Head Offices, Reading
John Player Building, Nottingham
Arab Hospital Centre, Collingham Gardens, Kensington
City of London Club

Flats and housing developments involving sanitary ware:

100 Luxury Flats, Barnes

Sittingbourne Estate for Abbey Homesteads – 250 bathrooms

Rushton Estate for Abbey Homesteads – 400 bathrooms

Linton Estate for Abbey Homesteads – 191 bathrooms

Bicester Estate for Abbey Homesteads – 300 bathrooms

Northampton Estate for Abbey Homesteads – 140 bathrooms

London Borough of Tower Hamlets – 1000 bathrooms

Etc., Etc.

Plus: there were a number blocks of flats in London where we supplied both bathrooms and kitchens.

Some of our contracts for kitchens – largely handled by Laurence:

136 Nobilia Kitchens for Wates, Pier House, Cheyne Walk, Chelsea

101 Nobilia Kitchens for Broome Manor Development, Swindon

72 Framford Kitchens for Federal Palace Suite Hotel, Lagos

30 Grovewood Kitchens, Jeddah

25 Wrighton Kitchens, Wellington Court, St. John's Wood

Nobilia Kitchens for several McClean Homes developments across the South West
Gatcombe Park, and much more besides.

Exports:

I have earlier mentioned our exports – mostly for Heat & Air Systems contracts. However, there were others but undoubtedly the largest was for a Government contract in Pakistan. The site was a new dam and the order included 822 WC suites, 471 washbasins with pedestal and taps, 210 baths, again with all fittings, 175 sink units, 535 shower fittings and many sundries. The baths were from British Bathrooms at Greenford and the sanitary ware from Twyfords who incidentally were also quoting for this very large contract. We beat all the others quoting (including Twyfords) simply because they had sourced their taps and shower fittings in the UK – whereas I purchased them in France at a much lower cost and shipped them direct via Marseille. Twyfords London Manager, the very likeable Don Nalder, was instructed by the factory to find out how I had managed to obtain this large order. However, I did not explain – even to a golfing partner like Don.

We also had orders from the Government for British Embassies abroad and we supplied goods to Helsinki, Delhi, Mauritius, Bagdad, Warsaw and others. My late brother Trevor (a long serving member of SIS) was taken ill whilst in New Delhi. He was astonished to see Humpherson labels on newly delivered sinks in the Clinic, within the High Commissioners compound.

**All this business – though sometimes taken at a low margin –
gradually enabled us to concentrate on the more profitable showroom trade.**

Appendix 9

A Separation is Made Between Works and Merchant Trade

When father took over running the business in 1946 he received advice from Lord Foster & Co. our Accountants and Auditor – that the business be split into two divisions – the Works (plumbing and heating contracting) and the Merchant trade supplying material to local plumbers and builders. The problem was explained to me when I came home in March 1947 and clearly it had been discussed since Grandfather's death. Finally, it was raised at the Annual General Meeting held on May 14th 1947 where it was decided to split the company to ascertain where the profit/losses were being made. The AGM was held in the dining room in the flat above the showrooms. My brother Ron and I had to sit in the hall outside, as we were neither shareholders nor directors at the time.

Humpherson & Co. Ltd.

Annual General Meeting held at the Registered Offices

188 Fulham Road. London. S.W.10. on Wednesday May 14th 1947

Present   S.A.Humpherson   Director
           E.A.Pidgeon   Director
           H.E.C.Pidgeon   Director & Secretary
           E.M.Humpherson   Shareholder

           Chairman   H.E.C.Pidgeon

Minutes of the Annual General Meeting for 1946 taken as read.

Auditors for the coming year   Messrs. Lord,Foster & Co.
Solicitors "   "   "   "   Messrs. Allward & Son.
Bankers   "   "   "   "   Midland Bank Ltd.
Directors   "   "   "   "   As at present.

The balance sheet for 1946 was read and approved and signed by S.A.Humpherson and E.A.Pidgeon (Directors)

Minutes of last A.G.M. were read and signed by the chairman.

The general business prospects were discussed. The Chairman pointed out that although no Dividends were payable on last year's figures a considerable profit was made. This had to be placed to the Profit and Loss account, leaving a deficit of £ 1,304.

The division of the Business Whereby the Works department was separated from the Firm, was discussed and approved. A further suggestion was made ,that to increase bussiness in general Ironmongery should undertaken. No definite date was fixed to start this side of the business but it was agreed that further information should be obtained on the matter. The Chairman arranged to do this and report in due course.

The Meeting closed.

We then formed 'Pidgeon & Co.' to handle the 'Works' and sent a notification to all our clients that Humpherson & Co. were no longer in the plumbing contract business. The notepaper for Pidgeon & Co. is below and you will see the directors are my mother, E. A. Pidgeon and E. M. Humpherson, Sidney Humpherson's wife.

Pidgeon & Company notepaper

Directors my mother E. A. Pidgeon and E. M. Humpherson

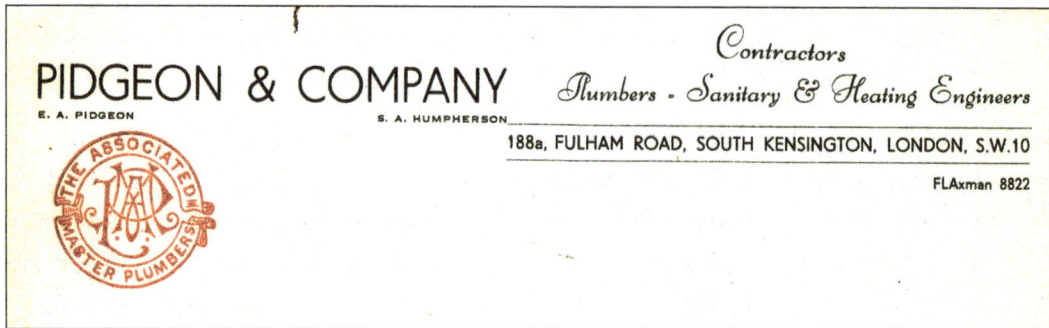

Humpherson & Co. Ltd notepaper:

Directors S. A. Humpherson, my mother E. A. Pidgeon and father H. E. C. Pidgeon.

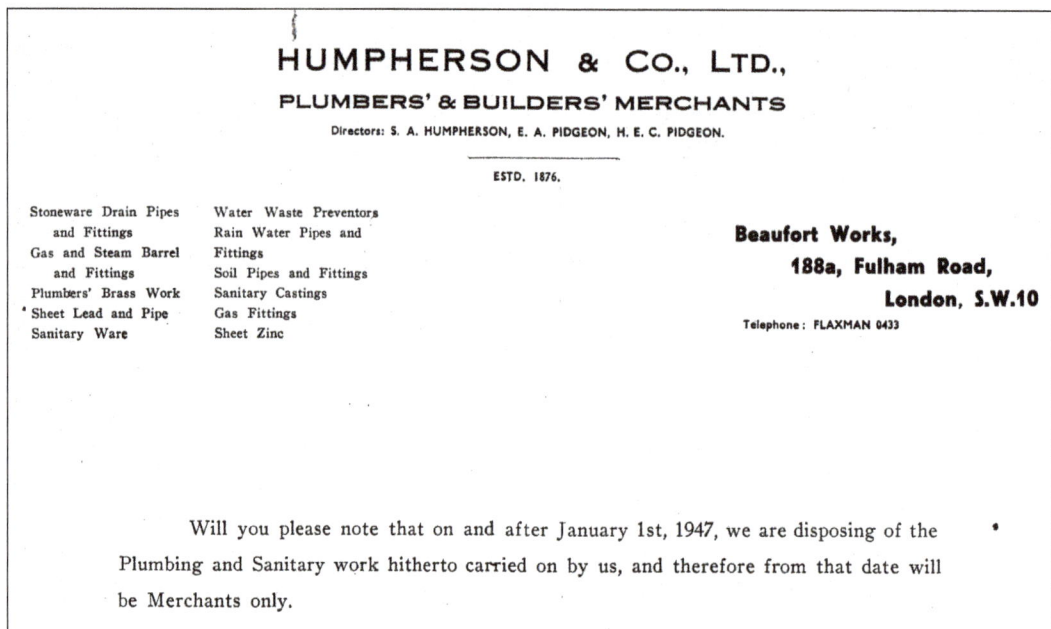

Note: This announcement by Humpherson & Co. is dated January 1st 1947 whereas the decision to split the two operations was only made on May 14th 1947. I can only think it is a misprint for June 1st 1947. I have no recollection of anyone picking up the point, or of them being reprinted.

However, for the first time instead of describing the company as 'Sanitary Engineers' Humpherson & Co. Ltd declared itself to be a 'Plumbers' and Builders' Merchants' a role that continued with variations, until 1981.

Appendix 10

My Appreciation of Italian Design

I first encountered Italian designs of bathroom fittings in the early 1960s, when Conex-Sanbra imported a small range of taps. Soon afterwards, the Delta Group, who brought in several ranges, including 'Silver Onyx' that we supplied to the Intercontinental Hotel in Park Lane – mentioned earlier.

We then decided we could and should import our own fittings from Italy. Laurence contacted Teorema in Brescia and we started to handle a small selection their taps and at the same time selected Cidneo sanitary ware – again from Brescia in northern Italy. Certainly, we were amongst the first to import a wide spread of Italian bathroom products in a substantial way.

You will have seen, in earlier parts of the book, some of the fittings we imported from leading Italian companies. However, from the many ranges – you may care to know my choice of the most outstanding.

First, my selection of taps

From the many Italian tap manufacturers, I believe Fantini Rubinetti S.p.A., are the most design conscious and consistent leaders of the market. The firm is in Pella – a delightful small town on the shores of the beautiful lake D'Orta – where the factory reaches right to the waters edge.

It appeared to me that some outstanding Italian products come from small towns and villages, in isolated and sheltered places, far away from the noise of major urban concentrations. It is as if creativity needs relative isolation to reach its full potential. Certainly that is true in Fantini's case. They have long continued to create brilliant new designs but my choice comes from the years I dealt with this company – and its inspirational CEO – Daniela Fantini.

This is Sfera and it caused a stir when first shown at the Cersaie Fair in Bologna. It is my choice of outstanding tap design.

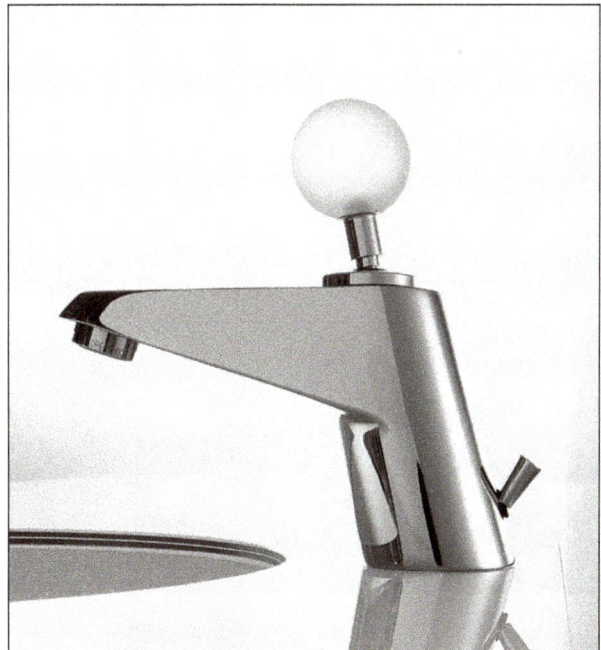

On opening day, Fantini had persuaded a number of sanitary ware makers to fit Sfera to basins on their own stands. It added to the rather dramatic launch of the fitting. Not surprisingly, other tap manufacturers made 'lookalike' taps for the following years exhibition.

However, Fantini had already taken the market with this very simple, tactile and pleasing design. There was a selection of different coloured heads available.

Secondly, my choice of sanitary ware

This was difficult because as with taps, Italy has many factories producing sanitary ware but unlike taps, they tend to be concentrated mostly in one area – Civita Castellana – an historic town some fifty miles north of Rome. We imported ware from a number of them but one was clearly outstanding, Ceramica Flamina.

Amongst their fine portfolio, several designs are worthy of my justly describing them as brilliant. They have been created by a man and wife team, Roberto and Ludovica Palomba based in Milan. Whilst they design in different fields – taps, furniture, lighting, kitchen products and so on – it is as designers of sanitary ware that I first encountered them. It was on the Flaminia stand at the ISH Fair in Frankfurt. Laurence accompanied me and we were both hugely impressed with their first project for Flamina the Aquagrande.

Aquagrande

This is the first model of what later developed into a range including 'semi-incasso'. A semi-shelf basin overhanging the edge of the work top and my favourite style of washbasin!

It was the first rectangular basin either of us had seen. Although others copied it later, nobody quite seemed to get the essential proportions quite right!

Later that year, I went with Michael to the Cersaie Fair in Bologna and met Ludovica and Roberto on the Flamina stand. We agreed to import the products on an exclusive basis.

It would be quite wrong of me to show only Aquagrande when it should be used in conjunction with their masterly design of a WC and bidet – 'Link'.

This is the initial design of Link but just like Aquagrande it was but part of a range. This wall-hung version was followed by 'Mini Link' and the 'Terra' design.

Link

Wall-hung version of Link on the right is to my mind, the outstanding WC design for many years. Possibly in all my working life in the industry.

What simplicity of line!

Opposite is the Terrra the floor mounted version of Link.

After nearly sixty years in the bathroom industry, I have seen the products of the major British and European manufacturers of sanitary ware and taps.

However, I do not hesitate to select these two products – Fantini taps and the Flamina sanitary ware designed by Roberto and Ludovica Palomba – as the best of Italian design.

I might add this selection also covers Britain and the rest of Europe.

Appendix 11

Humpherson's Advertising

Almost from the time of Peta Fordham's article in the Guardian, the media took an increasing interest in Humpherson's. There is little doubt that we had many 'firsts' and led the way with both products and displays. Indeed, we received so much coverage that larger merchants and some manufacturers assumed we had our own in-house PR staff!

However, whilst we enjoyed increasing press cover, we did not at any time forget the need for advertising. We went from simple inexpensive articles in the local press on to the nationals. Our standard became better – learning as we went along. One of our early 'firsts' – not mentioned so far – was to handle Alkathene plastic tubing used for water supplies. This was stocked mostly in ½" and ¾" for domestic use but in 1" for larger water supplies like that across the Loch to Castle Stalker (see Chapter 20). We advertised our lead in this field with the slogan *'Humpherson's for Plastic Tube'* and I recall the pleasure of the increasing trade resulting from such a simple and inexpensive advert.

We started the **HUMPHERSON'S NEWSLETTER** sent to existing and potential customers – by the hundred. I have one in front of me dated November 1967. I would reproduce it but I am afraid it is showing its age – by announcing our display of Shanks new colour 'Sun King' – before Shanks merger with Armitage.

It mentions our **'2000 Bathroom Suite'** delivered anywhere in the UK for £32.15.0 in white and £34.7.6 in colour. That really was anywhere in the UK – and cheaper for contracts. I recall supplying Wimpey to some of their developments in South Wales at £23.8.9d in white and £24.14.6 in colour.

The '2000' really was a complete bathroom suite with Perspex bath, taps and waste, a basin on brackets with taps and waste, and a low level WC suite with seat. Do not ask me how it was done – that's still a secret.

This was an age before photocopiers so the Newsletters were not printed but run off on a Gestetner copier using

A Gestetner copier similar to the one used for our Newsletters. How things have changed!

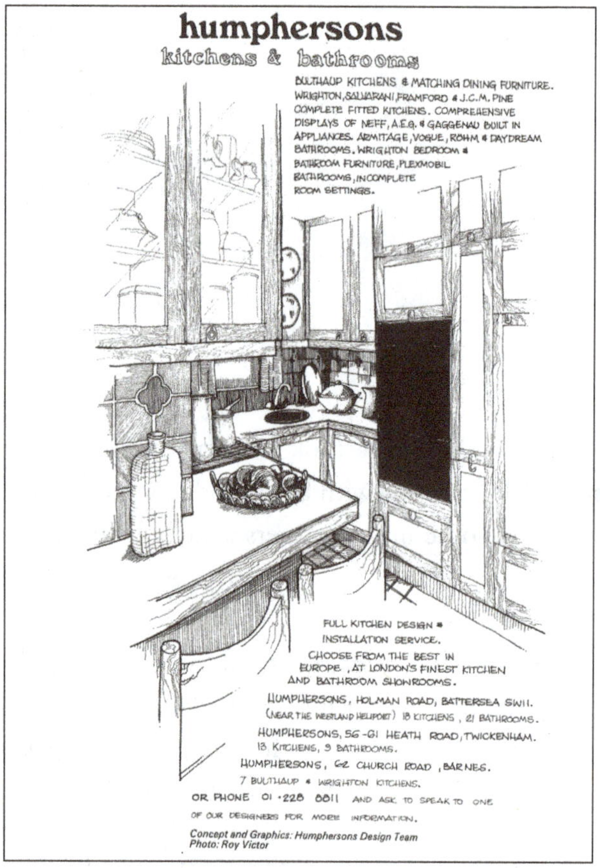
humphersons
kitchens & bathrooms
BULTHAUP KITCHENS & MATCHING DINING FURNITURE. WRIGHTON, SALVARANI, FRAMFORD & J.C.M. PINE COMPLETE FITTED KITCHENS. COMPREHENSIVE DISPLAYS OF NEFF, A.E.G. & GAGGENAU BUILT IN APPLIANCES. ARMITAGE, VOGUE, RÖHM & DAYDREAM BATHROOMS. WRIGHTON BEDROOM & BATHROOM FURNITURE, PLEXMOBIL BATHROOMS, IN COMPLETE ROOM SETTINGS.
FULL KITCHEN DESIGN & INSTALLATION SERVICE.
CHOOSE FROM THE BEST IN EUROPE, AT LONDON'S FINEST KITCHEN AND BATHROOM SHOWROOMS.
HUMPHERSONS, HOLMAN ROAD, BATTERSEA SW11.
(NEAR THE WESTLAND HELIPORT) 18 KITCHENS, 21 BATHROOMS.
HUMPHERSONS, 56-61 HEATH ROAD, TWICKENHAM.
13 KITCHENS, 9 BATHROOMS.
HUMPHERSONS, 62 CHURCH ROAD, BARNES.
7 BULTHAUP & WRIGHTON KITCHENS.
OR PHONE 01-228 8811 AND ASK TO SPEAK TO ONE OF OUR DESIGNERS FOR MORE INFORMATION.
Concept and Graphics: Humphersons Design Team
Photo: Roy Victor

humphersons
kitchens & bathrooms
WRIGHTON COTSWOLD DISPLAY KITCHEN FROM OUR BATTERSEA SHOWROOMS. JUST ONE OF THE 38 KITCHENS YOU CAN SEE IN OUR 3 LONDON SHOWROOMS.

humphersons
since 1876
kitchens and bathrooms
CHOOSE FROM THE BEST IN EUROPE ...
BULTHAUP KITCHENS & MATCHING DINING FURNITURE. THE FULL RANGE OF WRIGHTON FITTED KITCHENS AS WELL AS SALVARANI & FRAMFORD KITCHENS ALL IN COMPLETE ROOM SETTINGS. PROBABLY THE MOST COMPREHENSIVE DISPLAYS OF BUILT IN APPLIANCES IN THE SOUTH EAST. FEATURING NEFF AEG, GAGGENAU & MIELE. AT LEAST
2 LIVE DEMONSTRATION KITCHENS IN EACH SHOWROOM. ARMITAGE SHANKS, BALTERLEY, VOGUE, ROHM, POLLIACK & MAURICE HERBEAU BATHROOMS; BEAULINS, CZECH & SPEAKE; POLLIACK & VOLA TAPS. WRIGHTON BEDROOM & BATHROOM FURNITURE; STUKER BEDROOMS & PLEXMOBIL MODULAR BATHROOMS ALL IN FULLY FURNISHED ROOM SETTINGS. IN ALL, OUR FOUR LONDON SHOWROOMS HAVE A
TOTAL OF 92 KITCHEN & BATHROOM DISPLAYS BACKED BY A FULL KITCHEN DESIGN & INSTALLATION SERVICE & MASSIVE STOCKS OF ARMITAGE SHANKS, BALTERLEY & VOGUE BATHROOM FITTINGS
ALL PHOTOS AND ILLUSTRATIONS ARE OF OUR SHOWROOM DISPLAYS
CONTACT YOUR NEAREST BRANCH FOR FURTHER INFORMATION
HUMPHERSONS, HOLMAN RD. BATTERSEA, S.W.11. - 228 8811
HUMPHERSONS, 164/166 BROMPTON RD. KNIGHTSBRIDGE - 584 6062
HUMPHERSONS AT HEALS HEALS TOTTENHAM COURT RD.
HUMPHERSONS, 55/61 HEATH RD. TWICKENHAM - 892 2854
HUMPHERSONS, 227 HIGH RD. CHISWICK, W4 - 995 4172
HUMPHERSONS, KITCHEN STUDIO 62 CHURCH RD. BARNES - 748 0387

humphersons
since 1876
kitchens and bathrooms

green ink. It was a messy task – not the favourite job for junior office staff – but the Newsletter went out on a regular basis.

We progressed, always promoting the latest product but leap forward ten years, and the progress we made in the creation of our adverts is truly striking. The illustrations are examples of our high standard generated in-house by Laurence's design team.

Our adverts were run in all the leading Home Magazines (generally known as the 'Glossies') and were frequently changed to keep the interest high.

The pictures we used for advertising both kitchens and bathrooms were always taken in one of our major showrooms. The coloured picture was on the right hand page and the information about them facing it. These were sometimes printed in grey tones – as it counted as black and white – and thus reduced the cost.

**There can be no doubt that the high standard of our advertising
set a benchmark and played a substantial part in our growing success.**

Notes A

Frederick Humpherson – Photographer!

From a young age Frederick was keen on photography. I do not know how he managed in the earlier days but in 1902, when designing his flat above the new premises in Holmes Place, he included a dark room leading off from his extensive workshop. When he died, his brother Alfred inherited the business and moved into the flat. He was also interested in photography but perhaps did not have his brother's skill?

Frederick was a member of the Chelsea Photographic Society for years and this is an example of his work submitted for its annual competition. It is of Chelsea Reach with the Battersea Power station in the background. It was taken at sunset and though now somewhat battered – is still quite stunning. I have others and several are in their dark oak frames as submitted to the committee.

Frederick became a member of the Royal Photographic Society and was elected a Fellow of the Royal Photographic Society in 1911. I am told that gave him enormous pleasure. His many cameras were on shelves in his workshop, along with many hundreds (perhaps thousands) of glass slides in carefully marked boxes. I regret in turning the first floor into offices I was guilty of agreeing to the slides disposal – along with much else.

Frederick Humpherson was a talented man – one might say gifted – in many spheres.

Frederick's Profit Sharing Scheme

This letter was addressed to Mr Scott – Editor of 'The Plumber' – and refers to his decision to provide a profit sharing scheme for Humpherson's plumbing staff.

Dear Mr Scott,

I was in hopes to have seen you at the meeting last Wednesday as I was going to ask you if the enclosed was of any interest to you for The Plumber etc.

I believe I am the first to take up this profit sharing in our trade and I have no doubt in my mind that something of this kind will have to be done all round before long if we to maintain our trade. If you think it is of any value for print you may cut it up and also criticise it as you like as long as my intentions are not perverted.

Hoping that you are quite well, and it was not illness that caused your absence on Wednesday last. Wishing you a very happy New Year.

Yours faithfully,

Frederick Humpherson

Humpherson & Co. Ltd.

On Thursday January 2nd 1919 Messrs Humpherson & Co of Fulham Road S.W. the well-known & old established firm of sanitary Engineers & Plumbers called a meeting of the Employees.

Mr F. Humpherson addressing them that the business which he had carried on successfully for the past 43 years had that day been converted into a Private Limited Liability Company so as to enable him to bring in his brother & others into the firm.

He stated that for several years past he had contemplated that step in view of a scheme for profit sharing with the employees. The war unfortunately coming in 1914 had stopped that and put everything back for a time. Now that the war is practically over the scheme had been matured in the meantime he was now willing to give all the skilled employees a fair share of the profits.

We are given to understand the scheme is as follows. Supposing a profit is made of £600 is made *[Note: Today that is about £27,000]* after all out-goings, dividends in preference and in ordinary shares are paid, income tax at 6/0s in the pound. *[Note: The out-goings would also include all salaries and expenses].*

Then the profit will be divided in this way: Manager 4 points – Secretary 3 points – Foreman 3 points – Foreman 2 points – Foreman 2 points – 41 Skilled men 1 point each – 8 Unskilled men ¾ point each – 8 Apprentices ½ point each.

We should remember that the Armistice for World War I had only been signed some seven weeks earlier as a result Humpherson must still have men in the armed forces. He refers to the war being 'practically over' and that seems to confirm it. I also suspect the general contract business had not yet recovered so this scheme was a generous gesture on his part.

Frederick Humpherson died on 15th October in that same year and left the entire business to his brother – my grandfather Alfred Humpherson.

Product Names

Most leading merchants gave manufactures products their own name or figure number – irrespective of the factory description. It made it a little harder for customers to compare prices and gave an air of 'ownership' to the product. I suspect – indeed at the time of my close involvement with Thomas Crapper – they were merely adding the name 'Marlboro' to quite standard Twyfords or other makers merchandise. However, there was nothing wrong with the practice since Gosletts, Boldings, Froys and we were doing the same.

A different situation arises where the factory were manufacturing exclusive articles such as our 'Beaufort' pans. That had a direct connection from our Chelsea days. It was launched whilst we were still at 257 Fulham Road on the corner of Beaufort Street. Later, we used the name 'Beaufort' (or a derivative), for a number of our lines such as 'Beauseal' bath sealing tape, 'Beauline' taps although were standard taps badged in accordance with our design. 'Beauline Mixers' and so on. Another name we used was 'Flaxman' for a range of stainless steel sinks – taking the name from the then local telephone exchange.

Reyburn said that Crapper's used local street names such as Lennox, Onslow, Sloane, Cadogan and others, for his fittings. However, the 1888, 1935 and 1954 catalogues that I have – do not list fittings by such names. Others might – *but heigh ho!*

Humpherson's 'Drayton' Gully *(reproduced overleaf)*

This is one of Frederick Humpherson's designs. He describes is as '*..an improved stable gully*' – but I assume he did not regard is as sufficiently different to take out a Patent?

Remember, this would have been for sale in the 1880s and 1890s and everything was horse drawn. It was therefore necessary to provide stabling for tens of thousands of them in London alone.

In London and other big cities the carriages and horses were kept in mews and again stable gullies were essential.

In addition, this would have been in the heyday of our Police station contracts and I believe every station had stabling for horse. So overall there would have been a large demand.

STABLE-FITTINGS.

The "Drayton" Gully.

HUMPHERSON & Co., of 297 Fulham Road, London, S.W., have introduced an improved stable gully, known as the "Drayton," the construction of which is shown in fig. 11. Their claims for the article include efficiency and low cost. The quantity of water retained in the trap is small, and, while it fills its part, is not large enough in volume to form a nuisance should it stand some time. The iron-work—the perforated basket and the cast-iron frame and

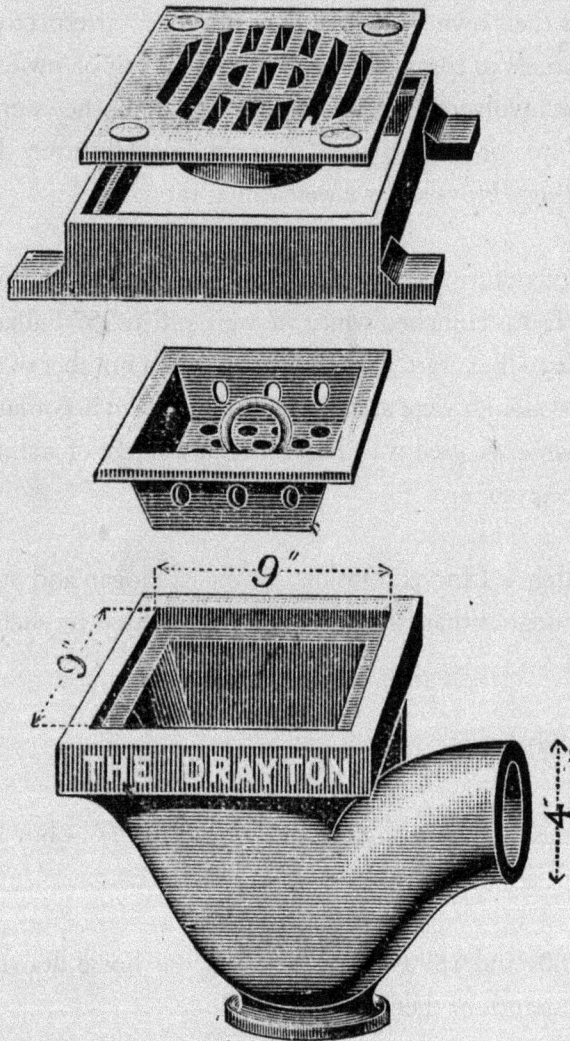

FIG. 11.

grating—is eminently strong and suitable for the rough use of a stable. The gully is made in glazed earthenware, either brown or buff, and list-prices, complete with the iron fittings described, are 13s. 6d. and 15s. 6d. respectively. One, two, or three inlets may be had.

Note: This Humpherson product, The 'Drayton' Gully is *actually* named after Drayton Gardens just across the Fulham road from his offices and works in Beaufort Street.

Notes D

Badges on Cisterns and Manhole Covers

There is considerable misunderstanding about merchants marking products with their name, thus implying that they manufactured it, whereas it was usually a form of advertising. This was quite common on cast iron cisterns, manhole and coalhole covers, even small domestic boilers. A few merchants had earlier and rightly, marked a product with their name because it was their own design or patent. However, as time went on there were fewer products that could boast exclusivity in that way and it became more a method of advertising.

Let us first deal with cast iron products. Across the country were many iron foundries but there were dozens – large and small across Scotland particularly in the Glasgow – to Falkirk region. They vied with each other for merchant trade and offered competitive prices for badging. In the case of manhole covers for example they could make up a name on a pattern to be let onto the mould. Thus it was quite simple and inexpensive to produce. Thus merchants like Humpherson & Co. and Thomas Crapper & Co., could offer builders the opportunity to badge their own name onto the products.

I well remember ordering 12 Burlington flushing cisterns from T. Ventom & Sons of Fulham for such as builders as **'Neville & Sons'** of Edith Grove Chelsea. Another was badged **'Godbolt & Sons'** of Kensington. Additionally, we ordered manhole covers and frames from Ballantines of Boness near Edinburgh badged for them and others.

In my early days with the company, my brother Ron and I often unloaded fifty badged with our own name, leaving a similar load on the lorry to go Crapper's stores nearby. Those were badged Thomas Crapper & Co. Both came from the same foundry and were identical – except for the name.

This illustration is from the 1888 Thomas Crapper & Co. catalogue, demonstrating that merchants could have their own – or a customers name – cast in. Therefore, there is no mystery in finding manhole covers, cisterns or indeed any flat casting with **Thomas Crapper's** name on it – or Neville & Sons, or Humpherson & Co. All one had to do was to pay the small fee involved to the foundry!

The fact that there is no particular mystery about 'badged' manhole covers or cisterns – does not reduce the fascination of spotting one!

Notes E

Everything Green!

Amongst the files and documents we found in the basement, was a framed Humpherson & Co. poster, advertising London pattern fireclay sinks showing our Beaufort Street address. Meaning they were produced before 1902. The London pattern sinks were cane colour, quite shallow and without overflow; unlike the Belfast pattern fireclay sink that largely superseded them in the 1920s.

Nothing very remarkable here, *except* that the sinks were printed in their natural cane colour on a light green background. Stranger still for period, the printing was in dark green over the light green.

When he took over the company books, my father used the existing Midland Bank cheques printed with our name Humpherson & Co in the usual Midland Bank colours. About 1949, he felt something different was needed to show that the company had changed direction away from plumbing contracts to become 'Wholesale Plumbers' and Builders' Merchants' even on our cheques.

The green poster for London pattern sinks was still lying about in the offices, when he recalled the green HSBC (Hong Kong & Shanghai Bank) Bills of Exchange I had sent home from Singapore during my six months spent there. At the time, I did not have a bank account in the UK, just a Post Office Savings account. So each month I sent my 'surplus' home to bank in his account until I could open my own. I have some rather tattered copies left but £20 a month (about £750 today) was the most I sent. I see another is for £12 (£450 today). The green is a little faded but it was 1946!

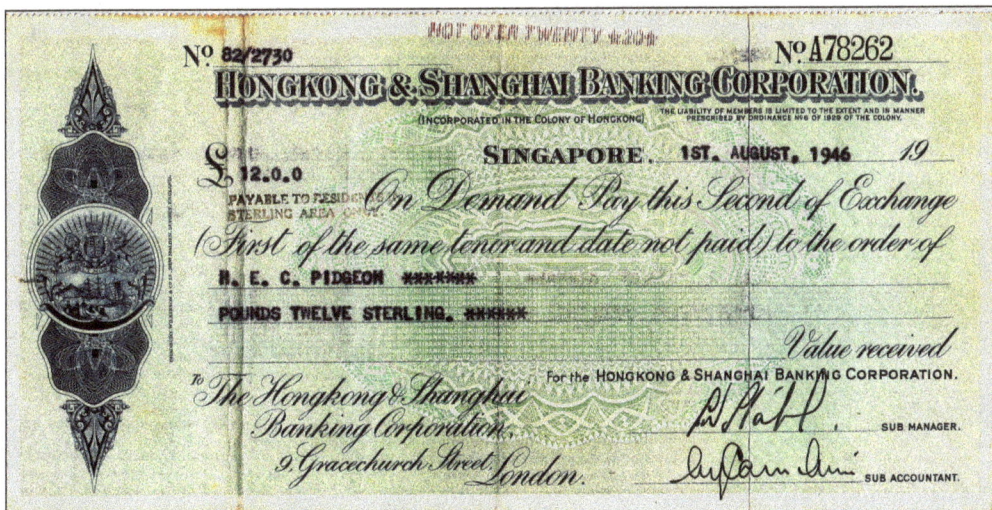

At that time, HSBC in Singapore printed their Bills of Exchange in green; these coupled with the green poster gave father the idea to should print our Midland Bank cheques in the same colour. Alan Day was the Midland Bank manager in their Onslow Square branch in South Kensington. He sought permission from his Head Office for this rather unusual request. After some deliberation, it was agreed and our quite splendid Humpherson & Co. cheques were the result.

I have a number of them still and the example below is a payment to Allward & Sons our Solicitors for £1.11.6. (£46 today). When father died in 1956, mother, my brother Ronald and myself were the only bank signatories but because this cheque was under £5, only one signature was necessary!

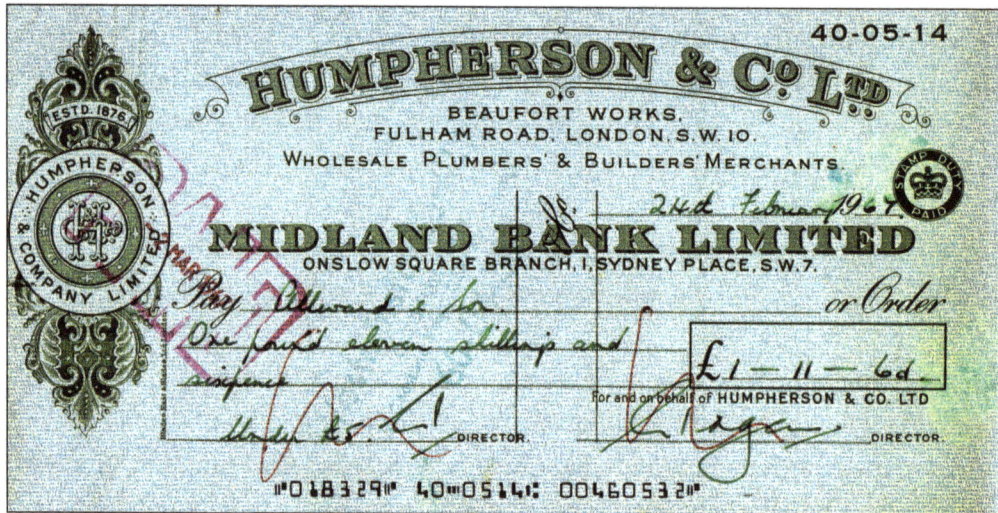

However, we were not content just with green cheques. We found green typewriter ribbons, so letters went out in what became known as **'Humpherson's Green'!** The staff were issued with green pens, invoices were printed green, as well as our letter headings. Later, we even painted the shop front and our newly acquired fleet of lorries were naturally painted green. It was positive and distinctive – yet another sign that Humpherson & Co were going in a fresh direction.

Catalogue covers were in green and our typists used green/red ribbons in their typewriters – we went even further and used green carbon papers so that even copies were in green.

Looking back it does seem 'over-the-top' but it made a considerable impact at the time.
That, after all, was the point of the exercise.

Notes F

Sanitary Ware – Any Colour so Long as it's White

Our main showroom at Holman Road alone contained 65 displays of kitchens and bathrooms. Many of the bathrooms were quite elaborate and most of the products on display were in one or other of the many colours then available. That was certainly true of other merchants that I knew at the time.

However, one of the largest displays featured white with gold fittings – then very popular. Yet we found that we were increasingly selling white bathrooms with **chrome** as well as gold and the trend developed.

In view of our substantial turnover, Tim Bennett sales director of Armitage-Shanks, made quite frequent visits to Humphersons in Holman Road. On one occasion, he asked why our orders for coloured ware – as a percentage of our growing turnover – were slowly decreasing? However, I think he already knew the answer from his representatives. We were promoting white more prominently, as customers found it easier to select the décor for white than colours, hence it was far less limiting!

He pointed out that they received a 40% premium for colour but admitted (though I already knew) – it was not costing them anything like that to produce. As a result, their margins were likely to fall if white became more popular nationally. It did, of course, reduce our profit but we made up for that by introducing more expensive designed taps and accessories from Italy.

The shift continued and when we started Original Bathrooms at Richmond – almost all the displays were white. One of our first customers said she chose us to supply her new bathrooms, partially because we were the first shop she had found who did not show Avocado!

Now when I look in bathroom showrooms – I notice the almost universal use of white!

Britain's water policy analysed

By-laws and fittings scrutinised as Mr. G. Pidgeon calls for new policy

Mr. G. Pidgeon

Mr. Geoffrey Pidgeon, who contributes this article is chairman and managing director of Humpherson & Co. Ltd., established by Edward Humpherson in 1876. One of his sons, Frederick, was closely interested in the improvement of the sanitary fittings available at that time, and his work at Beaufort Works and the Beaufort cistern became widely known. Mr. Pidgeon is a descendant of the Humphersons on the distaff side and says that as a plumbers' merchant he cannot ignore those things which gave him his business.

A member of NFBPM council, Mr. Pidgeon is also vice-chairman of the Building Regulations committee of NFBPM and of No. 14 Standing committee dealing with rainwater and soil goods. He also represents NFBPM on the British Standards Institution.

Model water by-laws: Suggested amendments

My comments on the Model Water By-laws divide broadly into two parts. Firstly specific criticisms of parts of the present by-laws, together with suggested amendments. This extends into a criticism of the present state of the water distribution arrangements in the country, and my views for the possible improvement headed — "Into the future."

Present By-laws

By-laws 2 (1) – Suggested amendment

(a) after the word "fitting" delete the semi-colon, and add, "and all fittings marked and/or marketed as being to the appropriate British Standard shall be sufficient evidence of their suitability for the purpose mentioned in these by-laws, without further examination stamping or testing by the Undertakings other than to satisfy themselves that, on a random basis only, samples conform to that Standard.

(b) add after the words "those matters" at the end of the paragraph ... "the Undertakings shall not withhold approval of such fitting if it has already obtained the approval of the British Waterworks Association."

Reasons for Amendment

(1) As a nation, we have evolved the highest standards for water fittings in the world. Indeed, they are so high that they are mostly considered too heavy and expensive for use in markets outside the United Kingdom and its remaining Dependencies. It is wasteful in terms of time, labour and costs for Undertakings to take each and every such British Standard water fitting and further test and stamp it for use in their own particular area. It is also wasteful in terms of imported raw materials for British Standards for taps, cocks and stop valves to be so unnecessarily high.

(2) The purely dimensional requirements of, for instance, BS1010 are not only too high, they are restricting in design. It is generally agreed that Continental patterns are more sophisticated and British makers will never produce fittings acceptable for world markets if fittings of such weight are persisted in. BS1010 should be examined urgently, but could remain a basically dimensional/performance Standard provided that other fittings that are introduced can be used if these conform to the performance standards. The new 1010 would then cover screw-down taps and stop valves as a minimum standard (and therefore most of the domestic market) but any other fittings would be acceptable provided it passed the tests laid down by the BWA. Standard dimensions for mixer centres, tail lengths, thread size, and so on, are obviously essential for all fittings.

By-laws 9 (and 33 to 41)

This by-law deals with the provision of a draw off tap for water and for the purpose of this article it is linked with storage cisterns by-laws 33 to 41 inclusive.

The time has come to change the system of domestic water distribution. The need for a drinking tap is obvious, and this is almost always in the kitchen. At this point there is clean fresh water—the remaining water points in a house can (in my view) be classed as "contaminated." The general layout of distribution is that all the draw off taps are fed from a storage cistern which will become foul and (I believe) non-potable in the strictest sense. Yet taps to washbasins, baths and the like are often used as drinking points where the public is not aware of the difference between fresh water from the main and that which has lain for a period in a storage cistern.

Worse still, it is common practice for the housewife to draw hot water from the kitchen tap for cooking purposes, and this water, too, has often lain in what is a foul storage cistern.

There is little serious illness that can be directly attributed to contaminated water supply. However, how many of the minor ailments diagnosed as stomach upsets could—if the facilities existed—be traced to water being drunk via a foul storage cistern? The link between some illnesses and the water drunk may go further, an area of medical research that seems to be neglected.

Changes should now be made over what I shall refer to as a "high pressure" system. For reasons of cost this may have to take place over a period of time, but a start could be made to improve matters now in two stages.

Stage one
Prevention of surge

All cold water taps to sinks, washbasins and baths to be connected direct to the main. The following points should be noted.

(a)i. A suitable apparatus should be fitted to the supply side of a mixer valve in order to prevent surge between the high pressure cold and the low pressure cold.

(a)ii. A suitable pressure reducing fitment be applied to the cold water system to reduce its inbalance with the hot.

(b) More use of suitable non-return valves should be made to prevent back syphonage (see comments on By-law 53).

(c) During this period the hot system will continue to be low pressure, and the public should be informed of the danger of foul water from the hot tap.

(d) All flushing cisterns should be classed as a non-potable storage cistern.

This reserve is only to cover the possibility of a break-down in supply, and need be no more than that necessary to flush the toilets over a short period. The importance of this reserve however, is to be doubted owing to the very infrequent shut downs that occur.

(e) This "stage one" (or something like it) is already in use in many parts of the country as standard practice. I ask that it be extended rapidly throughout all areas.

Stage two

All water fittings in the house should be direct to the main supply including the hot water system.

(a) It may be necessary to fit pressure reducing valves to the incoming mains to cope with fluctuating pressures in some areas.

(b) Hot water cylinders will have to be slightly heavier gauge to cope with increased pressures, and again, pressure reducing valves may be needed in some areas of exceptional pressure.

(c) Mains should be protected from possible contamination on the company's side of the stopcock by mechanical device to check backflow.

(d) This will give potable water throughout the house, even from the hot water tap. Nevertheless mechanical devices to prevent backflow may be needed on such fittings as bidets and halfvalves any point, indeed, where a hose pipe may be used, and so on.

(e) Every one of the new range of mixing valves can thus be used, since there will be no risk of imbalance in pressure or cross contamination.

(f) Almost all pipe sizes, taps and stop-valves can be reduced in size in a "high pressure" system with three outstanding effects: (i) much lower prime costs of pipe and fittings; (ii) lower installation costs; and (iii) an opportunity to link British sizes to ISO standards at this vital period of the metrication programme.

(There is a comparatively small export market for our current brass foundry range. A change along the lines indicated would make us more competitive, as I know our makers can be, and would reduce the increasing rate of imported fittings from the Continent.)

(g) In certain areas the use of storage vessels might be considered. A sealed pressure storage vessel would have the obvious advantage of providing a cold potable reserve in the event of a mains shut down.

(h) In high rise development, of course pumps will be needed.

Health menace of polluted cisterns

The change would clearly be beneficial to health, but in the meantime greater publicity must be given to the state of existing cold water storage cisterns. These are frequently foul-slimed—and polluted with bird droppings and worse. A cover, although mentioned in the by-laws is seldom used, and even this will not prevent insect or air-borne bacterial infection. It is vital that the public be made aware of the nature of the water at various points, and the need to regularly inspect and clean its storage facilities.

By-law 46

This needs to be extended to larger vessels and opens the way to equal pressure supply for mixer and shower fittings.

By-law 47

With greater use of mechanical devices to prevent backflow, it should be possible to simplify the regulations regarding mixing valves.

By-law 53

This is the most widely misinterpreted of all the by-laws.

Altogether too much concern has been expressed over the possibility of back-syphonage generally, and makers have too readily acceded to ill-defined requirements based on too little evidence. Almost all washbasins and most draw-off taps had to be re-designed, at enormous cost to the country!

There are undoubtedly conflicting views on how a bath-mixer with hand-shower should be installed, and the bidet appears to be liable to the personal whim of each inspector!

Back syphonage problems

Whilst the problem of back syphonage has been greatly exaggerated, the company's main should certainly be protected from each household. Considering the state of many storage cisterns this is essential. However, a mechanical device inserted on, or at, the company's stopcock, would prevent any backflow.

Within the home—if the problem can be shown as a genuine one — then again a valve to prevent backflow should be fitted where it is felt a threat can arise.

By-laws 54 to 57
Flushing Cisterns

One of the most wasteful aspects of the plumbing industry is the necessity for makers and merchants to make and stock flushing cisterns of varying capacities for different regions. There can be no case for the 2½ or 3 gallon flushing cistern where it has been proved that the 2 gallon flush is sufficient on a properly designed w.c. pan and immediate action is required to remove these other two sizes from manufacturers' ranges and to apply the 2 gallon as standard throughout the country.

Again some form of national code of practice should be considered for the supply to flushing cisterns.

BUILDERS' MERCHANTS JOURNAL SEPTEMBER 1969

Over the years there have probably been hundreds of press articles about the company and/or its products. As we had grown, so we had moved away from the usual builders merchant's approach to the sale of bathroom and kitchens – where they were only part of the business. We created showrooms exclusively for them but to a higher standard than had gone before. Our mixture of new products and quality showrooms created increasing media interest in the company.

Running alongside that were articles either by/or about me, in the press. These often followed my concerns on a number of major subjects. Raising the standard of merchant showrooms – hence my address to the AGM of the National Federation of Builders Merchants at Gleneagles. Our antiquated water regulations needed revision and considerable improvements have since taken place. I was a leader in the drive to change from fitting syphons in our WC flushing cisterns to the valve – thus saving vast amounts of precious water as well as energy. But dearest to my heart, was the work on 'Safety in the Bathroom'. My emphasis here, was on ensuring the disabled could safely use the bath, the shower or the WC – and preferably without supervision.

NFBPM Annual Conference
Gleneagles looks ahead to the '70's

THE organising committee did a thoroughly good job for Gleneagles again this year, the second occasion on which the NFBPM Conference has been held in Scotland. Quite obviously there, and at NFBPM Head Office, a concerted effort had been made to try to ensure that the proceedings would be well worth while, a thought which was admirably carried through by the chairmen for the various sessions.

As is now a well established custom Conference opened with a service on the Sunday evening at Dunblane Cathedral when Mr. J. B. Mathers (honorary treasurer) at the organ delighted the congregation with a tasteful selection of items in his repertoire. The lessons were read by Mr. A. W. B. Scott (Scottish Region chairman) and Mr. Cyril Norton, the President, with a most thoughtful address from the Minister, The Rev. John R. Gray.

How to progress in home improvements

THE session devoted to discussion of NFBPM Home Improvement Centres with Mr. J. B. Mathers (publicity committee chairman) presiding, began with Mr. C. A. Thompson recounting how his own company, Rycrofts Ltd., Bradford, had set about creating its own centre. Readers will recall that this was featured in our issue of May (page 109). Mr. Thompson emphasised that in his view, if merchants really did support the scheme as they should, they would find the results very much worth while.

Details of the 1968-1969 advertising proposals were given by Mr. Duncan McLeish (Murphy, McLeish Ltd.), public relations consultants to the Federation. The two principal home journals used in the first campaign had been retained but in an effort to reach a wider audience another had been added. Three-page insertions with the names and addresses of all Centres throughout the country would be alternated with single-page insertions. Full colour would be employed with actual product pictures instead of line drawings. The three magazines concerned had a total circulation of 1,530,000 with combined readership of about 7.5 m.

Mr. McLeish added that unfortunately makers had been somewhat slower in co-operating in the scheme than had been anticipated but if some of the larger firms set the example other would undoubtedly follow. Others who spoke were Mr. J. B. Jackson and Mr. A. Plowman (Editor, Display).

"I have no new thoughts to put before you today although the Press and magazines featured our new bathroom Boutique and Safety feature displays when they were opened last year. We have plans, quite extensive plans, for future development but these are still in the pipeline.

Sales pointers

"We have always based Showroom Presentation on certain principles. For example, before considering the showroom one must always first consider showroom staff. Showrooms will only be as good as the staff which man it. What then do we require of the staff? Personality, presentation, manner, are all important, but these can be subsidiary to

Mr. Geoffrey Pidgeon addresses Conference

Some of the delegates at the NFBPM Annual Conference

London merchant outlines a basic approach

"WHEN I was asked to speak to you I was not sure I could add much to the general fund of knowledge on showrooms. I felt that as plumbers' merchants in Kensington and Chelsea we are faced with special problems and, in addition, we have comparatively small premises. I realised however that these were not unique problems many of you handle kitchen and bathroom equipment and some have to manage with limited space. It is to these gentlemen that I address my remarks, and I hope these of you not within these brackets can find something useful in what I may to apply to your problems.

"As a company we were very pleased to join in the Home Improvement Centre scheme. For us it is an extension on a national scale of something we have tried to do locally. For example, if a certain pottery maker was about to show new bathroom suites in their advertisement in one of the Home magazines we 'got on the band wagon' so to speak, by having a bathroom display complete and, as near as we could, to the photograph that was to appear. Thus we linked our local display with the collective national advertising with little cost to ourselves. How much more we welcome this chance to participate in collective national advertising ourselves. The greatest potential, and in the long term, cheapest form of advertising, is to link in this way with the huge publicity budgets of manufacturers.

the paramount importance of the man knowing his material thoroughly, having a point of view to express which will guide the customer and, most important of all, product knowledge.

"Our showrooms are not Supermarkets where customers help themselves. They need guidance, firm if not strong views on the product before them and unlimited technical advice. Our showroom success stems from this; we are an Advice Centre (a word I have used before when talking of showrooms) and advice requires knowledge. So choose your showroom staff with that in mind. Also there should be in each company a showroom committee to include all senior showroom staff to discuss layouts and new products, and generally to foster a sense of involvement and the interchange of knowledge.

"In the showrooms themselves our company has some twenty bathrooms and five kitchen displays to which it is hoped to add in the next month or two. Accommodation is limited and in our case on one floor. Because of this limited space perhaps a small presentation must have greater impact than where there are acres to use. However, even with more space I would still apply the following points.

"They should look like bathrooms or kitchens. I wish

was not made in 8 ft. x 4 ft. panels. How often displays are built with these sizes and the greatest wall height is often just above the taps in the washbasin or sink. Consequently one display rams into the next. The eye cannot be concentrated on the particular suite being considered. One frequently sees impressive photographs of large showrooms in the trade journals where it is a veritable sea of jumbled boilers, kitchens, bathroom fittings, all from a distance running one into the other, screened only by 4 ft. walls. How much easier for customers to look into individual displays where at least one wall is full height. He is more able to mentally transpose that to his own bathroom, and your job is easier. It is undoubtedly this realism that accounts for our continued editorial mention. Your displays must be appealing to the eye. I always refer to the furnishing of a bathroom, never equipping it. Treat your bathroom setting as if it were in a home, add all the towels, soaps, bath salts, yes, even the toilet paper! Your kitchen should have a few jugs, saucepans and the other oddments that bring the thing alive. We do not leave the maker's name spread all over each display – these destroy the total impact and

should be available but not so as to spoil the realism of the setting. Of course these general remarks do not apply to our trade counter displays where 'bread and butter' lines such as sink units, closets and washbasins stand side by side. But after all this is for selection by tradesmen, whose main concern is price and suitability. Nevertheless my other comments apply equally to this area.

Colour, lighting and an up-to-date approach

"The majority of our displays are partially partitioned, after which we consider the individual impact to the eye. Here the most important feature is the colour scheme. I am sure that too much use is made of tiled hardboard or even tiles. Tiling is necessary to add realism to the water areas round a bath or shower, but the remaining walls can be papered. This has two effects. Firstly, it gives the bathroom that furnished look of which I have spoken and, secondly, it enables one to more readily change the colour scheme to keep the bathrooms up to date. The wall and floor coverings are selected with great care, and these

PROFILE: GEOFFREY PIDGEON

Enthusiasm - defined in one dictionary as ardent and lively interest or eagerness - is a quality possessed in full measure by Geoffrey Pidgeon (left), a leading authority in the UK and possibly the world, on bathroom products and design. His has been, in his own words, a full life and his joie de vivre is as tangible today as it has been throughout a long career.

Born in London, he joined the Army in 1943, aged 17 ½. He was attached to a special services unit which had a very wide and interesting brief, largely connected with secret communications, a part of

Returning to the austerity of post war Britain, he joined the old-established family business, Humpherson, in 1947. It was then based in Chelsea. Geoffrey takes great pride in the fact that his sons are the fifth generation of the family to sell bathrooms. This has been a continuous process since the mid-1870's.

The memory of his first day at work, 48 years ago, is still vivid, and he has amusingly recalled it: 'My father showed me my future working space which included a desk so high, that I was given a stool so that I could reach to work at it. I felt something out of a Dickens novel and was not pleased. Fortunately, my father listened to my expression of horror and allowed me to take a saw to the legs of the desk-and then to the legs of the stool!'

Eventually, the story had a happy ending, inasmuch as his father agreed to the pur...

which is now known as 'The Ultra Secret'. Today, the somewhat narrower field of work is broadly covered by GCHQ at Cheltenham. At the end of the war, he was serving with the unit overseas...

bludgeoned into it', he says smilingly. Later he became chairman and then its president.

While secretary of the merchants at Hammersmith college. Alongside such luminaries as Charles Golton and Bill Farrant, he was a member of the Builders Merchants Federation then the National Plumbers Mer chants) London area education committee-an experience he 'thoroughly enjoyed'. He was also on the national council of the federation and a member of several of its commodity committees.

In addition, he is a Fellow of the Institute of Builders Merchants, a founder-member of the Worshipful Company of Builders Merchants and for a time, was its Clerk.

Involvement in the industry also extended to British Standards work. Geoffrey recalls: 'For a number of years, I represented the industry on every single BSI committee connected with plumbing, sanitaryware and kitchens - something over 20 in all. I regularly attended about five of them and received, and commented upon, papers on all of the rest.

The largest meetings, and indeed work, were represented... UK merchants on

Fifth generation to sell bathrooms.

chase of a proper office chair.
...his father's suggestion, ...and the rudi...

MEET THE DESIGNER: 3
Geoffrey Pidgeon talks to Carol Tabbernor

Right: sanitary ware, fittings and tiles based on a 100 mm module bathroom. Siphonic wc, from £26·23; bidet from £9·14; washbasin from £13·09; bath from £75·90; towel rings, £1·94 each. Tiles: white, £6 per hundred; coloured, £7. Humphersons.

One does not usually associate designers with plumbers' merchants, but Geoffrey Pidgeon, chairman and managing director of Humphersons, is an exception. For many years, apart from running the family business, he has been the man behind the scenes advising some of the largest sanitary ware manufacturers about proposed new ranges. He is also a member of several British Standard committees for sanitary fittings and plumbing, and is deeply concerned with safety in the bathroom. As well as all these activities, he designs fittings.

He is the fourth generation—his mother's maiden name was Humpherson—to work in the firm, and two of his sons are continuing the tradition.

Humphersons have always been concerned with designing as well as selling. In fact, in about 1886, Geoffrey Pidgeon's great grandfather designed the original pedestal wash down closet which scarcely differs from the type in general use throughout the world today!

Apart from selling and designing, Humphersons also advise on bathroom planning. It was in this department that Mr. Pidgeon started his career, after gaining practical experience by working for a plumber. This period is probably responsible for his present interest in the appearance of bathrooms as well as their functional aspects.

He believes that sanitary fittings should be considered as furniture instead of equipment and finds it incredible that some people still leave the choice to their

builders, although they would not dream, for instance, of letting someone else choose their dining room table.

It is in keeping with this view that he displays sanitary ware in 20 room settings, which are well worth visiting for bathroom planning or decoration ideas, even if no new fittings are needed—it makes a pleasant change from the dreary looking rows of fittings that one usually finds. Naturally, all equipment shown is vetted for both function and good looks.

It is an eye opener to go round the showroom with Geoffrey Pidgeon while the good and bad features of various designs are pointed out, many of which most people might overlook. He is particularly impressed by the bath shown on page 171 and his reasons make a useful check list of points to look out for when choosing a bath: grab rails; side taps which are easy to use and which simplify plumbing; a wide shelf formed by the side as a seat near the taps, narrowing at the other end to give full bath width for shoulders; and a slightly sloping end for supporting the back comfortably.

Another range that he admires is shown on page 171 (top right). "I particularly like the sculptural look and the way in which the pedestals curve backwards boldly—both pleasing and imaginative. Also, the bidet has a good wide saddle and narrows at the back."

Another point about this range is that it comes in what Geoffrey Pidgeon calls "neutral colours" which, apart from being subtle and unusual, have the ability to

tone with a wide variety of shades so are less restricting in decoration schemes than most coloured sanitary ware.

He sees this as a trend—and he has been proved correct, for a deep olive green has recently been added to the apricot and yellow already introduced.

He was not responsible for these ranges, but he did design the one on page 171 (bottom right) which includes many useful features such as deep drainage troughs from the soap depressions, an anti-splash rim and inward sloping edges on the washbasin.

The patterned wc shown with the basin is also his design: here the aim was to provide an inexpensive fitting for a confined space. He has managed to design one which projects only 24½ in. and is close coupled (no flush pipe between the cistern and pan)—normally an expensive feature, but all for a very reasonable price.

His newest and most revolutionary project is a range of dimensionally co-ordinated sanitary ware, bathroom fittings, ceramic wall tiles and vinyl flooring. The idea started with the need for a metric range. The choice of a 100 mm module seemed obvious, as it is convenient and widely used in the building trade.

Instead of just designing overall sizes to fit into this module, Geoffrey Pidgeon has taken matters a step further to include everything from plumbing connections to tap holes. His interest in the overall appearance of bathrooms then

166

---

8 THE IRONMONGER · 1 July 1967 · 1 July 1967 · THE IRONMONGER 9

HARDWARE MERCHANDISER · HARDWARE MERCHANDISER · HARDWARE MERCHANDISER · HARDWARE MERCHANDISER · HARDWARE MERCHANDISER · HARDWARE MERCHANDISER

Bathroom comfort and safety featured by West London firm

Humpherson display of aids for the young, elderly and infirm

SUCCESSFUL merchandising of bathroom equipment obviously calls for showroom arrangement of complete bathrooms, hence the high standard of such displays by builders' and plumbers' merchants throughout the country. In their new showrooms at Beaufort Works, 186 Fulham Road, London, S.W.10, however, the ninety-year-old merchant firm of Humpherson & Co., Ltd., have gone a step further and given a new angle to this branch of merchandising.

To be more exact they have used two facets of the bathroom to spearhead their display scheme: (a) they have created a bathroom boutique, with emphasis on the furnishing of the room as a place to relax in; and (b) they have created a grouping of bathroom equipment entitled "For the Young—and the Not So Young" which also includes special arrangements for the elderly and handicapped. This is a marriage of the aesthetic and the practical which should, and indeed already has, captured the interest of both the trade and the public.

In the bathroom boutique not only the main items of equipment but also everything else for a completely furnished bathroom are on show and for sale: rugs, towels, cloths, curtains and all the smaller fittings that make for comfort and convenience. This showroom will also feature a special bathroom designed in turn by leading home magazines and architects. The first example, now on show, is a delight to the eye, colourful without flamboyance, and luxurious without ostentation.

Naturally such a bathroom is not cheap, but Humphersons provide for the more modest purse, too. In the older showroom behind they will show the customer a complete bathroom in colour (bath, basin, closet and low-down flushing cistern) for only £34 7s 6d. Moreover they display a remarkable plastic baths such as the quaint rainwater head...

Everything is priced, but not on cards or labels because these can fall off the article, get soiled, or look untidy. Instead, in every bathroom there is a small container mounted on the partition, holding a supply of folders. These are printed in the company's usual green ink and give the price of every item in that bathroom. Thus the customer not only has an immediate quotation but a list to be taken home for further study if need be.

The basement of the new showroom is the scene of what may be called the safety section with its devices "For the Young and the Not So Young". Our...

There are in fact only...

This quaint rainwater head, a fine example of the lead-worker's art, was made in 1890 by one of Humpherson's craftsmen, appropriately named Mr. Leadbetter. It hangs in one of the showrooms.

cistern devices for sufferers from arthritis or rheumatism; and, especially worth noting, a combined shower bath and sit bath that can be used for both elderly people and children, or as an ordinary shower tray by the rest of the family.

In a word, with these new developments of their premises, Humpherson are aiming at providing an advice centre on bathroom and toilet equipment. The chairman and managing director, Mr. Geoffrey Pidgeon, who has been a moving spirit in the enterprise says: "We examine all new products that come on the market, and with our long experience we try to judge, and then support, those we feel are worth while."

To enable all these displays to be accommodated in addition to the trade counter, a two-storey warehouse has been obtained in Tadema Road, Chelsea, providing open yards, covered bays and mechanised handling plants. Also this will have a display room for sanitary...

Above.—In the bathroom boutique: everything needed to complete the furnishing of a bathroom is shown on these wall panels as well as in the fitted suites.

Left.—In the section "For the young and the not so young". Bath fully fitted with grab rails, specially suited to the elderly and physically handicapped. Beside it we show the single control for water temperature in bath and basin. A turn of the knob pre-determines the maximum temperature of the water so that risk of its flowing too hot is eliminated.

Below.—Low level w.c. with press knob to control flush. Note no levers or other projections that could catch clothing. Next to it a narrow toilet to aid the handicapped and infirm. Grab rails within easy reach and so spaced to help as to make rising easier. Note also flush control set in wall at back needs only to be pressed by elbow or hand.

Plumbing, Heating & Air Movement News, February 1967

Opinion

The syphon versus the valve

Geoffrey Pidgeon, founder of Original Bathrooms, has long been an advocate of baths, sanitaryware and brassware and manufacture of the best in worldwide design. Here he gives his views on the current debate over the introduction of the flush valve to the UK.

There have been only a few major defining moments in the bathroom industry over the past 100 years and I would include the introduction of vitreous china, the plastic float (and ball), the acrylic bath and, possibly, the ceramic disc valve. However, we up with these is the pending and inevitable introduction of the use of the valve, instead of the syphon, in our WC cisterns.

At the end of November, I appeared on the "Big Breakfast" TV programme explaining the many advantages of the syphon over the syphon in our WC cisterns. Since then, the whole has hotted up. I believe there is inevitably going to be an acceptance of the use of suitable valves, and I intend to press for the change take place sooner rather than later.

I have written to Members of Parliament and I am encouraged by the response.

There are two main reasons for my interest in this subject. Firstly, I have long wanted to see good political ploy by the British sanitaryware makers, the main opponents of the 'Drop valve'. This is not about water conservation - though that is a good servation - though this is a good political ploy by the British Bathroom Council (B.B.C.) who are the main opponents...

We want to see less water - probably a lot less, instead of 7.5 - and the valve is an aid in this direction.

Secondly, I am rather tired of hearing, in the media about Thomas Crappers' role, incorrectly reported, as the inventor of our present cistern interior design.

Let us get some things clear from the start:

This is not about Brussels interference - though that is a common theme move into the modern era. It is the whole of sanitary ware as it is elsewhere.

Not only is the syphon out of date; it is also wasteful of water. A cistern fitted with a syphon can be used to control the amount of water descending into the WC. Many valves can be pressed so enough water that the user can see has cleaned the pan.

The main concern about jobs is from the pottery companies who are concerned that they may find more imports coming in...

outdated now!

The syphon design cannot even easily cope with the relatively new 7.5 litres requirement.

Many plumbers 'fix' the ball valve with a 7.5 litre cistern, to provide more water into the cistern to ensure it cleans properly every time.

The syphon was suitable for the 2 gallons (9 litres) for which it was designed, almost 100 years ago. But it is less effective with lower quantities of water. It will fail to regularly clean pans with 6 litres - unless pans are raised, (see below).

With 6 litres utilising a syphon, it may be necessary to actively 'crank' the lever to make the syphon action commence. It is likely that children and the elderly will have trouble in achieving a flush.

Preventing waste and flushing cleaner

The ground swell towards valves is actually more concerned with a common tense move into the modern era...

Valves flush the WC better because the water descends into the pan faster. There is a dynamic energy not available in the syphon where water has first to be directed upwards, in the wrong direction, before descending down the syphon action which gives it a flushing...

'Sluggish' is a good word to describe the velocity of water flow from a syphon when compared with a valve. Because of the greater water velocity entering the WC foreign potteries can design WC suites with cisterns having lower water capacity which leads to water saving...

generally overflow because the ball valve is defective in some way. It isn't shutting down, the float has dropped off, seating ruptured, etc., etc.

Warning pipes-why?

The peculiar UK requirement of having a warning pipe to the outside could be continued if you use a valve - but why? If you are supposed to be a warning, but in freezing weather, they are a nuisance. A dripping pipe quickly freezes and the water cannot escape. It then builds up in the cistern and has only one place to go - onto the floor - flooding the house.

It won't warn you if you are away on holiday or away for the weekend!

In internal bathrooms, and WC compartments, such as you find in hotels, at airports, and in some blocks of flats, we allow cisterns to have a standish (a sort of drip-pot). This Robinson contraption, with this handy little cup beside the cistern float, if the cistern over flows you can see it! (It is pretty also a breeding ground for germs since it cannot be easily cleaned.)

As alternative allowed, as seen at airports, is for the over-flow to be taken on so to the top of the WC then flattened to go under the seat and discharge over the back of the pan.

What a disgusting detail!

All this is unnecessary with a valve. The water should always valve. The water should never be seen discharging, from the rim into the pan.

In all this, we have been talking about properly designed valves manufactured by reputable firms and valves that can pass such tests as are considered necessary.

Nobody is advocating allowing the use of the sort of 'lush flapper valves' seen in the gents WC of some American Greek taverns! We are talking of high standards of manufacture and we are talking of high quality fittings only.

Out of step with the world

The world outside of the UK is using valves and tens of millions are sold each year - are we yet again to be the only ones in step?

Only Britain (and Hong Kong until China takes over) bar the valve - or if we alone are conscious of the need to protect water resources. What imprudence.

Nobody is advocating changing the syphon in cisterns already installed, nobody is suggesting that syphons be slaughtered. But, progress must be made and the valve must now be given equal status with the syphon, for our long term benefit.

Change will come - let us get on with it now and start the new millennium off right - at least in the bathroom!

SAFETY IN THE BATHROOM

An article by Geoffrey Pidgeon, Chairman & Managing Director, Humpherson & Co. Limited

'KEEP DEATH OFF THE ROAD' – We are continuously told, but for you your bathroom could be more dangerous than the M.I. It's true. Statistics show that more people are hurt by accidents in the Home than on the road and the bathroom is high on the list of black spots. But it need not be if a little thought is put into the lay-out and care taken with the choice of the fittings in your bathroom.

The problem facing us is two fold. Firstly to reduce the general risk for all of us and then to improve safety and comfort in the bathroom for the young and the elderly who are both more vulnerable.

Starting at the door, I feel most strongly that safety locks should be fitted which can be opened in case of emergency from outside. This lock is very simple and can be opened with a screwdriver or a small coin but it gives a sense of independence to youngsters and very elderly people who are then able to lock the door in the sure knowledge that in the event of an accident they can be easily helped.

Then there is the use of electricity in the bathroom. So that there is no risk of electrocution, lighting fittings should all have pull cords and shaving points should be of an approved pattern. Any electric heating used in the bathroom should be chosen with very great care and only installed by a competent electrician. This is not a field for the handy man! Under no circumstances should portable electric heaters be used in the bathroom and, of course, there should be no other power points.

As a general rule, I like to see three sides built round a W.C., a shower, a bath, or a bidet. This not only makes for more interesting room but does reduce the directions in which one can fall. Each of these partitions should have grab rails placed so that one is fully under control at all times.

This is particularly good where there are elderly people in the house as the rails help them to raise and lower themselves and are an added safety factor should they slip.

Many baths today have a grab rail fitted but all too often this is only on the far side of the bath. As one has to reach across the bath before it can be used, it is seldom any aid to getting into the bath. It is hardly of any use in getting out! Choose a bath which has grab rails on both sides. They should be as unobtrusive as possible but long enough for one to reach when in the fully reclined position.

It is possible to add a simple cross rail either hinged from the tap or permanently attached to the bath. This is of very great use to people suffering with stiff joints or one of the many afflictions of old age. For existing baths, grab rails can be fitted to the wall quite inexpensively and with care they can even be fitted to the bath itself.

Most falls in the bathroom are due of course to a wet and slippery floor. The increasing use of suitable carpets in the bathroom will help reduce accidents caused by slipping, but in the area of the bath, and particularly when young children are involved, carpeting is not everyone's choice. Here I would choose one of the textured vinyls of which Marley, Gerland and Amtico offer a considerable choice. There is a special 'safety flooring' called 'ALTRO' which is made in a restricted range of colours but if coupled with carpeting would give you the best combination.

Ideally, all the water in the bathroom should be thermostatically controlled. This can be achieved by either bringing all the supplies through one thermostat where they can be mixed, and delivery made at a predetermined temperature, or individual thermostat can be used for the bath, shower and washbasin. But an absolute MUST is that the shower be thermostatically controlled when children are involved – the consequence of not having one could be a painful scald leaving an ugly scar for life. For people who have rheumatism or arthritis, easy action taps are a boon. Most of us have seen the lever taps in hospitals but these are seldom allowed in the Home as waterboards will only permit their use under special circumstances. However, we have levers to fit to our shower controls and there is a patent lever action valve called the 'Levertap' now coming onto the market which is the nearest we are likely to get to those magnificent elbow action taps used by surgeons in television programmes about hospitals.

Some manufacturers have the mistaken belief that you create safety in the bath or shower tray simply by putting a row of ridges or knobs on the base during the casting and then enamelling over the top.

Continued overleaf

Notes H

Valves *versus* Syphons

In the period 1870 – 1880 water consumption in London increased dramatically, due mostly to the rapid rise in its population. Demand also developed as a result of the rapidly increased use of water closets connected to the main drainage, replacing the wide use of earth and ash closets. Whether this ended up in the river in the early days is not relevant here. I suppose this to some degree was exacerbated by the affluence of the rising middle-class, able to have piped water to washbasins and baths in their homes.

All this led to the need to find ways of reducing consumption. Perhaps the biggest culprit was the crude valves used. The 'valve closet' was truly unreliable and the various devices used to shut off the water equally at fault.

The syphon cistern was the answer to the need for a 'water waste preventer' or 'WWP' and Frederick Humpherson's Beaufort was one of the earliest. Though details varied, they all had one thing in common. The water was drawn up over a standing pipe within the cistern and once it tumbled over the top it 'syphoned' out the remaining water with it and let it fall into the pan. There was always an air gap, so that providing the inrush of replacement water was not too fast, the syphon action was broken and only the contents of the cistern used. Early on, this was set at 2 gallons but 2.5 gallons and even 3 gallon cisterns were allowed in parts of the country.

Basically there were two methods used in 'Syphon' cisterns and both are illustrated below.

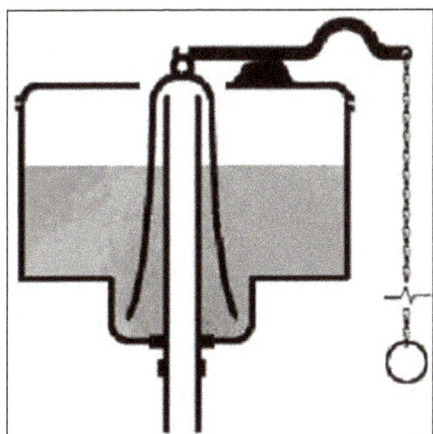

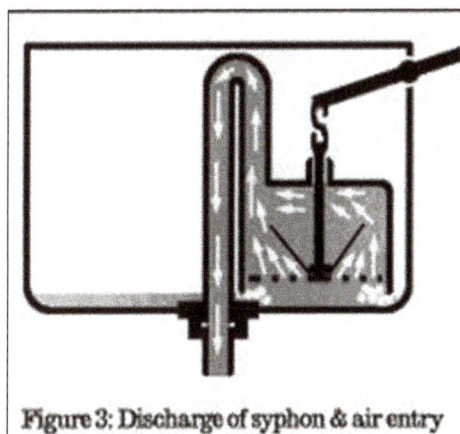

Figure 3: Discharge of syphon & air entry

The water is 'sucked' up and the velocity of the resulting flush is limited when compared with the modern valve. As one operates the lever on a valve (more often these days you press a button) then the whole contents

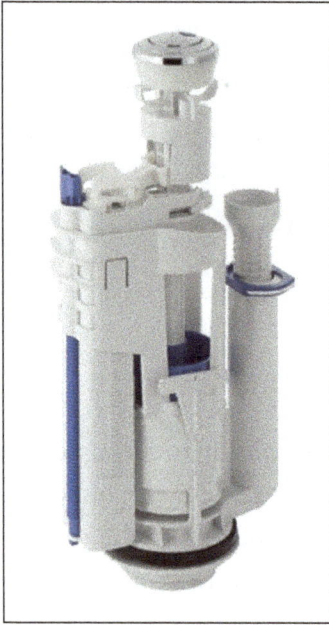

goes out with a rush. It is rather like taking the plug out of a basin with the immediate discharge that occurs – but I hasten to say the modern valve is rather more complex.

I was asked how, as the great-nephew of Frederick Humpherson, I could now advocate the use of the valve? I pointed out that over a hundred years had passed and manufacturing technology had moved on. I wrote several articles on the subject that had wide press coverage. I was asked to appear on TV in the 'Big Breakfast Show' on Channel 4. A taxi picked me up from our home in Richmond at 4 am and took me to the studios in East London. Another appearance on the subject was one Sunday on BBC1 – after the One o'clock news. It was filmed in our showrooms that made it easier for me – unused to TV studios.

The picture shows a modern valve fitting – typical of those being used throughout the world today.

I took great heart when I learned years ago – that South Africa was approving the use of the valve – to gradually replace the syphon fittings of old. If a country like South Africa changed over it spoke volumes for the benefits arising – now appreciated worldwide.

I wrote to MPs but the biggest battle was with the British pottery industry. They were keen to keep the syphon, with its low-pressure discharge, since that hopefully kept foreign competitors out. European manufacturers were making WC pans with the water supplied via a 'valve' in the cistern.

To export to the UK – using its low velocity syphons - involved them in making the rim of the WC pan in a different way to pans supplied to the rest of the world. But slowly, more and more did just that!

Gradually, those like me wanting a better performance – coupled with very substantial water saving – won the argument. However, it was a hard fight against outdated practices and the self-interest of UK pottery makers. It is amusing for me to read their sales literature today, making claims for the water saving that has arisen from the use of the valve!

One such reads *'.... WCs that flush on either 4 or 2.6 litres of water, a saving of up to 52%.*

That would not have been possible with the low-pressure discharge from a syphon. The valve gives this greater velocity meaning that a well-designed WC will flush with much less water.

The standard cistern capacity for use with a syphon used to be 7.5 litres or 9.5 litres for a full flush – *'when required!'* The use of the valve has achieved a massive saving in water.

We finally joined the rest of the world – but it was a real fight!

Notes I

Humpherson's Lead Rainwater Head and 10 Downing Street

This magnificent example of the plumber's craft was made in Frederick Humpherson's workshop on the corner of Beaufort Street Chelsea. It was shown at the Leicester Health Exhibition in the 1880s and received much acclaim. The head itself measures 80cms x 60cms and even then was regarded as outstanding workmanship. The rainwater pipe leading from it further demonstrates the great skill of the plumber and you will notice he put the joint at the front, for all to see. Remember, both head and pipe were worked up from sheet lead.

The head later adorned Frederick Humpherson's office but after the move to Holmes Place in 1902, it was affixed to the wall just inside the entrance. It stayed there, until long overdue redecoration took place, just after World War II.

It was understood that only a family member should handle it. In spite of offers by my brother and myself – uncle Sidney Humpherson insisted he could do it. However, after he removed the screws, he could not hold on to its great weight. Standing at the foot of the ladder we were able to slow its fall and that prevented too much damage. Its nose is dented and we decided to leave it – in memory of Sidney!

Years later, after major alterations in the 1970s, it was put in an even more prominent position, near the main staircase leading to the offices. I should add that the fourth generation named him 'Fred' after great uncle Frederick Humpherson and the name has stuck.

Around that time, work was proceeding on rebuilding parts of 10 Downing Street. One day, George Emmerton, a sales representative for the Associated Lead Company, asked to see me on 'a private matter.' Apparently the Lead Federation knew of 'Fred' and asked if he could be offered to the Ministry of Works as a supreme example of lead work. It was to adorn the back of 10 Downing Street overlooking its gardens and Horse Guards Parade. Though unwilling to part with 'Fred' I felt duty bound to ask mother whose reply was, and these are her exact words

'Thank them very much Geoffrey – but no!'

Perhaps it was because Harold Wilson was the incumbent at the time?

Notes J

More Crapper Myths From Wallace Reyburn

1. **'Pull and Let Go is Born.'** In 'Flushed with Pride' chapter 3 is entitled 'Pull and Let Go is Born.' It goes on to describe the work of Thomas Crapper – implying that he was responsible for the principle of the valveless water waste preventer. On page 13 it states *'…he perfected the cistern as toilet users throughout the world know it today.'* This 'marvel' is illustrated on the opposite page 12 – and is the Patent 4990 granted to Albert Giblin in 1898 that he *sold* to Thomas Crapper & Co.

These fourteen appear as pages 62 to 75 in the 'Bijoux' catalogue of William N. Froy of Brunswick Works, Hammersmith of 1885. That was well before Crapper's 4990 cistern saw the light of day leading to Wallace Reyburn's pronouncement that *'pull and let go is born!'*.

All this ignores the fact that were many cisterns requiring a chain to pull – not the least of which was Frederick Humpherson's 'Patent Syphon Cistern' shown at the International Inventions Exhibition of 1885. However, some ten years later there were a multitude of 'pull and let go' cisterns on the market. Below, are no less than fourteen different models shown in just one merchant's catalogue.

2. **Stair Treads. Reyburn says** '... Patent No. 6,029, March 16, 1903 – T.P. Crapper, Stair Treads, which on investigation at the Patent Office are seen to be not unlike a type still installed in modern homes.' First of all, (a) the stair tread application was shared with a George Wiggins (whoever he was) and (b) Thomas Crapper and George Wiggins did not obtain an actual patent for the stair treads, the would-be patent being abandoned. The Patent Office have reported no copy of it exists.

3. **Patent for house Ventilation.** Much is also made of Thomas Crapper's two patents for house ventilation but these too were shared. This time with George Edward Mineard, a well-known builder of fine homes in Kensington. This is an extract from a recent study of Victorian house builders called 'The Origins of Lexham Gardens and Lee Abbey' by David Weekes, first published in 1996.

"George Edward Mineard was a builder of some of the finest buildings in Kensington and Chelsea in the period 1875 to 1890. His close friend Sir Henry Cole was the founding Director of the South Kensington Museums was also a builder but obsessed with the dangers of sewer gases. After touring houses under construction in Kensington, he purchased houses built by Mineard in Philbeach Gardens. One should note that Cole was impressed by a system of ventilation invented by Mineard to prevent sewer gas dangers, and Cole encouraged him to patent this. Cole also secured for Mineard the contract to overhaul the sanitary arrangements at Sandringham, then one of the newer Royal residences."

Note: It says the system of house ventilation was the invention of Mineard and Cole *'encouraged him to patent this.'* Nowhere does it mention Thomas Crapper. The invention and patents (No's 1628 in 1881 & 1282 in 1883) were then presumably shared with Thomas Crapper who had to provide, or more likely manufacture, the fittings? Incidentally, the good offices of George Mineard – and especially Sir Henry Cole with his strong Royal Court connections – may also explain how Thomas Crapper first obtained the work at Sandringham. That in turn, led him to receive his 'By Royal Appointment' awards – so beloved of Robert Gillingham Wharam when I attempted to purchase Thomas Crapper & Co., from him.

4. **Trough closet story!** Wallace Reyburns trough story on page 55 of Flushed With Pride is puzzling. The illustrations referred to are actually a 'range' of separate closets and in no way can be referred to a 'trough'!

Still, in the words of his Editor – it made good reading!

Notes K

Thomas Crapper & Company Today

As I related in Chapter 18 'Crappers for Sale' – I failed in my attempt to purchase the company. This was due to my inability to grasp how important the staff was to the owner Robert Wharam – even his two cleaning ladies. Shortly afterwards, he sold it 'lock-stock-and-barrel' to Boldings of Davies Street Mayfair, for exactly 40% less than I intended to offer, if I had been allowed to make it!

Having purchased the firm – Boldings gaily went on to sack some of the staff – including its MD my good friend Robbie Barratt. Then in 1966, they closed the Kings Road operation and moved what remained to Davies Street. In 1969 Bolding & Sons were declared Bankrupt. Mr Stephen Cowell, an Englishman residing in South Africa, purchased the group and sold it on, except he kept the dormant Thomas Crapper & Co.

Whilst the company was clearly not trading it remained registered at Companies House. Enter Simon Kirby an antique dealer based in Stratford-upon-Avon, who delighted in collecting antique sanitary ware. He went to South Africa and finally persuaded Stephen Cowell to relinquish control – thus becoming the proud owner of a venerable but defunct company – Thomas Crapper & Co.!

Simon with several stalwart friends set about relaunching Thomas Crapper onto the British market – some 30 years after it had disappeared from the bathroom scene. The company chose to make a small but authentic range of high quality products – based on the old models. There is a continued demand for 'period' ware and Crapper's range is made to the highest standard. I am bound to say Simon has succeeded in his aim to bring the Crapper name alive again and he has a number of thriving outlets across the country displaying the range. His outlets show the authentic Crapper Badge.

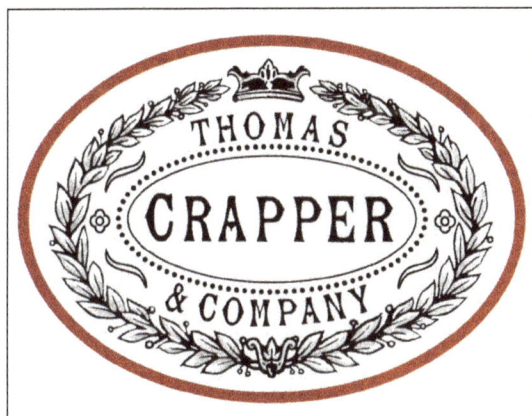

I wonder – *what if Robert Wharam had listened to my offer* – all those years ago?

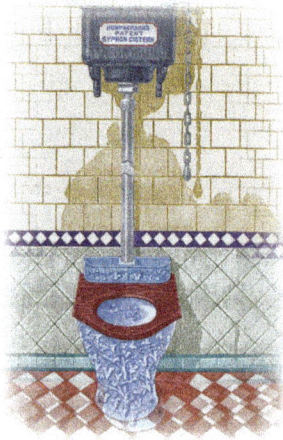

Acknowledgements

Since finding the old catalogues in 1947, I knew I had to write 'The Bathroom Book' eventually. My resolve hardened when 'Flushed with Pride' was published in 1969 with a number of inaccuracies but I still did not start to put anything in writing more than just rough notes until1994.

However, during a visit to Bletchley Park in 1996, I met David White then the Curator of its Wireless Museum. On hearing that I had worked in MI6 (Section VIII) at nearby Whaddon Hall, he asked me to write about our wartime work. This ended as being 'The Secret Wireless War' and launched at Bletchley Park in 2003. I later wrote two other books but all the time had kept notes and pictures that might be useful for the 'Bathroom Book' that I intended to follow them.

Now, I am deeply conscious of the debt I owe to numerous writers and friends in the creation of this book – some going back to those early days. In preparing my acknowledgments – I find I have photographs and information – but no idea of the source!

However, one person stands out, the late Dr Andy Gibbons from the University of North Colorado – in Greeley. He had read 'Flushed with Pride' and was intrigued by the story to such an extent that he formed 'The Smallest Room Press & Thomas Crapper Society.' He came to see me at Humphersons in Holman Road, Battersea and we formed an instant friendship. He went to see Crapper's grave and spent time researching his history – but slowly coming to realise Reyburn's book was inaccurate – to say the least!

Later, he introduced me to Ken Grabowski from Chicago who was similarly fascinated and who decided to fully follow Andy's work for himself. Suffice it to say, on his first visit he called on us and came again – no less than twenty two times! He was not only interested in Reyburn's fanciful story but more in Thomas Crapper's family history and that of the Wharam family, who played such a big part in Thomas Crapper & Company's success.

William Humpherson – the following were helpful in providing information on Frederick Humpherson's brother William. George Hampshire, Felicity Cole, Nigel Canham (the local newspaper), and Richard Harris.

Sue Ridley and Julie Merrick both of Ideal Standard and Sara Johnston of Geberit UK, were of great help with the story and/or photographs.

Bruce Eadie and his crew who made a film about the 'Beaufort' pan for the Science Museum. It was great fun making it. I think because of our frequent outbursts of laughter, it took twice as long to make as intended. It can be found on: https://www.youtube.com/watch?v=2NjuUoWCTO0a

Some years ago, I donated one of the last four 'Beaufort' WC pans to the Science Museum. They have since heartily supported the idea of launching my book there and I wish to express my grateful thanks Helen Peavitt, Alison Hess, Laurie Michel-Hutteau and Mark Johnson.

In my research, I discovered that Frederick Humpherson spent a great deal of his time in Woodhall Spa in Lincolnshire. I was helped to put the story together by Sarah Town from the Woodhall Spa library; Roger Pickavance and Jacqueline Goodhall of the Woodhall Spa Cottage Museum and most especially by Patricia and Nicholas Duke-Cox. These have helped me find my way around the mystery of Frederick Humpherson's – 'other life'!

Paul Dobson, is the grandson of Albert Dobson. Albert designed the Patent flushing cistern and sold to Thomas Crapper, who offered for sale as 'Crapper's Valveless Water-Waste Preventer Patent No. 4009.' Paul gave me the true story about his grandfather's work. His information is much appreciated and it is now recorded in this book.

Amongst the authors who helped me I must thank, Lucinda Lambton, David Eveleigh, John Ragland, James Denley, Munro Blair and the late Roy Palmer. Their books are mentioned in Chapter 7 'The Beaufort WC.'

Lynn Hainge is a member of the Allward Family and sent me a fine selection of photographs of Castle Stalker used in Chapter 20. They brought back memories of a hectic weekend's plumbing alongside my brother Ron and our son Michael.

Iris Collins is friend from our Bowls Club. She kindly edited the first few chapters and was of great help in pointing out a number of mistakes. She also advised me to have the book professionally edited. Lo-and-behold, it turned out that our neighbour Dr Christine Pickard – in addition to being a medical doctor – edited the British Medical Journal. She has kindly read through and corrected the book. Thank you Christine. However, I suppose inevitably, I rewrote whole passages. Therefore, any faults in grammar or spelling are entirely due to me!

Michael Dever of 'Snappy Snaps' Richmond. In spite of its odd name, I found the company to have the range of skills I would normally associate with a leading photographic laboratory. I am grateful to Michael for all his help in so cleverly bringing some old prints 'back to life'!

In Bristol City Council – David Emeney in the Records Office and Graham Tratt of Bristol Archives. Alan Patient of Blue Plaques of London. Jay Roos, Manager of Brompton Cemetery London, for his great help in seeking Frederick Humphersons's grave and the supporting information he provided.

Acknowledgements

I am grateful to James Froy of N. Froy & Sons with his help with the flushing cisterns shown in the 1895 copy of William N. Froy's 'Bijoux' catalogue.

Richard Harris of the Kingsteignton History Society has been most helpful in providing me with more information about my great-uncle William Humpherson of Hexter-Humpherson.

The fine picture of a Neo-Classica washbasin in Chapter 25 has been sent to me by Valentina Fulgenzi of Sanitosco Sanitari, the manufacturers in Civita Castellana, Italy. The taps shown in Appendix 10 are by Fantini Rubinetti of Pella northern Italy and I thank Daniela Fantini for sending the photographs. I am also grateful to Ludovica and Roberto Polomba for their pictures of the Flaminia range of sanitary ware they designed – for Ceramica Flaminia whose factory is in Civita Castellana.

Aneeta Pidgeon: Our daughter-in-law Aneeta is an interior designer but also an accomplished artist. I should add she is a very good bathroom designer. She made the pictures of the archer and the firewatcher for the book.

I have received excellent ideas and much support from Sarah Wyndham Lewis and Jenny Hildreth of ArcPR and I am truly grateful to them both.

The super pictures of a Victorian washstand and china fittings were kindly sent to me by Lisa Griffiths aka 'Victoriana Lady' who lives in Rockport, MA. Lisa is an author and historian – especially on all things from the Victorian period.

I owe much to our three sons, Laurence, Michael and John, who have had to put up with my many questions about people and events from their time in the company. I find it strange, how I can remember so many details about the early days, and need prompting over more recent events!

David Pearman: Last, but by no means least, I want to thank my friend David who has been so helpful from the outset of this project. He is the proprietor of Prestige Press who are specialist publishers and book designers. His knowledge and understanding of the publishing world have been of immense benefit on this and my earlier books.

I have made every effort to acknowledge correct copyright and/or origin of material and images where applicable. However, much information and pictures came via friends over a long period of time so it has proved impossible to establish the original source or author. Any errors or omissions are unintentional and should be reported to me and I will arrange for corrections to appear in any reprint.

Finally, I do sincerely apologise to anyone that I may have missed in these acknowledgements.

Index